The Khmers

The Peoples of South-East Asia and The Pacific

General Editors
Peter Bellwood and Ian Glover

Each book in this series will be devoted to a people (or group of associated peoples) from the vast area of the world extending from Hawaii in the north to Tasmania in the south and from Fiji in the east to Cambodia in the west. The books, written by historians, anthropologists and archaeologists from all over the world, will be both scholarly and accessible. In many cases the volumes will be the only available account of their subject.

Already published

The Peoples of Borneo
Victor T. King

The Khmers
Ian Mabbett and David Chandler

In preparation

The Melanesians
Matthew Spriggs

The Vietnamese
Jeremy Davidson

The Malays
*A. C. Milner and
Jane Drakard*

The Bugis
Christian Pelras

The Fijians
*Nicholas Thomas and
Victoria Luker*

The Peoples of the Lesser Sundas
James L. Fox

The Balinese
*Angela Hobart, Urs Ramseyer
and Albert Leeman*

The Lapita Peoples
Patrick Kirch

The Maoris
Atholl Anderson

The Khmers

Ian Mabbett
and
David Chandler

BLACKWELL
Oxford UK & Cambridge USA

First published 1995

Blackwell Publishers, the publishing imprint of
Basil Blackwell Ltd
108 Cowley Road
Oxford   OX4 1JF
UK

Basil Blackwell Inc.
238 Main Street
Cambridge, Massachusetts 02142
USA

British Library Cataloguing in Publication Data
A CIP catalogue record for this book is available from the British Library.

Library of Congress Cataloging-in-Publication Data
Mabbett, Ian W.
The Khmers / Ian Mabbett and David Chandler.
p.   cm. – (The Peoples of South-East Asia and the Pacific)
Includes bibliographical references and index.
ISBN 0–631–17582–2 (alk. paper)
1. Cambodia. I. Series.
DS554.3.M33   1995
959.6 – dc20   94–28125
CIP

Typeset in 11 on 12½ pt Sabon by Best-set Typesetter Ltd.
Printed in Great Britain by Hartnolls Ltd, Bodmin, Cornwall
This book is printed on acid-free paper

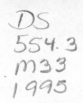
Contents

List of Plates

List of Maps

Preface

Chapters 1–15 were written by Ian Mabbett, and chapters 16 and 17 by David Chandler, but all chapters were revised in the light of extensive discussions, and the authors share responsibility for the book as a whole.

The many people who gave the authors valuable help cannot be held responsible for any defects in the present work. The authors are glad to thank them: Professor Claude Jacques, who offered the fruits of his ongoing research on Cambodian inscriptions; Professor Charles Higham, Dr Donn Bayard and Dr Helmut Loofs-Wissowa, who patiently examined parts of the manuscript and made available the results of recent archaeological research; Dr R. Hill and Dr T. T. Chang, who commented upon the history of rice-growing; Dr Peter Bellwood, who as Series Editor examined the whole work and made important contributions to the thinking behind the sections on archaeology; Associate Professor Walter Veit, who allowed the authors to select freely from his substantial collection of illustrations; and Richard Engelhardt, who made available some of his photographs of Angkor.

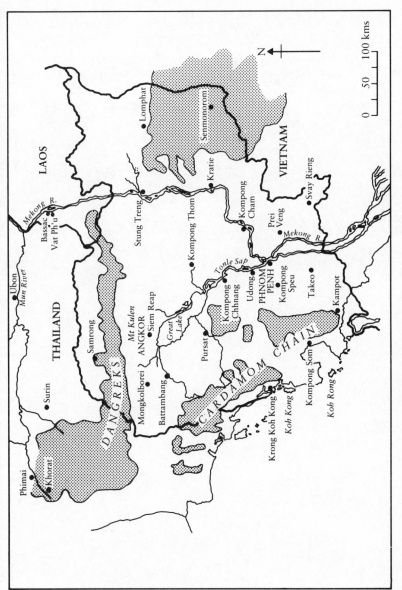

Map 1 General map of Cambodia

1

Introduction

There is a poignant contrast between Cambodia today and Cambodia as it was in ancient times.

In modern times – and especially in the 1970s – the country has been a passive victim of history. It has been beset by powerful neighbours, mastered by an imperial power, ravaged by war, devastated by a boiling tide of savagery, colonized by ancient rivals, and subjected to the vagaries of international politics.

In ancient times, from the ninth century to the thirteenth, Cambodia was a power to be reckoned with. Chinese merchants knew it as Cambodia the Rich; early Portuguese visitors who came before the flickerings of antique glory were quite extinguished considered that it had been one of the wonders of the world. The remains of Angkor remind us of its assertive grandeur: the confident serenity of temples that brought the gods to earth, the bombast of royal inscriptions declaring the invincibility of kings, the massive feats of organization that remodelled the landscape and mirrored the heavens in a web of bright waterways – it is all designed on a scale too vast to be readily conceived of in the Cambodia that we know today.

What we perceive is not just what is registered by our eyes but also what we know about the objects before them, what we expect and what we remember. When we look at Cambodia, we seem to perceive, like a landscape dimly seen through a patterned curtain, the shapes of the country's past greatness; but the two realities refuse to blend, they cannot easily be fitted together in one image.

Early western visitors to Cambodia, finding the ruins of ancient temples slumbering (though not lost and forgotten) in the forest, were at first unwilling to believe that they had been built by the Khmers themselves; and the Khmers, however much or little they knew about their past, produced myths about the construction of Angkor by divine agency – myths that were perhaps designed to protect the truth from the foreigners rather than to reveal it to them.

Accordingly, marvellous theories were propounded to account for the ruins. The first-comers from Portugal and Spain in the sixteenth century thought that the monuments must have been built by Jews, or perhaps by Alexander the Great, or by Romans under the Emperor Trajan. The Portuguese traveller Diogo do Couto thought they must have been built by Indians.

We have, then, two Cambodias: the misremembered Cambodia of centuries long past, whose history was lost, and which was built by the gods; and the modern Cambodia, which has a history of its own and whose fate has been determined by all-too-fallible human beings. The concern of this book is primarily with the first. We shall be looking to see through what mundane instruments of history and environment the gods did their work. What factors shaped the rise of Khmer civilization? How did this civilization come to be identified with such a powerful state? Then, more briefly, we shall look at the factors which wrought such a transformation upon it, replacing the majestic empire of Angkor with the Cambodian state which we know today.

In this chapter we shall be considering the question of Khmer identity. Language is one of the most important ways of identifying the people of Cambodia: there are minority racial groups with different languages, but the Khmers are numerically dominant. They identify themselves also by descent, culture and history.

Language

The English 'Cambodia' represents the Khmer word *Kampuchea*, which in turn represents the Sanskrit *Kambuja*, 'born of Kambu'. The word 'Khmer' denotes both the language of Cambodia and the people who speak it.

Various forms of the name *Khmer* appeared; they include *Kvir* in Cham sources, and *Kamar* and *Kimer* in Arab ones. The Chinese renditions *Ko-mieh* (*gemie*)[1] and *Chi-mieh* (*jimie*) appear, though the most generally used Chinese name for the kingdom, *Chen-la*, was first used in pre-Angkorian times and stuck thereafter; it is unclear what indigenous name it represents.

The Khmer language was first written in the period of Indian influence, which provided the Khmers with written characters as well as institutions of court culture. The language of Indian court and temple was Sanskrit. This language left a clear impression in the vocabulary of the temple inscriptions remaining from the period of Angkor and before. It was not just the terminology of court ritual and religion that experienced its influence – many Sanskrit words for everyday things found their way into the old form of Khmer. A random sampling from the Old Khmer passages of some of the inscriptions yields Sanskrit words for fruit juice (*phalodaka*), clarified butter (*ghṛta*), molasses (*gula*), milk (*kṣīra*), camphor (*bhīmasena*), unguent (*lepana*), cooking pot (*kaṭāha*), incense (*dhūpa*), bowl (*bhājana*), and oil press (*suti*).[2]

Sanskrit was not the only source of foreign influence upon Khmer vocabulary. Another very important one (closely related to Sanskrit) is Pāli, the sacred language of Theravāda Buddhism, which from the thirteenth century became increasingly influential and largely ousted Hinduism and other forms of Buddhism. There has been renewed borrowing from Pāli in modern times. Further, one should add the substantial influence of French during (and since) the period of the French protectorate.

Yet these foreign intrusions are superficial; the Khmer language retains a structure and a basic vocabulary quite different

[1] Chinese terms will be given here according to the Wade–Giles transliteration, with the Pinyin transliteration in parentheses after the first occurrence.
[2] These examples may be found among expressions recorded by Judith Jacob, The ecology of Angkor: evidence from the inscriptions. In *Nature and Man in South-East Asia*, ed. P. A. Stott, London: School of Oriental and African Studies, 1978, pp. 109–27, at pp. 125–7.

from those of the languages that have influenced it in historical times. It is a structure similar to those of many other South-East Asian languages, with a stock of basic one-syllable root words whose meanings are varied or modified by the addition of prefixes and infixes. Polysyllabic words not formed by inflexion of root monosyllables are usually Sanskrit or Pāli borrowings.

Beneath the layers of later borrowed vocabulary, the Khmer language is to be identified by its membership of language groupings indigenous to South-East Asia.

Languages fall into clusters and sub-clusters with presumed common origins. They can be arranged like a family tree. The study of relations between clusters can yield information about the origins and migrations of the ancestors of those who speak them.

There has been much recent study of the prehistory of Asian languages, and the implications of this sort of study for our understanding of Cambodia will need to be noticed further (see chapter 4). Here we are concerned simply with the nature of the Khmer language and its relations with others.

Attempts to divide languages into such families are still beset by doubt and debate. A widely used categorization of eastern Asian languages recognizes the following families: the Miao-Yao (spoken by minority hill peoples especially in southern China), Tai-Kadai, Austronesian and Austro-Asiatic. The Khmer language belongs in the last of these. Theories linking the prehistory of this Austro-Asiatic family with the others will be noticed below.

The Austro-Asiatic family includes Mon, Khmer, Vietnamese, the Munda and related languages of north-eastern India, the Aslian group of Malayan languages (Senoi, Semang, Negrito and others), Nicobarese, and Khasi in Assam. There are about 150 of these languages. The ancestors of the speakers of them were scattered over a large part of Asia in prehistoric times.

The Mon-Khmer sub-group is one major cluster within Austro-Asiatic. Mon and Khmer themselves are spoken by comparatively large and dense populations of agriculturalists, but there are many other closely related languages, spoken for the most part by small minority communities on the fringes of

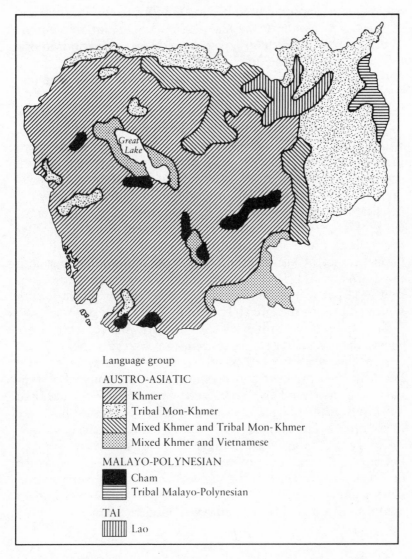

Language group

AUSTRO-ASIATIC

Khmer
Tribal Mon-Khmer
Mixed Khmer and Tribal Mon-Khmer
Mixed Khmer and Vietnamese

MALAYO-POLYNESIAN

Cham
Tribal Malayo-Polynesian

TAI

Lao

Map 2   Ethnic-linguistic groups, early 1970s

agricultural society; commonly they practise swidden farming and foraging in the hill regions. Mon-Khmer languages are spoken in Vietnam, Thailand and Laos as well as Cambodia; upland minority communities include the Khua, May, Ruc,

Sach, Khmu, Lamet, P'u Noi, T'in, Yumbri, Lawa, Palaung and Wa, as well as the Khasis of Assam.[3] Some of the upland 'montagnard' peoples practising swidden cultivation in the hill areas of Cambodia, particularly to the north, speak Mon-Khmer dialects, notably the Bahnar, Mnong Sedang and Loven.

The precise relationship between Khmer and other languages in the same sub-group is not clear. Khmer appears to be somewhat isolated.[4] D. T. Bayard suggests that the line between prehistoric speakers of Mon and Khmer lay through northeastern Thailand, with Mon speakers inhabiting the Khorat plateau and Khmer speakers elsewhere.[5]

The Mon speakers, like the Khmers, had an advanced agricultural society in ancient times, and there were Mon city-states dotted about in parts of Burma and Thailand. By the happenstance of history, the Mons were mostly absorbed into the Burmese and Thai empires. Mon speakers are now concentrated particularly in Tenasserim (the great majority), with scattered groups in central Thailand.

The ancient city-states of the Khmers, by contrast, were eventually consolidated to become an empire, Angkor, and despite the vicissitudes of history that unity has survived, and has tended to preserve and promote the uniformity of a standard language used by the citizens of successive Cambodian kingdoms. Khmer has long been established as a major language in the area. It has been subject to change through the centuries; the language of the inscriptions, from the earliest ones extant to the time of Angkor, is known as Old Khmer, while the language of about the fifteenth to the eighteenth centuries, surviving in chronicles, is called Middle Khmer, and the much better known language of the last two centuries is Modern Khmer.

---

[3] See F. Lebar, G. Hickey and J. Musgrave, *Ethnic Groups of Mainland Southeast Asia*, New Haven, Conn.: Human Relations Area Files, 1964.
[4] H. L. Shorto, The linguistic protohistory of mainland South-East Asia, with a comment by D. T. Bayard. In *Early South East Asia: Essays in archaeology, history and historical geography*, ed. R. B. Smith and W. Watson, New York: Oxford University Press, 1979, pp. 273–80, at p. 277.
[5] D. T. Bayard, Comment. In ibid., p. 279.

Plate 1   Cambodian farm women

Khmer Identity and Myth

The Khmer people can readily enough be identified from the outside, as it were, by the criteria of language, political organization and history. But what about identification from the inside? How do the Khmers identify themselves?

If we search Cambodian lore for clues to the origins of the Khmer identity, we find myths. These often contain the answers to important questions about culture and society, though not necessarily the questions which most interest us. 'Khmer', the

name used in the Khmer language itself, was perhaps responsible for the invention of a celestial being, Merā, to go with
Kambu in an early legend. (Thus 'Khmer' = 'Kambu–Merā'.)
First recorded in an inscription of AD 947, it tells of the holy
man Kambu Svāyambhuva. In Hindu myth, the latter name is a
title for a creator or progenitor figure. Kambu Svāyambhuya
married the nymph Merā, who came to him as a gift of the great
god Śiva. From this union descended the ruling house of the
Khmer people, the solar dynasty.

Another myth added a lunar ancestry to the solar. The notion
of a ruling house that originated in a sort of eternal dreamtime
from the union of sun and moon gods also played its part in
Indian lore. In the Hindu *purānas*, Ilā was a daughter of Manu,
the originator of humanity and founder of the solar race, who
was actually making a sacrifice to obtain sons but made a
mistake in the ritual and had a daughter instead; there are
various legends about her, but in one version she married
Budha (Mercury), who was the son of Soma the moon goddess;
this union of the lunar and solar lines appears in a number of
myths with adaptations to different sectarian needs. Similarly,
some kings of Angkor traced their descent to the union of a
solar line with a lunar one, with Kambu and Merā figuring as
founders of the solar line and Kaundinya and Somā, mythical
founders of the kingdom of 'Fu-nan' to the south, inaugurating
the lunar. In India, the sun was associated with the north and
the moon with the south. Felicitously, this mythical pattern
could be mapped upon the sacred geography of the lands of the
Khmers.

Geographical Environment and Myth

Whatever the historical links between the Khmer communities
and the kingdom near the coast known to the Chinese as 'Fu-
nan', we should not lose sight of the fact that the Khmers
themselves were not originally a coastal people. Their written
traditions may indeed owe a great deal to the commercial
culture laid down in the delta of the Mekong river where the
Indian traders came, but the Khmer civilization that received
these traditions probably took shape further north. It was a

civilization of the forested uplands. Before history began, it is likely that the closest links of the Khmers with neighbours were with the Chams of the Annamite Cordillera.

This is the direction indicated by another Khmer legend, that of Preah Thong, described as the exiled son of a king of Indraprastha, 'Indra's Palace'. This prince settled in Kok Thlok, the 'Land of the Thlok Tree'. He married a female serpent spirit dwelling beneath the waters (a Nāgī) who helped him to conquer the Chams. In one version, he seized the throne of the Cham king and changed the name of the kingdom to Kambuja. Variants of the story make the first king of the Khmers a Cham whose ship ran aground at Kok Thlok, perhaps in the area of Phnom Penh, which is accessible by water from the sea. The myth is kept alive by modern custom, playing a part in the ritual of weddings. It is possible that a Khmer kingdom was indeed founded by conquest from the Chams in the vicinity of the ancient sacred site of Vat Ph'u, near Bassac, although the evidence is very hazy. For the purpose of inferring historical fact the myths are of little value.

The Indian Connection

Now, it would be wrong to imagine that these sons of Kambu came from India, or even that they obtained their culture and identity from any sort of Indian colonization. The connections between the land of the Kambuja and any Indian prototype are equivocal and obscure.

One intriguing theory is that there was a connection with the Scyths, a central Asian people. We might seek an Indian original for the Kambuja in the ancient Kamboja, a warrior tribe of Scythian descent from far up in the north of what is now Pakistan.[6] These people, regarded as degraded by the brahmanical tradition, had the custom of shaving their heads, and Indian idiom knew the expression 'bald as a Kamboja'. There is some (very slight) support for the theory of a Scythian connec-

[6] One proponent of this view is E. Porée-Maspero; see her *Etude sur les rites agraires des cambodgiens*, 3 vols, Paris: Mouton, 1962–9, esp. vol. 3, pp. 701–819.

Plate 2 Cambodian bride and attendants. The bride is about twenty, as is the groom. Her costume shows Chinese influence

tion in C. Jacques's speculation that an early embassy sent from 'Fu-nan' to India may actually have found its destination in the very area that was occupied by the Kambojas.[7]

However, it must be acknowledged that the evidence for a Scythian impetus to the emergence of the Khmer kingdoms is too thin and conjectural to warrant more than passing notice. A knowledge of Kamboja throws no real light on the beginnings of Cambodia. The ancient Khmers were not regarded as a degraded warrior tribe; they were not bald; and they did not know anything of a Scythian ancestry that they have passed on to us. Above all, they were not Indians.

The Unification of the Khmers

In the earliest recorded times, there was no unified kingdom of the Kambuja. There was a multitude of chieftaincies or principalities dotted about what is now Cambodia, and beyond it into neighbouring countries (particularly Laos); they did not begin to feel themselves to be one people, the Kambuja, until a series of powerful rulers had created a unity that was at first fragile and fitful but eventually came to underpin a durable sense of peoplehood. The very name Kambuja was not, so far as is attested, in use until the period of Angkor – the earliest surviving mention comes in a Cham inscription dated AD 817, and the earliest mention in Cambodia itself dates from AD 947.

It is not legitimate to project the notion of Khmer nationality back to the beginning of history. The creation of such a nationality is something that must be accounted for historically. The unity of the Khmers as a group is not an irreducible *datum*, but came about for particular reasons. Somehow, a particular slice of humanity came to feel itself to be one people, and has so remained (in spite of the odds) ever since.

On the surface level of the historical record, the building of Khmer unity was the work of kings. No one ruler built it in one go, but the reign of Jayavarman II (*c*.770 – *c*.834) came to be remembered in subsequent reigns as the legitimizing foundation

---

[7] This suggestion is offered by C. Jacques, in Histoire préangkorienne du pays khmer. Unpublished MS.

of the Angkorian state. 'Angkor' is the name nowadays used for the place where most of Jayavarman's successors (though not Jayavarman himself) had their capitals – leaving their monuments for the admiration of an incredulous posterity – and for the empire that was ruled from these capitals. The name 'Angkor' represents the Khmer *Nokor* and is derived from the Sanskrit *nagara*, 'city'. In post-Angkorian times, the word came to mean more than just any city: it meant a royal capital, a centre of power over a kingdom or empire. Hence 'Angkor' has come to stand for the whole imperial achievement of the Khmers in the period of their greatness. What began as a constellation of small principalities has in modern times become a community, a people. It is with the shaping of this community that we shall be concerned here.

2

Images of the Khmers

Much of what we know about Cambodian history, particularly in the earliest times, comes from the writings of outsiders. Here is what a Chinese visitor recorded about the people he saw in the Mekong region: 'The men are of small stature and dark complexion, but many of the women are fair in complexion. All of them roll up their hair and wear earrings. They are lively and vigorous in temperament.'[1] These words, based on an observation originally recorded in the seventh century, describe the people of the Khmer kingdom known to the Chinese as Chen-la (Zhenla). In the thirteenth century, these small dark Khmers were redescribed by a later visitor, Chou Ta-kuan (Zhou Daguan), who did not care for some of their customs, as 'large and black'; but the women of the nobility were 'white as jade'. This whiteness, noticed long before by the earlier Chinese observer, is an interesting continuity, pointing to the way in which ladies of leisure were kept sequestered in the shadowy recesses of their homes, away from the bruising glare of direct sunlight. Later still, the Portuguese visitor San Antonio commented that the many wives of the Khmer nobility were white, while commoner women were brown.[2]

Let us take another foreigner's words:

[1] Ma Tuan-lin, *Ethnographie des peuples étrangers à la Chine*, tr. Marquis d'Hervey de Saint-Denys. Geneva: Georg, 1883, vol. ii, p. 479.
[2] Gabriel Quiroga de San Antonio, *Brève et véridique relation des événements du Cambodge*, tr. A. Cabaton. Paris: Leroux, 1914, p. 98.

The people have no knowledge of [advanced] agriculture, using picks and hoes. . . . All these shortcomings stem from the laziness of the Cambodians . . . my instructions to you are these; teach them to use oxen, teach them to grow more rice, teach them to raise mulberry trees, pigs and ducks. . . . If there is any outdated or barbarous custom that can be simplified, or repressed, then do so.[3]

These are the words of a Vietnamese emperor in 1838. For him, as for the Chinese, the Cambodians were barbarians, and their customs were a matter for reproach – all the more so, perhaps, because they stood so close to the Vietnamese in point of geography and civilization.

The Vietnamese emperor's concern to civilize the Cambodians was interestingly similar to the policy of the French, when their turn came. A Frenchman, working in the service of a benevolent colonial government, could afford to be more forgiving, though: in the eyes of Jean Delvert, author of the classic study of Cambodian farm life, the Khmer peasant is indeed indolent, but this is no more than a natural response to the physical conditions in which, unlike the womenfolk of the aristocracy, he has to work; and this influence converges with the tenets of his inherited Buddhist faith. His indolence is a form of wisdom. What struck Delvert particularly was not the Cambodian's laziness but his light-heartedness – '*Le paysan cambodgien est* gai' (Delvert's emphasis).[4] He continues:

In the aggregate, the physical type is *handsome*. The man is well constructed, his shoulders broad, his waist and hips narrow. The woman is comely: she has well-modelled shoulders, a fine bosom, a depth to her eye and a radiance to her smile; the habits of going barefoot and of carrying things on her head have braced her posture, so that in some cases she has a superb carriage; some women are thick-set, some on the other hand are tall and slender.[5]

He goes on to cite the opinion of G. Groslier: 'The dark skin of the peasant is partly due to the sun, for the skin of the stomach,

[3] *Dai Nam Thuc Luc Chinh Bien.* Cited by D. P. Chandler, *A History of Cambodia*, Boulder, Col.: Westview Press, 1992, p. 126.
[4] J. Delvert, *Le Paysan Cambodgien*. Paris: The Hague, Mouton, 1961, p. 137.
[5] Ibid., p. 135.

Plate 3 Young women selling birds in Phnom Penh. Purchasers earn Buddhist merit by setting the birds free immediately

pelvis and upper thighs, always covered by the sampot, is paler
than the rest of the body.'[6]

For another and more recent perception of Cambodia, we can
turn to other sorts of foreigners, who have come as pilgrims
since the colonial oficials have departed. They are not confronted so vividly by the largeness or smallness of the men, the
whiteness of the women, or the laziness or wisdom of the
farmers; they notice, rather, the *ambiance* of ancient ruins that
seem designed to give added meaning to the overworked word
'picturesque', and which for so many have distilled the essence
of Cambodian civilization. Around many of these monuments,
battered by time, the forest has come crowding. Galleries of
beetling dipterocarps strain upwards into the hot sky, their
trunks making a nave where bird cries echo in the cathedral
stillness.

Yet nothing is more certain than that the romance of crumbling ruins is no better as a witness to the reality of Cambodia's
past than the partial observations of transient foreigners. Gentle
melancholy and poetic confusion have nothing to do with the
Khmer civilization that gave birth to these monuments. In the
great days of Angkor, the true message of the architect's creation
was one of stern order and dynamic conquest, an imposition of
ideas as abstract as Plato's upon the microcosm of nature. It was
a world dominated by an obsessive cosmology that sought to
banish the dark profane forces of the wilderness to the further
side of a protected boundary, setting up an antithesis between
disordered, demon-haunted nature and the meticulously symbolic domain of divinely consecrated enclosures.

This is the image that we should recognize if we wish to
understand how the Khmers themselves saw their civilization –
an image of order, clarity and purpose mediated by divine
power.

For the Khmers of old, the contents of the world we inhabit
are but blurred and imperfect imitations of archetypes which
exist in eternity, pure and uncontaminated. Thus, heavenly
forms can be realized on earth by perfect actions and perfect
constructions. The Angkorian city, with its obsessive attention

[6]   Ibid., citing G. Groslier, *Recherches sur les Cambodgiens*, Paris: Challamel,
1921.

Plate 4   Ruined tower, Ta Prohm

to ritual design, was quite literally and practically a sacramental creation, making the ideal forms known from Hindu and Buddhist myth real and concrete in the world: the temple at the centre of the kingdom really became the centre of the universe and the home of the gods; the king at the centre of the government realized his identity with the impersonal ideal king in heaven; he became pure kingliness.

These are just ritual ideas, not delusions; the Khmers were practical people who dealt with the real world. But, not having our modern 'scientific' knowledge, they found it natural (like their contemporaries in western Europe) to suppose that they could tap in to some of the divine energy of the heavens by this sort of ritual mimesis. Each building was *imitating* the ideal form in heaven in order to realize it on earth.

This way of looking at the Khmer image of Khmer civilization helps us to make sense of a paradox: the way in which the creations of Cambodian art, architecture and ritual strove not to be themselves but to be *images of themselves*, like endless reflections in a hall of mirrors.

The notion is contradictory, for if the thing imaged is itself an image, what can the original reality be? It is a philosopher's conundrum. Yet there is nothing whimsical about this notion: it makes perfect sense if we recognize that each particular earthly form was trying to purify itself and become the ideal heavenly one. The logic of this aspiration is clearly enough at work in the art of the craftsmen who designed and chiselled the monuments that lie open to our inspection today. A simple example, characteristic of the earliest period of Khmer architecture, is the lintel which is not content to be a simple lintel, but which is sculpted as a fanciful image of one; its bas-relief carvings depict a series of arches whose ends are swallowed by sea monsters (*makaras*), themselves represented as supported by the capitals of columns quite distinct from the actual capitals of the columns which support the lintel.

Again, there are the characteristic false doors. The standard shrine construction associated with a temple is a square one-storey tower, with an open doorway on one side, and false doorways faithfully carved on the other three in imitation of the carpenter's craft. Or there are the tiered temple roofs, each tier a diminished version of the main structure below it; or the

Plate 5 False door at the Preah Koh (on tower dedicated to Jayavarman II), showing kāla *motif on the lintel*

miniature versions of temple towers that stand at the corners of terraced roofs. A temple thus constantly repeats and reduplicates itself. To be sure, the Indian prototypes from which these principles of temple design were derived had these features, but the Khmer genius pursued the logic of self-imaging relentlessly, even to the extent of sculpting false windows on some stone temple walls, with false stone curtains equipped with false stone draw-cords.

Conspicuously Khmer, too, are the 'flying palaces' characteristic of 'Chen-la' temple architecture: panels on walls decorated with relief carvings of structures that fly through empty space;

figures can be seen at the windows looking out at us from their looking-glass world.

In all this we see how a design may imitate itself. Perhaps there are parallels in other departments of culture. Perhaps we can see the emperors of Angkor as images of emperors, much as temples are images of temples. For the mighty rulers of this Ozymandias realm, lost by their own descendants and resurrected from the inscriptions that recorded their deeds, very rarely offer up to us any spontaneous display of their personal characteristics. On the contrary, every inscriptional record is an exercise in apotheosis: the king is portrayed, not as the real individual he is, but as an imitation of an ideal king in heaven.

Gladdening the sphere of his dominion with his talents, levying taxes that were imbued with lenience, causing hearts to expand, agreeable, he was appropriately lauded on account of his kingly virtue.[7]

The remarkable thing about this typical verse from an inscriptional *prasasti* (a conventional eulogy of the ruler in Sanskrit poetry) is that, like the false doors and lintels of Khmer architecture, it is not what it appears to be; or, rather, it is not only an overblown account of King Udayādityavarman's virtues but something else as well. The point is that by a deft use of words with alternative meanings the poet has contrived an extended pun, and the whole stanza can be read in a second, quite different, way:

Gladdening his orbit by his beams, sending out rays imbued with softness, causing the lotus to expand, agreeable, he was appropriately lauded on account of his lunar quality.

These words are in glorification of the sun god. This in no way diminishes their aptness to the praise of King Udayādityavarman, however, for 'Udayāditya' means 'Risen Sun'. The conventions of the poet thus presuppose an identification of the royal with the divine. It is worth noticing further that the combination of the ruler's solar identity with 'lunar quality' neatly evokes the genealogical myth which helped to cement the legitimacy of the rulers of Angkor: that they were descended from the union of two semi-divine lineages, the solar and the lunar.

[7] The stele inscription of Sdok Kak Thom, stanza XXI; G. Coedès and P. Dupont (eds), *Bulletin de l'Ecole française d'Extrême-Orient*, 43 (1943–6), pp. 57–134, at p. 78.

The task of a *praśasti* was sacramental: it was to superimpose the image of the divine upon the earthly king and kingdom. Little in the way of genuine biography will sneak into the eulogistic record; but it would be a mistake to see the *praśasti* as evidence merely of royal megalomania or the poet's sycophancy. The sacrament was part of the ritual that perpetuated Khmer psychological and cultural identity.

This is not to say that, because the ritual apparatus of Khmer royalty assimilated kings to gods, the subjects of the realm were deliberately and successfully deluded into mistaking their rulers for beings of a substantially different order. Symbolism and ritual were important and necessary to the state, but not as instruments of psychological control or levers upon subjects' loyalty. They were important and necessary in providing a conceptual framework within which people could recognize themselves as Khmer citizens.

In order to understand this, we need to take account of the pattern of social and political relationships that existed among the Khmers before the development of an imperial ideology to legitimize their submission to a single ruler.

As we look back at the history of this empire, it is easy to overlook the psychological and cultural stresses that attended its creation. There had to be a transitional period – and perhaps it was never entirely superseded – when rulers came from particular families well known to belong to, and to have vested interests in, particular communities, yet had beneath their rule majorities of subjects from other communities with no natural bonds of loyalty. Inscriptions refer to regional capitals such as Bhavapura, Indrapura, Aninditapura, Amoghapura. The actual sites of such cities are often in doubt, but they all had their great families, and many of these had supplied more or less independent rulers in one period of history or another.

Some recent scholarship has helped us to see how strong were the continuing traditions of the localities, former little principalities whose lordly families harboured ancient royal claims and waited for opportunities to reassert their independence.[8] Several times, when succession was disputed, rival monarchs

[8] For example, M. Vickery, The reign of Sūryavarman I and royal factionalism at Angkor. *Journal of Southeast Asian Studies*, 16, no. 2 (1985), pp. 226–44.

based their campaigns upon those territories where they could command the ancient loyalties of local tradition. There is no doubt that emperors had to struggle constantly to assert and maintain their authority.

The earlier kings of Angkor had beneath their rule conglomerations of people, many of them recently enslaved, who lacked inherited traditions of shared identity. The actual basis of power lay in practical considerations such as commercial advantage, distribution of population and access to scarce resources. If the institutions of Khmer political unity were to persist, people needed a vocabulary to describe it, a set of terms that would give the king a role transcending the traditions of locality and making of his kingdom an image of a transcendent city of the gods. Hence the obsessive cosmological symbolism that made nearly every detail of metropolitan art an evocation of the divine.

None of this means, of course, that kings were worshipped as gods and given unquestioning obedience by all their subjects. It would be a mistake to imagine that 'god-kingship' in that sense was ever practised in Cambodia. Rivals for the throne led armies into battle; kings slept uneasily, never knowing whom they could trust. Beliefs about the world of the gods provided a vocabulary to describe royal power, and ritual for augmenting it; but no royal destiny was proof against being superseded.

The notion of a Khmer kingdom, a throne that commanded the loyalty of all Cambodians, did not serve as the instrument of a totalitarian state; what it did, rather, was to serve as the focus or symbol of an increasingly durable community. As time went on, however, the fall of a Khmer ruler was less and less likely to signal the fragmentation of Cambodia into independent principalities; even after years of war, it was increasingly likely that the Khmer state would be reconstituted. In the following chapters we shall be examining the various factors that played a part in the evolution of this state.

3

The Land

Sometimes faraway countries are known best by the rare products which are imported from them; sometimes a product is known by the name of the country which exports it (such as 'chinaware'). The name of Cambodia is enshrined in 'gamboge', defined as 'a gum-resin obtained from trees of the genus *Garcinia*, natives of Cambodia, Siam, etc. It is largely used as a pigment, giving a bright yellow colour, and also as a drastic purgative.'[1] These applications do not suggest anything symbolic (though there is an obvious appropriateness of the image of catharsis to the tragic history of the 1970s); significantly, though, the fact that the country should be embodied in the name of a forest product is a reminder of something easily overlooked about the Khmer environment: the Khmers, throughout much of their history, were forest dwellers. As a French missionary described the country in the 1850s:

The illustrious Khmer realm is still a wild country despite its ancient civilization. It could be described as a huge forest. Only here and there, beside the rivers or within the interior, around a few ricefields, there have sprung up groups of wretched huts whose inhabitants exert themselves no more than is needed to avoid dying of hunger.[2]

Father Bouillevaux, who wrote these words, has incidentally the best claim to have 'discovered' the remains of Angkor for the west after their long silvan hibernation.

[1] *Shorter Oxford English Dictionary*, s.v. Gamboge.
[2] C. E. Bouillevaux, *L'Annam et le Cambodge*. Paris: Victor Palmé, 1874, pp. 92f.

Plate 6   Rural houses

To be sure, Cambodia was not always the sparsely inhabited wilderness which he describes. Bouillevaux lived in a Cambodia decimated by a long period of war. But we must remember that a hundred years later, when the population had grown to about 4.6 million, the Khmers were distributed over an area of roughly 70,000 square miles or about 180,000 square kilometres; the capital, Phnom Penh, had a population of about a quarter of a million. There are only approximate estimates of the population before and after the savage depredations of the 1970s; probably there were over six million Cambodians at the beginning of the decade, and about four million by the end of the Pol Pot regime. By the early 1990s, the estimated population of the country was thought to have climbed beyond six million.

During most of their history, the Cambodians have been distributed sparsely over their territory, most of them living in small agricultural settlements. Their traditions were those of the small, face-to-face community; when institutions of kingship appeared, they were probably remote and wonderful to most Cambodians. In the twentieth century, a Cambodian could write:

Plate 7   Ox carts with straw

In former times . . . there were no canals, and no paths; there were only forests, with tigers, elephants, and wild buffaloes; no people dared to leave their villages.

For this reason, hardly anyone ever went to the royal city. If anyone ever reached it, by poling his canoe, the others would ask him about it: 'What is the king's appearance like? Is he like an ordinary man?' And the traveller, seeing all these ignorant people asking questions, would reply: 'The king has an elegant, beautiful appearance, unstained by dust or sweat; he has no scars . . .' But of course often he had never seen the king at all.[3]

This describes a period of decline, when the Cambodians were struggling for survival in isolated rural settlements. But the wilderness or forest has always figured prominently in the awareness of Cambodians. Trees are a feature of the environ-

[3]   Institut Bouddhique, Phnom Penh, Commission des Moeurs et Coutumes Cambodgiennes, Archive no. 94004, cited by D. P. Chandler, *A History of Cambodia*, Boulder, Col.: Westview Press, 1992, pp. 47–8.

ment in a way that they are not, for example, in the intensively farmed areas of China. Khmer farmers have not been so short of space that everything wild had to go. Trees and bushes are tolerated or deliberately planted. Quite often they are revered as the abodes of watching spirits. Further, they give shade to workers toiling beneath the unforgiving Cambodian sun; and their fruit is often a useful addition to the daily diet.

It is a civilization that grew up with trees. In woodland clearings, or along the upper courses of forest streams, the Khmers lived first in isolated settlements that were surrounded on all sides by the dark disorder of nature. Angkor, the zenith of their art, was a culminating assertion of order all the more strident because its authors knew nature so well. The wilderness was never far away, and a polarity of wild and tamed, of dark haunted bushland versus inhabited open spaces – *brai* and *sruk* – runs like a leitmotiv through Khmer cultural consciousness. In the wilderness were unknown and therefore dangerous spirits; being wild, their unpredictable powers could work greater good or ill than the familiar, measured energies of the local divinities that were patrons of cults in the settled environment. The immortal and invisible spirits that dwelled everywhere in the natural environment are fundamental to an understanding of the mental universe of the Khmers.

In the nineteenth century, it was estimated that an elephant journey in the dry season from Battambang to Siemreap (about 50 miles as the crow flies) would take five days; the scholar-administrator Etienne Aymonier described a journey from Battambang to Mongkolborei (no more than 30 miles) as taking two days. In 1895, a French official described the Kampong Thom region as wild grassland; during the seasonal floods, wildfowl and boars would wander into the precincts of the new Residency. At Angkor, no life stirred but enormous birds that strutted solemnly among the ruins.

Wild animals too were always familiar tokens of the wilderness, outnumbering the scattered groups of humans. These have included parrots, black and white ibises, kingfishers, vultures, crows, egrets, sparrows, cormorants, storks, cranes, wild ducks, canaries, peafowl, and iridescent birds that haunted the tree-tops. Elephants, important in the court traditions of Indian kingdoms, used to be valued engines of war or vehicles of state.

Plate 8 Sugar palms

One Angkorian inscription referred to the damage done to the embankments of a reservoir by the trampling feet of elephants, which should henceforth be kept off. A Chinese source records a mission sent from China in 1320 to buy Cambodian elephants. Tigers haunted the dark forest; ancient toponyms recorded in inscriptions reveal the presence of pythons, bees, crocodiles, wild boar, tortoises and leeches; there were hills named after lizards and ants, as well as deer and buffalo.[4] The rhinoceros was hunted for the medicinal properties of its body parts, as well as its horn. The thirteenth-century Chinese visitor Chou Ta-kuan mentions tigers, panthers, bears, wild boar, stags, gibbons and foxes; he reports that there were no lions or camels, that the horses were only small, that oxen were used for draught, and that there were crocodiles which seemed to him like dragons.[5]

When we turn to the physical surroundings of the Khmers, this ancient inland environment of wilderness and forest should be kept in mind. The Khmers are an *inland* people, at home in an upriver environment. No major river runs through Cambodia to the Gulf of Siam. The historical main artery of commercial and cultural traffic, and axis of settlement, has always been supplied by the Mekong River and its main tributaries. The Mekong enters Cambodia from the north and leaves by the south-east to flow through southern Vietnam to the sea. For parts of their history (and as late as the seventeenth century), the Khmers dominated the Mekong delta area, but it was far from the centre of Khmer power and came, rather, under the influence of the Cham kingdoms of central and southern Vietnam, permanent rivals of the Khmers, who never became known as sailors and traders on the international routes. The line marking the historical limit of Khmer settlement runs southward from the Dong Nai, approximately through Bien-Hoa, Saigon (Ho Chi Minh City), Baria and Cap St-Jacques.[6]

---

[4] On the evidence of inscriptions, see J. Jacob, The ecology of Angkor: evidence from the inscriptions. In *Nature and Man in South East Asia*, ed. P. A. Stott, London: School of Oriental and African Studies, 1978.

[5] Chou Ta-kuan, *Mémoires sur les coutumes du Cambodge de Tcheou Takouan*, tr. P. Pelliot. Paris: Ecole française d'Extrême-Orient, 1951, p. 28.

[6] B.-P. Groslier, Pour une géographie historique du Cambodge, *Les Cahiers d'Outre-Mer*, vol. 104 (1973), pp. 337–79, at p. 354.

Plate 9   Mekong River – sunset

Further, the coastal area of Cambodia is quite sparsely inhabited and hilly. The Cardamom Hills occupy much of it. The
port of Kompong Som or Sihanoukville, a modern city, marks
a new orientation unrelated to the past.

The natural vegetation of Cambodia can be divided into
zones of forest and grassland. A wide strip along the coast
favours evergreen hygrophytic woodland; further inland, the
areas of mountain grassland are surrounded by deciduous
monsoon forest. The dichotomy of wet, coastal lowland and
forested upland, south-east versus north, marks an important
duality in the ecology of Khmer settlement. Prehistoric Khmer-
speaking people probably inhabited the uplands, while the
trade-orientated civilizations of the coast, perhaps peopled by
speakers of Indonesian-related languages, developed around the
beginning of the Christian era. Later on, under the kingdom
known to the Chinese as 'Chen-la', the centre of civilization in
what is now Cambodia shifted toward the Great Lake, in the
vicinity of Siemreap. During a long history of migration and
expansion, both zones have contributed to shape the experience
and culture of the Cambodians.

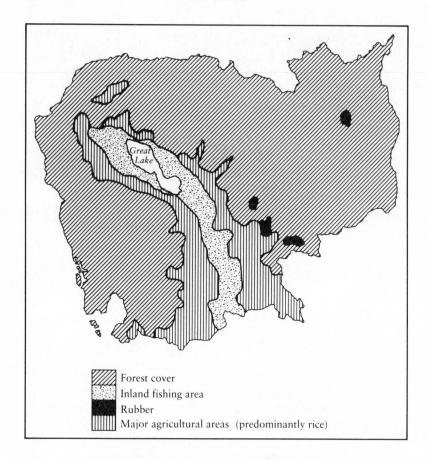

Forest cover
Inland fishing area
Rubber
Major agricultural areas (predominantly rice)

Map 3   Economic activities

Much of the territory of Cambodia is occupied by scattered communities of minority peoples who derive their living from hunting, collecting forest produce or simple farming (often slash-and-burn agriculture). These people are to be found in the hilly regions – primarily the Cardamom Hills to the south and the Dangrek Mountains to the north, between the Lakes area and the Mun River.

Between these two zones, and southward to the Vietnamese border, runs the corridor of agricultural Khmer settlement. It is specifically this area, which occupies only about a third of the total territory of the country but contains the overwhelming majority of its inhabitants, that is studied by Jean Delvert in his work on the Cambodian peasant; all his maps draw a line around it, ignoring the rest of the country. It looks like a pistol aimed at Thailand, an image that reverses the relationship of relatively recent times. Within this area, most people outside the cities follow occupations that connect them closely with the land, usually as rice farmers. So have their ancestors from time immemorial.

The life of the farmer has always been rigorous, but in some ways Cambodia is worse off than other parts of the region. The soil is shallow; sandy soils of some parts are very poor, and the clay soils of other parts typically consist of a mere 0.3 metres (about 12 inches) on a hard infertile bed.

Plate 10   Rice fields, Siemreap

The precipitation, nowadays about a metre a year, is only just what is needed for the cultivation of the main rice crop. Often, after a false start to the monsoon, there is a miniature dry season in June and July, or at the other end of the season the rains (which have a higher acid content than is good for the crop) may end prematurely, in October, and the local pattern of rainfall can be very irregular, with some small areas favoured and others left dry. In the 1950s and 1960s, groups of Chinese would assemble on the roof of a hotel in Phnom Penh and place bets on where the rain would fall.

Water is of course essential to settlement; communities cluster along river courses or around lakes. A village situated any distance from a river must have a reservoir, called a *beng*. Hamlets cluster (as in the past) around collective ponds, *trapeang*, which are shared by several families. Wells are dug with a primitive technology, wherever they are practical, but it is notable that over a substantial area to the west of Phnom Penh there is no accessible water table and hence no potable water on the spot. In other areas. particularly in the sandy alluvia and in much of the lowlands, water can be reached at only a few metres' depth.

Plate 11   Typical field system, seen from the summit of Phnom Bakheng

There are several different sorts of agricultural environment, all dependent upon their position in relation to the rivers and lakes. Generally speaking, and for obvious reasons, the closer to water the better. Particularly favoured are the seasonally breached banks alongside a river, both the top surface and the slopes that are exposed as the water level declines with the onset of the dry season; riverside villages with orchards and intensively cultivated strips of paddy extend in ribbons along the river banks. When the floods come, a large area to either side of the river is under water, and close around this are the wetlands where paddy can be grown with little difficulty. Further away, agriculture is carried on upon a low platform of clay soil, wherever there are lakes, ponds or streams. Clay soils are retentive of water and good for rice. Humus-rich soils such as occur to the south of the Tonle Sap lake are good for agriculture, but many parts of the shore of this lake, though inherently fertile, are not much used because of drainage problems. Alluvium is best of all, particularly if it is poorly drained, for this provides the right conditions for rice so long as the water is not excessive. Further away still are the sandy soils that rise to the higher plains and the zones of grassland and light forest.

Plate 12 Ploughing and planting

Everything depends upon the monsoon rains. They come in
May and end in November; very little falls in other months. In
Phnom Penh, for example, there is precipitation of about 1.2
metres in the period from May to November, only 0.22 metres
from December to April. The rains, at their height, come dramatically, in fierce deluges accompanied by thunder and sudden
gusting squally winds.

The dry season, by contrast, is very dry and hot. The mean
annual temperature on the plains is 27°C (hotter than southern
Vietnam or Bangkok); Phnom Penh has 35°C in April.[7] The
conditions are much more unpleasant in the dry season than
such figures suggest because of the combination of heat and
aridity. In comparison with the rest of Indochina, Cambodia
has more hours of sunshine and thus a much higher ratio of
temperature to rainfall. The soil cannot very well be worked in
these conditions, and the farmer would prefer, if the pressing
needs of survival permit, to devote himself as far as possible to
indoor work.

Parched and enervating, the Cambodian dry season seems to
dry up the springs of life itself:

In March and April, the beds of the rivers are almost all dried out; the
grass plains and the ricefields under stubble are like one great straw
mattress, which is frequently set on fire. The open forest is baleful with
its yellowed grasses, its wizened trees with their splitting trunks, its
floor bestrewn with great red gleaming leaves that crackle beneath the
feet. The whole country, man and beast, suffers from want of water:
the ponds are dried up. In Phnom Penh, the drawers of water come in
long processions to the few water outlets to fill the drums which they
carry all round the town.[8]

This, then, is the environment in which the Khmers manage
today to find their ecological niche.

How did history bring them to fill it in the first place? It
will help if we take account of the particular character of
the zone where Angkor arose. The success of Angkor as a centre
of empire needs to be attributed in part to its situation in a
relatively fertile zone capable of supporting a substantial population, and with good access to resources elsewhere.

[7]   J. Delvert, *Le Paysan Cambodgien*. Paris: The Hague, Mouton, 1961, p. 35.
[8]   Ibid., p. 42.

Satellite photography reveals a large trapezium-shaped area between the western Dangreks and the north-west shore of the Great Lake that was once subject to a massive erosion which was possibly the cause of the formation of the lakes. The region around Siemreap, however, was protected from this erosion by the Kulen hills, and thus stood in an island of fertile soil.[9] (How far the agricultural productivity of this soil was enhanced by irrigation is a sensitive question which will be noticed further, in chapter 12.) In historical times it came to enjoy the advantages of an environment suitable for agriculture, access to the rich stocks of fish in the lake, and a good strategic location.

The significance of the location can be brought out by considering the pattern of Khmer settlement. When written records first provide evidence, there appear to have been communities along the course of the Mekong, as far north as the area of Bassac in Laos and probably along the Mun river. These settlements also extended downriver to the great confluence near Phnom Penh known as Quatre Bras. The 'Four Arms' of this great confluence of waterways are marked by the junction of the Mekong and the Tonle Sap. The latter connects the Mekong with the Great Lake to the north-west. This route has historically been a main artery of communication.

A study reported by R. C. Ng sought to identify the ecological conditions which shaped the patterns of Khmer migration and settlement, using three major criteria to identify the places where, all else being equal, settlement would be favoured. These were terrain suitable for paddy growing (not too steep), inherent fertility of the soil, and the presence of drinkable water. The combination of these criteria, used to eliminate all areas that were unsuitable for agricultural settlement, leaves us with two major favourable zones: one is a corridor with Angkor at its northern end that broadens out as it runs south-eastwards to the Mekong and to the coast of Vietnam; the other is a belt running east–west with its ends at Vat Ph'u and Phimai.[10]

[9] B.-P. Groslier, La cité hydraulique angkorienne. Exploitation ou surexploitation du sol?, *Bulletin de l'Ecole française d'Extrême-Orient*, 66 (1979), pp. 161–202, at p. 162.
[10] R. C. Ng, The geographical habitat of historical settlement in mainland Southeast Asia. In *Early South East Asia: Essays in archaeology, history and historical geography*, ed. R. B. Smith and W. Watson, New York: Oxford University Press, 1979, esp. map, p. 271.

These are precisely the areas of Khmer habitation from very ancient times. Perhaps, indeed, the pattern of Khmer settlement is part of the explanation of the eventual success of the Khmers in creating a durable empire: the zone of settlement just described was so configured that most of the population could quite cheaply be reached by armies sent out from the capital, and therefore were relatively easily controlled.

It is not only the geographical distribution of settlement that gave rulers an advantage in asserting their authority; it was also the bounty of nature that helped to sustain a relatively concentrated urban population around the flood plain of the Great Lake. Every year, the melting of the Himalayan snows which feed the Mekong combines with the coming of the monsoon rains in May to send a huge surge of floodwater downstream. This surge is so great that, after some months, it causes the Tonle Sap to reverse direction and carry the waters back up to the Great Lake, which increases in area from 2,700 square kilometres at its minimum in the dry season to 10,000 square kilometres in the wet; a third of the cultivable lowland area of Cambodia is flooded. The rate of flow of the Mekong itself increases from a minimum (dry season) of 1,700 cubic metres a second to a dramatic 34,000 cubic metres a second – and it carries 10,000 kilograms of silt a second.[11]

So far as agriculture in Angkorian times went, this made available two ways of supplementing the basic rainwater-fed main crop. One was the option of planting 'floating rice', a long-stemmed variety which grows rapidly to a great height and keeps pace with slowly rising floodwater. This could be cultivated wherever the floodwaters did not rise so fast as to drown it. The other, not favoured by independent farmers because of the onerous toil involved but effective enough for employers of organized labour, was the growing of a dry-season crop in water temporarily trapped from the retreating floods by small-scale earthworks built around three sides of a miniature reservoir (a *tanub*) or across the course of a stream.

The teeming fisheries of the Great Lake made a great contribution to the Cambodian diet. Among the Khmer, the technol-

[11]   C. F. Higham, *The Archaeology of Mainland Southeast Asia*. Cambridge: Cambridge University Press, 1989, pp. 6–9.

ogy of fishing, the taxonomy of species, the craft of fish cuisine and the science of garnishes and seasoning for fish dishes are all brought to a high pitch of scientific refinement.

Innumerable varieties of fish live in the lakes; the flooded forests make a particularly good breeding ground, providing a protected environment for spawning and abundant supplies of plankton to feed on. Every year from November to April – principally January and February in the Tonle Sap – the fish migrate in droves during monthly periods of seven or eight days in a rhythm governed by the moon. In these periods especially, they can be hauled out of the water by the basket-load. Fishermen have devised a formidable array of rods, traps, barrages and baskets to lure the fish into their hands; there is a whole armoury of basketwork devices – the *trou*, the *lop*, the *angrouth*, the *chneang tram* (a hand-drawn trawling or dredging apparatus), and many more. The fish are used fresh or they are dried, salted, smoked, or made into a pinkish fermented paste called *prahoc*. They are made into soups; they are eaten with onions or herbs or a variety of seasonings. They are a

Plate 13   Fishing, Siemreap

valuable source of protein and constitute perhaps the most basic and regular sauce to garnish the staple bowl of rice.

The abundance of the Tonle Sap's resources was one factor that helped sustain the rise of the Khmer population, and hence the power of the Khmer kingdom. One teasing question is whether that abundance is the same today as it was in the days of Angkorian greatness. Some think that the men of old were better off than their modern descendants: it may be that the Great Lake of the Tonle Sap is actually shrinking, and this may be a result of reduced rainfall. An inscription of AD 850 associated with a temple a little way to the north-west of Siemreap refers to a shore and a ferry in its vicinity.[12] Possibly the extensive deforestation that attended the construction of Khmer settlements through the long history of the old kingdoms actually affected the precipitation.[13] Apart from that, the whole area may have been affected by a climatic shift that brought a diminution of rainfall.[14]

The effects of deforestation may indeed have been disastrous in the long run. As Groslier has argued, the needs of Angkor for timber and fuel must have caused considerable deforestation; this would encourage leaching and compacting of the soil, with large-scale erosion and cutting of ravines; convection rains would diminish.[15]

We cannot at present know for certain. But the suspicion must linger that maybe the destiny of the ancient Khmers was more securely tied to the fate of their spirit-haunted forests than they ever knew.

[12] Groslier claims this in La cité hydraulique angkorienne, at p. 163. The inscription is that of Prasat Cak, K521 (south tower); see G. Coedès, *Inscriptions du Cambodge*. Paris and Hanoi: Ecole française d'Extrême-Orient, 1937–66, vol. 4, pp. 168f, 'Inscription de Prasat Cak', referring to an endowment by Jayavarman III.

[13] Groslier refers to Chou Ta-kuan's statement that the dry season lasted for six months as evidence of a change that has taken place in the climate since the time of Angkor: La cité hydraulique, p. 186.

[14] See ibid., and J. Needham, *Science and Civilisation in China*, vol. III. Cambridge: Cambridge University Press, 1959, p. 463. The latter offers only weak support for Groslier's claim, since the climatic amelioration it suggests is largely confined to northern China during the first millennium BC.

[15] Groslier, La cité hydraulique.

4

Before History Began

History is known from written sources. Before the Khmers had any writing, what were they doing? How did they acquire the civilization that they possessed when they appear in the earliest written records?

Such questions lead us far back in time, and enlarge the geographical scope of our concern to embrace the prehistory of mainland South-East Asia as a whole. The ancestors of the modern Khmers were not a self-contained group. In this and the following chapters, we shall be concerned with the lessons to be drawn from the archaeology of the surrounding parts of South-East Asia.

Rapid strides have been made in the progress of archaeology in the region, and ideas about its prehistory have altered radically. Further strides remain to be made, and our notions will alter correspondingly in the future, but the insights to be gained from recent research are beginning to engage with hard facts about the earlier occupants of South-East Asia. In the past, on the other hand, much of what was inferred about prehistory was largely guesswork.

It is not only archaeology that is bringing about this progress. Other disciplines, such as linguistics, are contributing. When we looked at the Khmer language in chapter 1, we noticed that it belongs to the Austro-Asiatic family, which spread across parts of Asia in prehistoric times. There is debate about the nature of its relations with the neighbouring language groups, such as the Austronesian which spread very widely across Asia and into the Pacific.

One hypothesis seeks to relate the evolution of these language groups to developments in prehistoric cultures. It proposes that the geographical spread of a language family is likely to reflect the expansion of an agricultural population. The assumption made is that a language spreads to new territories either because its speakers migrate there or because it is adopted by people living there. In the latter case, the people who adopt it must have a reason for doing so, such as that the language is associated with economic strength and political dominance.

Using these principles of interpretation, some prehistorians have sought to map the movement of people and agriculture in prehistoric Asia from the evidence of language distribution; the conclusion to this line of thought is that one original home of agriculture, based on rice cultivation, lay in southern China, in a zone extending southwards from the Yangtze valley. The earliest sites known are in the area of P'eng-t'ou-shan (Pengtoushan) on the shore of Lake Tung-t'ing (Dongting) in the Yangtze valley. Another, separate, home lay further north in the Yellow River valley, with millet as the staple. One main family of languages carried far and wide by the farmers from southern China was the Austro-Asiatic, which is the one to which Khmer belongs.[1]

What the migration theory of origins proposes for South-East Asia is that by about 3,000 BC the agricultural civilization of southern China, with its several families of languages, had spread along the coast of China to northern Vietnam and across to Thailand; perhaps also it reached India (as the presence of 'Austro-Asiatic' languages there suggests), absorbing local people and cultures on the way. A site which is thought to represent an early stage of this development in South-East Asia is Phung Nguyen in the Red River valley; people there cultivated rice, and a variety of artefacts has been recovered, including

---

[1] On the postulated links between Asian languages, migrations and agriculture, see P. Bellwood, The Austronesian dispersal and the origin of languages, *Scientific American*, 265 (July 1991), pp. 88–93 (this is the pagination of an edition consulted in Australia); idem, Southeast Asia before history, in *The Cambridge History of Southeast Asia*, ed. N. Tarling, Cambridge: Cambridge University Press, 1992, vol. 1, pp. 55–136. The other major language groups which have been said to come from early farmer origins are the Austronesian and the Tai-Kadai. This hypothesis is not universally accepted, however.

stone arrowheads, knives, baked clay spindle whorls and bow pellets.[2]

Although prehistorians, by and large, agree on the origin of rice-based agriculture in an area extending southwards from the Yangtze valley, there is room for debate about the manner in which it spread south and the extent to which autonomous developments in the southern lands contributed to the process. Some argue that contact with the incoming culture with origins in south Chinese populations might have been a stimulus, but that local ecological factors were more important conditions of the transition to agriculture. In order to identify some of these local ecological factors, we need to narrow the focus to the prehistoric environment within South-East Asia.

The evidence of human habitation in Cambodia itself goes back a long way. Pebble cultures from the old stone age are attested at a number of sites; in eastern Cambodia, between Snoul and Chep, there have been found pebble implements in deposits thought to date to as early 600,000 years ago. Comparable finds in northern Thailand have been judged older still.[3]

For a long period after 13,000 BC the mainland of South-East Asia was home to a variety of stone-using cultures in which various improvements in technology took place. These cultures are collectively labelled 'Hoabinhian' after the province in northern Vietnam where many of their sites are found. By the third millennium BC, settlements of people practising hunting, gathering and simple agriculture were appearing in the Khorat plateau, the Tonle Sap area and the Mekong delta. Some of these were probably the ancestors of the Khmers. We know about them from a number of archaeological excavations, particularly on the Khorat plateau.

The places favoured by these communities were mostly near the banks of streams, tributaries rather than major rivers, and in the intermediate levels between the higher uplands and flooded plains. Rice could be adequately watered but not drowned in such localities. Various animals were domesticated, including

[2] Ha Van Than, Nouvelles recherches préhistoriques et protohistoriques au Vietnam, *Bulletin de l'Ecole française d'Extrême-Orient*, 68 (1980), pp. 113–54.

[3] E. Saurin, Le paléolithique du Cambodge oriental, *Asian Perspectives*, IX (1966), pp. 96–110.

cattle, pigs and dogs. Possibly all of these were eaten. Large game, including deer, was hunted; the diet included a great deal of fish, as well as chicken and frogs. Shellfish were also collected. People may also have eaten many things not actually represented by remaining evidence – including dung beetles, wild yams, bamboo shoots or mushrooms.[4] Starvation was not a common cause of death (but some people suffered from anaemia or arthritis). As C. Higham remarks, 'the prehistoric occupants of Ban Na Di were as robust as Finnish farmers and modern inhabitants of the State of Ohio'.[5]

In Cambodia itself, the site of Laang Spean has yielded important evidence. The oldest cultural level claimed for it has been dated to a period from about 6,800 BC, and provides evidence of Hoabinhian hunters and gatherers who made no pottery. The second level, dated to about 4,290 BC, was marked by various scraping and grating tools, made by people who had a varied diet and made a cord-marked type of pottery; from this level came remains of many animals including cattle, deer and reptiles. It provides evidence of 'Hoabinhian'-style industry as early as the fifth millennium BC, with polished stone artefacts from about 4,000 BC; it was inhabited over a very long period.[6]

To the north of modern Cambodia, the Khorat plateau sites, excavated in recent years, are particularly important; some of them have occasioned a great deal of debate. So far as the evidence goes, it is not provable that agriculture arrived earlier in the region than about 3,000 BC, and one interpretation of this development is that its appearance in the archaeological record probably represents the direct effect of newcomers who already had agriculture and were linked with northern Vietnam and southern China. This fits in with the migration theory based partly on linguistic evidence that was reviewed above. However, there is a rival interpretation of the evidence from upriver mainland South-East Asia: that the agricultural and later

[4] C. F. Higham, *The Archaeology of Mainland Southeast Asia*. Cambridge: Cambridge University Press, 1989, pp. 86, 130–3.

[5] Ibid., pp. 139f.

[6] Three later levels are dated to the late third millennium BC, the mid-first (not rich in artefacts but with plenty of pottery), and the late first millennium AD. See R. Mourer, Préhistoire du Cambodge. *Archéologia*, no. 233 (March 1988), pp. 40–52.

Map 4   Prehistoric sites

bronze-using sites such as those of the Khorat plateau represent influence arriving from the coast to the south, where, on this theory, agriculture developed close to the swampy shores that provided a favourable environment for it. On this second view, any influence produced by the extension of early farming from southern China would be much less direct.

The sites themselves do not, in the present state of scholarly belief, provide clear evidence one way or the other. The Spirit Cave site in northern Thailand (with occupation dates approximately from the eleventh to the sixth millennia BC), though attesting an interesting range of plants and once thought to be the home of very early agriculture, is now recognized as offering no evidence of plant domestication. Not far from Spirit Cave is the Banyan Valley site, which evidences the gathering of wild rice some time after 3,500 BC.

Non Nok Tha, in north-east Thailand on the western side of the Khorat plateau, also gives evidence of agriculture in the floodplains. Its dating has proved problematic; on current opinion the habitation it evidences likely does not date to before 2,000 BC. As will be noticed below, the chronology of Non Nok Tha is bound up with the problem of dating the appearance of bronze technology in the region.

Skeletons from some sites, notably Non Nok Tha (which yielded 188 complete or partial skeletons), tell us something about life in these ancient settlements. The average life expectancy seems to have risen over the course of the centuries, suggesting steady improvement in the control of the environment. People were shorter than their modern descendants; at Non Nok Tha men grew to between 162 and 178 centimetres (5 ft 3 ins to 5 ft 8 ins) and women to between 142 and 157 centimetres (4 ft 6 ins to 5 ft 1½ ins). Their teeth show the marks of a rough diet; possibly they chewed areca nuts (a custom that has survived to modern times).

About 120 kilometres (75 miles) east of Non Nok Tha is the site of Ban Chiang, which has yielded evidence of habitation over a long period. In its early phase, beginning about 3,000 BC, its occupants domesticated various animals such as chicken and cattle, and ate a meat diet including shellfish and turtles. Fish predominated. They ate rice. Some time after 2,000 BC they used bronze, a development to be reviewed below.

This is the picture offered by archaeology. In summary, agriculture is seen to have spread across much of mainland South-East Asia in the third millennium BC; there is disagreement about the route by which it spread.

What sort of factors are likely to have favoured the development of rice agriculture? One long-held view is that domestication is likely to have occurred where a good variety of wild rice was available to communities of gatherers. South-East Asia had this variety in prehistoric times; the core area where rice species occurred naturally lay in Assam, Bengal, Burma, Thailand and Cambodia, and is now recognized to have extended well into southern China, with probable widespread availability in a wide marginal zone around this area. One species, *Oryza fatua*, an ancestor of the modern cultivated *Oryza sativa*, was still found wild in the 1930s in Cambodia, near the Tonle Sap.[7] It has been claimed, further, that wild water rice was independently domesticated in the Red River delta area as early as the fifth millennium BC.[8] Remains of rice husks have been found in potsherds dating from about the third millennium BC at Ban Chiang, and milled kernels at Ban Na Di dating from about 1,500–900 BC.[9]

On this view, then, mainland South-East Asia was a favoured location for the development of agriculture. Long ago, Carl Sauer enunciated the principle that plant domestication is likely to occur where wild species abound,[10] and some prehistorians are inclined to see agriculture in the region as almost entirely a local development. Others, however, emphasize the contribution of outsiders. They argue that the major shift from a foraging lifestyle to agriculture is not likely to be undertaken except in special conditions, and rarely happens within a stable environment unless there is a stimulus from outside.[11]

---

[7] See R. Hill, On the origins of domesticated rice. *Journal of Oriental Studies*, 14 (1976), pp. 35–44.

[8] Nguyen Phuc Long, Les nouvelles recherches archéologiques au Vietnam. *Arts Asiatiques*, XXXI (1975), pp. 1–154 (special number); Ha Van Tan, Nouvelles recherches préhistoriques et protohistoriques au Vietnam. *Bulletin de l'Ecole française d'Extrême-Orient*, LXVIII (1980), pp. 113–54.

[9] T. T. Chang, Domestication and the spread of the cultivated rices. In *Foraging and Farming*, ed. D. R. Harris and G. C. Hillman, London: Unwin Hyman, 1989, pp. 408–16; since this publication, the date for Ban Chiang has been revised.

[10] C. O. Sauer, *Agricultural Origins and Dispersals*. New York: American Geographical Society, 1952; 2nd edn, Cambridge, Mass.: MIT Press, 1989.

[11] The interpretation of the evidence is complicated by the possibility that rice can make genetic leaps from domesticated to wild and back again within a few decades: Helmut Loofs-Wissowa, personal communication, citing the view of Douglas E. Yen.

The area was, indeed, always well endowed by nature, and it was not until our own times that human population became so dense as to endanger its own subsistence (and even now the shortages of resources, where they exist, are often the artefacts of political or social conditions as much as of sheer population size). As C. Higham wrote, 'One of the main points about Southeast Asia . . . is the relative ease of obtaining food, particularly in the coastal estuarine areas, but also in the inland marshy river valleys.'[12] A variety of cereals was available growing wild; game was always there for the hunting. Fruit, nuts, roots, fish and fowl were placed considerately within reach in the earth, in the waters, in the surrounding air.

By whatever mechanisms agriculture in the region was initiated, conditions were favourable to its development. Wild rice is not easy to harvest because the connective area between grain and stalk shatters quickly, and there is only a short period in which it must be gathered. Cultivation techniques would have overcome these disadvantages, but need not have been intensive. Early techniques for growing rice in flood or swamp water could have been very simple, without any irrigation. Wet rice cultivation is likely to have come before dry.

The most favourable environments for the first domestication might well have been swampy grasslands in monsoon areas, in sites where seasonal flooding would not have been abrupt but where there were frequently shifting watercourses that discouraged the forest from taking hold. There was no need to develop co-operative and labour-intensive farming techniques, or to settle in large sedentary communities, in order to exploit the rice. It could be protected and sustained by elementary procedures, such as weeding out competing plants or diverting water channels to encourage growth. Such procedures were the first steps in agriculture. They could be carried out at need by small groups living in simple dwellings that could be casually abandoned whenever people wished to move.

Once a community had acquired such techniques of cultivation, it had the means to stock its larder all year round, for, if regularly sun-dried, rice is easily stored for relatively long periods without deterioration. The same goes for the fish that

---

[12] Higham, *Archaeology*, p. 29.

could easily be found in lakes and ponds and the waters of streams; salted, smoked or fermented to make fish sauce (*prahoc*), it provided a range of ingredients that could be stored for long periods. (Tiny fishbones inside small vessels from Non Nok Tha suggest the possibility that fermenting was practised there.)

Given these facts, some prehistorians have argued that the most favourable sites for early domestication were on the coasts. Agriculture could have developed first in mainland South-East Asia, they consider, in areas with access to fresh water near the mangrove swamps of the coast and river-mouth areas. When the coastal locations were well settled, people began to move to the upriver sites that suited their lifestyle, with access to swampy riverside areas where flooding was not too deep for rice to grow; it is in such environments that further steps could be taken in the domestication of rice. Though these inland regions did not offer the same sort of year-round resources as the coasts, stored rice and preserved fish (for which salt was important) could tide people over the dry season. Gradually a network of inland communities took shape.

C. Higham and his colleagues have studied the recent evidence of late third millennium BC sites in the Bang Pakong Valley, part of the Central Plain of Thailand. Such sites, the argument goes, may have been typical of the process of transition to agriculture. At Khok Phanom Di there is evidence from pollen in core samples indicating the presence of various plants that flourish in ricefields from about 4,700–4,000 BC, although convincing evidence of agriculture at the site begins only in the second millennium BC. There was a particularly long period of continuous occupation, and Higham and Maloney are inclined to see the settlement as a locus of early social advance, with a measure of stratification.[13]

However, other prehistorians consider that the agricultural activity actually attested by such sites (from about 2,000 BC) is not early enough to demonstrate that rice cultivation evolved locally, on the coasts, before there could be any influence from

[13] C. Higham and B. Maloney, Coastal adaptation and domestication: a model for socio-economic intensification in prehistoric Southeast Asia. In *Foraging and Farming*, pp. 650–66.

the north. The dates of the earliest agricultural sites do not so far demonstrate that agriculture in the region began on the coasts. Sites in the Lopburi region, as well as Ban Chiang, show agriculture further inland in the third millennium BC.

What is clear is that agriculture developed in South-East Asia in the third millennium. Metal-using cultures appeared shortly after agriculture. Early evidence of copper smelting (a major step towards bronze manufacture) has been found in Lopburi province, Thailand; it includes ores, ceramic moulds, smelting slag and crucible fragments. The date of the beginning of bronze industry has proved problematic; recent finds have suggested to some scholars the possibility of copper or bronze production before the end of the third millennium BC, but at present it is safe only to claim on the evidence of the Lopburi Province sites that metallurgy was established by 1,500 BC.[14]

The evidence of bronze increases in the course of the second millennium. There are bronze finds from several places; they include arrowheads, spearheads, knives, fish-hooks and axes from about 1,500 BC in Vietnam, and from late in the second millennium BC in Thailand have been found evidences of a flourishing bronze industry; in the first millennium BC there was smelting carried on at Ban Na Di, and axes, fish-hooks, bells and bowls have been found.

Simultaneously with the region's bronze age, from the second (or on some views latter third) millennium BC to about 600 BC, there is some evidence of increasing social stratification in the way that cemeteries sometimes have zones of privileged burial. At Ban Na Di, for example, interment with finer ornaments (and in one instance with a crocodile-skin shroud) distinguishes some burials; at Non Nok Tha there is some, but rather less clear-cut, evidence of differential burials: Bayard has suggested from an analysis of eighty-seven burials there that the settlement was occupied by at least two groups of people distinguished by

[14] Surapol Natapintu, Archaeometallurgical studies in the Khao Wong Prachan Valley, Central Thailand. In P. Bellwood (ed.), *Indo-Pacific History*, vol. 2, 1990, in press. Cf. H. H. E. Loofs-Wissowa, The rise and fall of early bronze in Thailand. In *Proceedings of the XXXII Congress for Asian and North African Studies*, ed. A. Wezler and E. Hammerschmidt, Stuttgart: Steiner, 1992, pp. 117–28.

higher and lower status.[15] Khok Phanom Di illustrates differential burial of rich and poor; some of the more affluent had elaborate sets of grave goods. One woman was buried with about 120,000 shell beads; a child was buried with a toy potter's anvil.[16] This sort of evidence, equivocal though it may be, suggests the development of social ranking.

Cambodia is not rich in sites thoroughly excavated with modern scientific techniques. The site of Laang Spean in Battambang province has been mentioned above; it provides evidence of habitation over a very long period, from the fifth millennium BC to late in the first millennium AD. Polished stone and pottery date from early in the period and ceramics from the latter part of it. At three sites near Mlu Prei have been found polished stone tools including a few scrapers, along with evidence of a developed bronze industry in the form of bivalve moulds and crucible fragments. Iron slag has also been found there. However, these are all just surface finds; it is not clear how far back into the first or second millennium BC the histories of the sites extend. One of the sites has delivered up stone and clay bangles and clay stamps; from another has come pottery in abundance.[17]

Meanwhile, to the south, bronze-using communities are attested in Dong Noi valley sites in southern Vietnam from the middle of the second millennium BC; similarities of tool types (axes, chisels, arrowheads and spearheads) to finds in northeastern Thailand have suggested to some archaeologists a network of bronze-using cultures in a zone running from the coastal reaches of the Mekong to the region of Ban Chiang.

If this interpretation is correct, we should expect to find

[15] D. Bayard, Rank and wealth at Non Nok Tha: the mortuary evidence. In *Southeast Asian Archaeology at the XV Pacific Science Congress*, Otago, University Studies in Prehistoric Anthropology no. 16, Otago, 1984, pp. 87–128, cited by Higham, *Archaeology*, pp. 156f.

[16] Higham and Maloney, 'Coastal adaptation', p. 662.

[17] The sites are O Yak, O Pie Can and O Nari. See J. P. Carbonnel, Recent data on the Cambodian neolithic: the problem of cultural continuity in Southern Indochina. In *Early South East Asia: Essays in archaeology, history and historical geography*, ed. R. B. Smith and W. Watson, New York: Oxford University Press, 1979, pp. 223–6; R. Mourer, Préhistoire du Cambodge.

further artefacts of similar types in sites within the interior of the network. Samrong Sen on the Chinit River (30 kilometres from the Tonle Sap) constitutes a significant intermediate site.

Samrong Sen yields shouldered and rectangular stone adzes like some from the lower Mekong area, and miscellaneous artefacts such as metal armbands, polished stone tools, ornaments, bones and stone beads. There is evidence of hunting. Possibly dogs were domesticated. Fish-hooks and net weights provide evidence of fishing, and there are remains of water turtles and shellfish. Shells found at the site have been given a carbon dating of about 1,230 BC. The presence of a bronze industry is shown by a crucible, and bronze items include bracelets, spearheads and a bell. The composition of some of these indicates that they are likely to have been cast later than 500 BC. The site is distinctive for its hand-fashioned bowls, with decorations of triangles and comb-marked lines; there are similar wares from Vietnam (Sa Huynh), and some have postulated connections further afield, notably with the Philippines.

The pottery is characterized by various wares, particularly open bowls on broad pedestal bases. The people of Samrong Sen appear to have been inclined to an aquatic diet, which is typical in South-East Asia.

The site of Samrong Sen no doubt accords with the notion of a network of cultures subject to influences from the coast, but the archaeology of prehistoric Cambodia is undeveloped, and the record is scant and hard to interpret. In the vicinity of Angkor itself, there is little to flesh out the record of prehistoric settlement, though work by B.-P. Groslier has indicated the presence of a 'neolithic' site at the foot of the Phnom Bakheng, the very centre of the imperial capital, and others near the north shore of the Great Lake and at Sambor Prei Kuk.[18] Systematic work, in the sense of digging, has not been carried out extensively in the Angkorian region. Excavations currently under way at the twelfth-century site of Preah Khan, however, may well reveal a continuum of occupation in the region from 'Fu-nan' times until the construction of the temple.

[18] B.-P. Groslier, La cité hydraulique angkorienne: exploitation ou surexploitation du sol? *Bulletin de l'Ecole française d'Extrême-Orient*, LXVI (1979), pp. 161–202, at pp. 165f.

Here, then, we see a picture of mainland South-East Asia in the bronze age which has been interpreted by some pre-historians to accord with their emphasis upon the autonomy of local cultures. On their view, networks of exchange extended upriver from the coastal settlements which occupied the most favourable locations for agriculture; the inland communities were increasingly involved in this pattern of exchange and were stimulated to develop their own resources, including bronze-working.

On the other hand, there are others who are sceptical about the coastal origins of agriculture and about the idea that local economic development occurred independently of the south-ward spread of agriculture or of the later spread of metal-working from southern China. These people would emphasize that clear evidence of bronze in the region before 2,400 BC is lacking. The evidence for the priority of coastal sites of trade and agriculture is fragmentary, and its implications are debated. The coastal sites which are presumed to have been the power-houses of economic advance have yet to yield satisfactory evidence that they produced the initiates and innovations that acted upon the sites of the interior. Their agricultural under-pinning, the argument goes, has yet to be convincingly shown to predate that of the communities further north. Clearly, then, different views are possible, and decision must wait upon the further progress of archaeology.

One thing that is clear, however, is that, from about the middle of the last millennium BC, there was a major develop-ment in the patterns of social organization in some parts of the region. Even before the rise of states, with the apparatus of kingship, Indian ritual and Sanskrit culture, a number of inland sites show that much larger settlements were emerging, with presumably centralized and organized populations. These settlements demand to be recognized as the earliest cities, and they furnished the necessary social matrix for the subsequent development of the indigenous state. We shall look at the emergence of these larger settlements in the next chapter.

5

The Rise of Cities and Indian Influence

Some time after 500 BC, important changes began to occur in the region. A sophisticated bronze industry, iron tools, larger settlements with major fortifications, relatively long-distance trade or exchange and (as we can reasonably infer) social institutions of centralization and authority all appeared.

Let us take metal culture first. The region possessed an impressive bronze industry of its own by about 600 BC – the famous Dongson culture, named after its type-site in northern Vietnam. Links have been postulated between this bronze industry and that of the late Chou (Zhou) culture of the Yangtze River valley, and some discern connections with Yünnan, where the Tien (Dian) culture of sites such as Shih-chai-shan (Shizhaishan) offers close artistic parallels. However, for others, the style and character of the Dongson productions suggest local origins, with an ancestry that has been traced by the Vietnamese to the cultures represented by the Phung Nguyen, Dong Dau and Go Mun sites.[1] This is another area of disagreement, where some scholars emphasize the role of outside influences and others the role of local development.

The best-known products are the large bronze drums; they weigh up to about 100 kilograms and stand 1 metre high. They are likely to have had a ritual or ceremonial function, possibly

[1] Trinh Sinh and Ha Nguyen Diem, The shapes of pottery vessels from Phung Nguyen to Dong Son [in Vietnamese]. *Khao Co Hoc*, no. 2 (1977), pp. 50–67, cited by C. F. Higham, *The Archaeology of Mainland Southeast Asia*, Cambridge: Cambridge University Press, 1989, p. 192.

as part of the legitimizing regalia of chiefs or in funerary rites as the dead were ferried to the after-life in boats pushed out into the river. H. Loofs-Wissowa has argued that the drums were regalia objects, possibly bestowed by a religious authority in Vietnam.[2] The early type of drum, known as Heger I, is now represented by over 200 examples. They are richly decorated, the top surface being covered by angular motifs in zones about the centre; represented are houses, birds, people in distinctive costume. Such drums have been found in many parts of South-East Asia and are well known as symbols of antiquity. A tourist can take coffee at a smart Bangkok hotel from an occasional table exactly modelled on a Heger I drum.

The origin of iron-working in South-East Asia is another topic that has been the subject of debate between proponents of importation from outside the region and those of independent development within it. It is, of course, possible that an initial stimulus came from outside, but that the industry developed thereafter autonomously.

To some scholars, it appears probable that the first outside influence would have been from China. Bennet Bronson finds it 'hard to believe that indirect Chinese influence is not involved.'[3] Some disagree. For example, Anna Bennett's work in the Khao Wong Prachan valley in Central Thailand indicates that the prehistoric copper smelting methods were quite different from those used in China and elsewhere.[4] Wrought iron appeared in China early,[5] but the predominant method was casting; the fact

[2] H. Loofs-Wissowa, Dongson drums: instruments of shamanism or regalia? *Arts Asiatiques*, 46 (1991), pp. 39–49.

[3] B. Bronson, Patterns in the early Southeast Asian metals trade. In I. Glover, Pornchai Suchitta and J. Villiers (eds), *Early Metallurgy, Trade and Urban Centres in Thailand and Southeast Asia*, Bangkok: White Lotus, 1992, pp. 63–114, at p. 106.

[4] Anna Bennett, Prehistoric copper smelting in Central Thailand. In *Prehistoric Studies: The Stone and Metal Ages in Thailand*, ed. Pisit Charoenwongsa and Bennet Bronson, Bangkok: Thai Antiquity Working Group, 1988, pp. 125–35. Iron smelting, it has been thought, could have developed easily as the result of the use of a haematite flux in copper reduction; C. Higham, personal communication.

[5] See Donald B. Wagner, *Ancient Iron and Steel in China*. Leiden and New York: Brill, 1993, p. 146.

that South-East Asian iron was forged is one objection to a Chinese origin for the industry. However, the present evidence does not permit any firm conclusion.[6]

At all events, claims have been made for the use of iron in South-East Asia by the seventh century BC. The evidence includes, for example, iron bracelets from graves at Nil Kham Haeng, in Lopburi Province, Thailand, datable to about 700 BC.[7] Claims have also been made on the basis of finds at Ban Chiang Hian (a site described further below). By the earlier part of the fourth century BC, iron was used in the manufacture of numerous weapons and tools found at Ban Don Ta Phet. More problematic is the case that has been made for early iron on the evidence of finds at Thaungthaman.[8]

The possibility of a Chinese connection is hinted at by the Tabon caves in the Philippines, where there is evidence of iron tool export from China about 180 BC. This may well illustrate a process that had begun much earlier, but the interpretation of iron finds from the Philippines is complicated, and various routes have been proposed for it.[9]

[6] On the origins of iron working in China, see ibid.; Wagner dates the earliest known non-meteoric iron artefacts to the fifth century BC (pp. 60–80, 95); a dagger blade perhaps substantially earlier is of meteoric iron (p. 96).

[7] A burial belonging to Phase 2 of the sequence revealed by the excavation and said to be dated securely to the period 700–500 BC contained a number of metal bracelets, one of them iron. Iron bracelets occurred in other burials also. Surapol Natapintu, Archaeometallurgical studies in the Khao Wong Prachan Valley, Central Thailand. In P. Bellwood (ed.), Indo-Pacific History, vol. 2, in press.

[8] Ban Chiang Hian yields evidence of iron technology along with domesticated buffalo after 500 BC. In Burma, the site of Thaungthaman knew iron in the middle of the first millennium BC; see J. Stargardt, The Ancient Pyu of Burma, vol. I: Early Pyu Cities in a Man-made Landscape, Cambridge: PACSEA, in Association with the Institute of Southeast Asian Studies, 1990. There are problems in the chronology of this site. Cf. P. Bellwood, Early Burmese urbanisation: inspired independence or external stimulus? Review of Archaeology, 13, no. 2 (1992), pp. 1–7; H. H. E. Loofs-Wissowa, Taung Tha Man In site, northern Burma, unpublished manuscript; three samples were dated, the earliest being assigned to the third century BC, although it was a substantial distance from the middle sample dated only thirty-five years later.

[9] See H. H. E. Loofs-Wissowa, Prehistoric and protohistoric links between the Indochinese Peninsula and the Philippines, as exemplified by two types of ear-ornaments. Journal of the Hong Kong Archaeological Society, 9 (1980–1),

Another sort of development that occurred in the middle of the last millennium BC, particularly significant for the subsequent formation of the states known to history, was the appearance in inland sites of cities with a degree of administrative centralization and manpower control.

Upon the Khorat plateau, the Mun-Chi river drainage area was home to a number of important settlements that typify the trend, probably from about 400 BC. The ancestors of the Khmers were certainly affected by the social and material developments that were taking place in this area.

The site of Ban Chiang Hian displays a settlement, occupied in about the fourth century BC, which was fortified by moats and ramparts. Recent satellite photographs indicate that there was an elaborate system of water reticulation, with canals discharging from the moats on the northern side.[10] The construction work would have involved the movement of 100,000 cubic metres of earth; assuming that one man would be able to dig 2 cubic metres a day with the help of two more men to move the earth, the undertaking would have required a full year for 500 well-fed adults.[11] The population of the settlement would have been something like 2,000, and these would have required about 450 hectares (1,100 acres) of agricultural land. Such a site, with its evidence of control of manpower and centralized public works, irresistibly suggests some degree of urbanization.

Another site, not far to the west, is Non Chai; its location places it within range of iron deposits exploited after 200 BC, and its population is likely to have been close to 1,000. Dating of charcoal samples shows that the site was occupied in the later first millennium BC. Bronze spillage and iron slag suggest that

pp. 57–76, at pp. 59f. In the second century BC an attempt was made to halt the export of iron goods to the south, evidence that the Vietnam region depended upon imports; it has been suggested that iron-working could have been carried from Vietnam to the Philippines by refugees from Chinese encroachment. Another view is that Vietnamese iron finds before about the first century AD are all imported. Loofs-Wissowa distrusts claims for Vietnamese iron-working before the period of the Oc Eo site (c.2nd–6th centuries AD).

[10] C. Higham, personal communication.

[11] P. Chantaratiyakarn, The middle Chi research programme. In *Prehistoric Investigations in Northeast Thailand*, ed. C. F. W. Higham and A. Kijngam, Oxford: British Archaeological Reports, 1984, pp. 565–643, at p. 633.

both were worked on the site. Bronze manufactures included bracelets, ring fragments and bells;[12] iron objects included nails and tools. There were also blue glass beads (types of which were widespread in the region), and manufactured objects possibly used in silk weaving. There were remains of cattle, pigs, deer, dogs (eaten), fish and turtles. Comparison with other sites indicates its involvement in an extensive trade network across the Khorat plateau; salt, iron implements, bronze ornaments and possibly silk and fermented fish were now trade commodities in addition to the bronze and other goods that had been distributed through the region since about 2,000 BC, and it has been observed that this trade must have played a part in the apparent moves to 'some form of centralization' over much of the Khorat plateau.[13]

Further south, up the Mun river in the vicinity of Phimai (now in Thailand), there is evidence of early settlements, expecially Ban Tamyae, dated to a period roughly 600 BC–AD 600; iron was known, and there were growing communities likely to have acquired increasing social and political centralization.[14]

In the Mun valley there are many large circular settlements with multiple concentric moats and embankments, covering areas up to 68 hectares, with an average of 25. Elizabeth Moore has reviewed the information so far available about these sites. They occupy various environments, upland and lowland; in the hills, they were in a position to exploit timber, salt and iron. They represent a considerable expansion which took place between 500 BC and AD 500. Within the moats there were earthworks 10 metres high, topped by thorn-bushes and perhaps palisades. The moats, of limited value for defence outside the wet season, could have been adapted as reservoirs for the irrigation of neighbouring fields, and the management of them could no doubt have been manipulated to favour

[12] Bronze technology showed significant advance: unlike the bivalve moulds in the middle phase of Non Nok Tha and Ban Chiang, Non Chai bronzes were made by the 'lost wax' method.
[13] D. Bayard, Pisit Charoenwongsa and Somsuda Rutnin, Excavations at Non Chai, Northeastern Thailand, 1977–78. *Asian Perspectives*, 25, no. 1 (1982–3), pp. 13–61; phrase quoted at p. 57.
[14] Higham, *Archaeology of Mainland Southeast Asia*, p. 215.

families with higher status. The ready availability of alternative resources, Moore suggests, would have inhibited the long-term development of centralized institutions of power.[15]

In eastern Cambodia, there are many circular earthworks; locally they are known as Moi ('savage') forts. Dates for material from these include one late in the first millennium BC and one late in the first AD. Eighteen have been mapped so far. Typically they consist of two concentric circular embankments with a moat between and an interior diameter of 100–200 metres. One at Mimot near the Vietnamese border, excavated by Groslier, yielded fourteen cultural levels.[16]

All in all, it is evident that, from a period roughly datable to the fourth century BC, substantial advances took place on the mainland of South-East Asia. Chiefdoms arose, commanding denser settlements with elaborate fortifications and deploying iron age technology. On the Khorat plateau, for example, settlements had previously not occupied sites larger than 5 hectares; subsequently, sites well over 20 hectares were occupied. There was a substantial shift in the pattern of social organization.

What brought this about? Many factors are likely to have been involved; the difficulty is in determining which of these factors were crucial.

One type of interpretation emphasizes that the development took place at the same time that iron culture was disseminated through South-East Asia. One way of accounting for the rise of large, more complex societies is to attribute it to the consequences of the more intensive agriculture made possible with iron implements, particularly ploughshares.

It is very likely that iron implements did indeed have much to do with the process of social and cultural change, but the chain

[15] Elizabeth H. Moore, *Moated Sites in Early North East Thailand*. Oxford: British Archaeological Reports, 1988. British Archaeological Reports, International Series 400.

[16] Of these sites, some are in Kompong Cham, some in the areas of Mimot, Chalang, Krek and Peam Cheang. In 1980, Groslier pointed to the coincidence between the area occupied by the 'civilization of the circular cities' and that of Khmer occupation, particularly from the end of the sixth century AD with the conquests of the king Citrasena/Mahendravarman: B.-P. Groslier, Prospection des sites Khmers du Siam, cited by R. Mourer, Préhistoire du Cambodge, *Archéologia*, no. 233 (March 1988), p. 52.

of cause and effect is not clear. Consider, for example, the suggestion that iron ploughshares were crucial in making possible greatly increased production. It is true that the Vietnamese acquired iron ploughs from their contacts with Chinese culture, but there is nevertheless no evidence of iron ploughs elsewhere in the region, and it has been argued that, anyway, in the particular circumstances of wet-field rice agriculture in monsoon Asia, the introduction of the iron plough did not have the potential to increase yields dramatically.

One view is that a combination of relatively simple developments in agriculture – ploughing, bunding and transplanting of shoots from nursery fields – could have stimulated the process in some areas. D. Welch, who studied the Phimai region, suggested that improvements in rice yields brought about by such developments could have made possible surpluses beyond the needs of the farmers, the chief limit upon production being labour.[17] Population growth would then have followed upon agricultural advance, rather than the other way round. The chronology of these postulated developments is uncertain, however.

There are others who would consider population growth to be a *cause* of the other changes. One idea is that there is a certain critical size above which a community can no longer retain its earlier pattern of more or less egalitarian relations among the families that compose it – friction and competition are so great that the community must either fragment into a number of separate settlements or acquire a new, more centralized structure, with institutions of authority embodied in leading families. When this happened, the emergence of chiefs, incipient rulers, brought about a redistribution of resources. There were now institutions by which labour and surplus produce could be manipulated for new purposes: buildings, rituals, ornaments and feasts which all marked the elevation of a chief's status. Demand for labour and produce provided the motivation for more intensive farming.

Again, according to yet another theory, these developments could be attributed to conquest: when a population had grown

---

[17] D. Welch, *Adaptation to Environmental Unpredictability: Intensive Agriculture and Regional Exchange at Late Prehistoric Centers in the Phimai Region, Thailand*. University of Hawaii, PhD thesis, 1985.

to the point where, given a particular subsistence pattern, there was no more land that could easily be colonized, the defeated groups in clan conflicts were unable to move away and clear new fields for themselves, so they remained as servants of the victor families; patterns of authority and control could emerge from the development of super-communities, with subordinate groups in a position of servitude to the families of chiefs.[18] Before agricultural technology had advanced very far, easily exploited sites for settlement were relatively sparse, and new lands might become difficult to find even while there was plenty of empty space. So far as warfare in South-East Asia is concerned, it is sometimes suggested that finds of quantities of metal spear-heads necessarily indicate warfare (and therefore armies and political control).

Another way of looking at the process is to appeal to the effect of involvement in growing networks of exchange. Any new demand for the resources of a particular place, or even an increase in an existing demand, could bring decisive advantages to the communities living where the resources were found. Leaders of these communities would be in a position to acquire power and authority. Ritual positions of seniority could turn into practical control and lead to a clear elevation of status, with chiefs commanding labour and resources. An important change could take place in the society of people living well inland, up the Mekong and Mun rivers for example, as a result of a demand for local products arising from trading activities taking place far away on the coasts.

If major social changes were stimulated by the political dynamics of a trading or bartering network, did the network need newcomers, with a different culture, from outside the region? The evidence that the changes were brought about largely or solely by immigrants from outside the region is not clear-cut. Certainly there were major discontinuities consistent with this inference; at Ban Chiang and Ban Na Di, new types of pottery and the appearance of iron may represent new arrivals, but it is also thought possible by some that local people were responding to new features of their relationship with their en-

---

[18] This theory follows Carneiro's 'circumscription hypothesis': R. Carneiro, A theory of the origin of the state. *Science*, 169 (1970), pp. 733–8.

vironment, and that such migrations as are evidenced were within the region. Ban Na Di, for example, may well have acquired its cultural innovations from newcomers from nearby. If exchange of valued goods played a part, it could have been within the region. Evidence of such exchanges can be found in the bimetallic spearheads and cowrie shells from Ban Chiang Hian.[19]

Clearly, there was a complex process of adjustment which produced agricultural intensification, the use of iron, the appearance of different levels of society, and the establishment of larger settlements. This process is likely to have involved a number of interacting elements such as access to iron, the intensification of agriculture to produce surpluses, the pressure of an expanding population, larger and denser settlements with more impressive fortifications and other structures, enhanced trading and craft activity making more goods available, social hierarchy with vertical relations of authority and subordination and the clustering of bands of followers around chiefs, control of valued resources, differential wealth, and political subordination of smaller communities to a central one where a chief lived. There are various different theories attributing varying weights to these elements, and it will be some time before scholars reach general agreement about the way in which the process worked.[20]

So far we have been concerned with the evidence of prehistoric change, before the rise of Indian-style states. A lesson suggested by the evidence reviewed here is that we need to distinguish between two processes and recognize that they were not a single event. The first was what we can call 'proto-urbanization': the rise of substantial settlements with populations of over 1,000 and at least some elements of social hierarchy, based upon economic advances. This process, as we have seen, began in areas populated by ancestors of the Khmers, in about the fifth to fourth centuries BC.

---

[19] Chantaratiyakarn, The middle Chi research programme, p. 642.
[20] P. Wheatley, *Nagara and Commandery: Origins of Southeast Asian Urban Traditions.* Chicago: University of Chicago, Department of Geography Research Paper nos 207–8, 1983, reviews some of these theories of incipient urbanization. See especially pp. 276–85.

The second process is state formation. The word 'state' is used here to identify a structure of authority which employs a corps of officials and soldiers to enforce order and collect economic resources. Such a structure requires a surplus-producing economy capable of supporting various classes, such as the families of rulers or nobles, warriors, officials, merchants, craftsmen, scribes and priests. Society is stratified and complex, with a variety of economic specializations and division of labour. Whenever writing develops, its adoption is likely to be mediated by leisured or non-productive classes such as the nobles, merchants or priests.

What the evidence seems to suggest about the relationship between these two processes is that proto-urbanization developed as a distinct stage before the rise of states. The earliest knowledge we have of genuine centralized states in the Mon-Khmer area comes from the evidence of kingdoms already professing Indian religions and using Sanskrit. Relations of trade or exchange with Indians date at least a century or two BC, and there is even evidence (from Ban Don Ta Phet in Thailand) suggesting contacts as early as the fourth century BC,[21] but the development of indigenous states with Indian court culture is hardly likely to have occurred for long after that, perhaps not until about the fourth century AD. The rise of proto-urban settlements, on the other hand, took place in the middle of the last millennium BC, as we have seen. Therefore, although new finds are constantly making us revise our judgements about the evolution of ancient cultures, the weight of evidence and opinion requires us to insert a gap between the proto-urbanization evidenced by the rise of large settlements and the rise of kingdoms with Indian cultural professions, and to identify, well *before* the rise of the 'Indianized' kingdoms, a major phase of economic and political advance.

This is the background against which we must assess the rise of states in the region. When mainland South-East Asia emerges into the light of history, we see its rulers professing the trappings of Indian culture. How were these acquired, and what part did they play in the establishment of centralized states?

[21] Ian Glover, *Early Trade between India and Southeast Asia*. Hull: University of Hull Centre for Southeast Asian Studies, 1990, pp. 36f, n. 5.

The nature of the Indian contribution to the process of state formation in mainland South-East Asia, like so much else, is subject to debate. Some interpretations emphasize the role of outsiders (in this case, Indians), and others emphasize the indigenous features of the process.

For lack of evidence, we can rule out the idea that states with Indian-style court cultures appeared as the result of Indian imperial conquest. What we are seeking is, rather, a description of the way in which the Indians – initially traders, later from all walks of life – acted as a catalyst for change. No ancient source actually describes it, and we are reduced to speculation.[22]

Some historians have proposed that the process was the result of Indian initiative, the work of merchants, warrior adventurers or priests. Others have preferred to emphasize local initiative: the Indian court culture that figures in the sources was, on their view, not a dominant culture imposed from outside but the creation of local rulers who invited Indian brahmans to serve them and selected what they wanted of Indian ritual, lore and literature.

These ideas have long been mulled over in the scholarly literature. Recent archaeological research has yielded more and earlier evidence of Indian trading contact. Links between South-East Asia and the southern parts of India, particularly Andhra on the east, may go back to before the Christian era;[23] and sites in Thailand, notably Ban Don Ta Phet in the lower Menam Chao Phraya valley, have yielded carnelian and glass beads of likely Indian provenance from perhaps the last centuries BC; from Chansen, in the same area, comes an ivory comb with possibly Buddhist symbols engraved on it that has been tenta-

---

[22] For a review of the historical evidence, see G. Coedès, *The Indianized States of Southeast Asia*, tr. S. Cowing. Canberra, Australian National University Press, 1968, pp. 14–35. For a review of the varieties of scholarly interpretation until 1977, see I. W. Mabbett, The 'Indianization' of Southeast Asia. *Journal of Southeast Asian Studies*, 8 (1977), pp. 1–14, 143–61, and The 'Indianization' of mainland South-East Asia: a reappraisal. In *Jean Boisselier Felicitation Volume*, ed. Natasha Eilenberg et al., in press.

[23] H. P. Ray, Early maritime contacts between South and Southeast Asia. *Journal of Southeast Asian Studies*, 10, no. 1 (1989), pp. 42–54.

tively dated to the first or second century AD.[24] An intriguing piece of evidence is provided by a pottery sherd found in Bali, inscribed in Indian characters, which may attest an early connection between India and the archipelago.[25]

Whenever exchanges with India began, there is good evidence of well-established traffic by the beginning of the Christian era. At U Thong was found a third-century copper coin of the Emperor Victorinus (*r*.268–70); first-century Indo-Roman rouletted ware sherds come from Java, and in southern Thailand have been found a number of Indian etched beads; the ancient city site at Beikthano in Burma yields coins and etched beads from the early centuries AD.[26]

Given such contacts, it is easy to imagine how a ripple effect might have operated from the coasts towards the inland communities such as those of the Khmers, as Indian traders established settlements at river mouths and initiated a demand for gold and forest products obtainable from the hinterlands.

It is important to distinguish between coastal settlements occupied by Indians and regular South-East Asian states with indigenous rulers and Indian-influenced culture. Several centuries of commercial contact may well have passed by before the latter appeared. When this happened, the early states lacked dense agricultural hinterlands. A model proposed by B. Bronson to describe rivermouth trading states may apply to them: they were essentially mercantile principalities, highly vulnerable to changes in trade patterns and to piratical attacks by rivals; but

[24] B. Bronson, The late prehistory and early history of central Thailand with special reference to Chansen. In R. B. Smith and W. Watson (eds), *Early South East Asia: Essays in archaeology, history and historical geography*, New York: Oxford University Press, 1979, pp. 315–36.

[25] The characters were originally identified as Kharoṣṭhī; this script is associated with north-western India between the third century BC and the fourth AD: W. Ardika and P. Bellwood, Sembiran: the beginnings of Indian contact with Bali, *Antiquity*, 65, no. 247 (1991), pp. 221–32. It appears however that the script may be Brāhmī, which is also ancient.

[26] Glover, *Early Trade between India and Southeast Asia*, see esp. pp. 4, 9. The evidence of Indian influence is discussed more fully in Mabbett, The 'Indianization' of mainland South-East Asia.

when one of them conquered others there were no means to establish durable imperial control.[27]

This is an economic perspective. Paul Wheatley, while giving weight to various theories of urbanization, emphasizes the role of religious culture. He proposes a central role for 'thearchic kingship' in the rise of the early 'Indianized' principalities: chiefs used Indian cults to promote their households to a new, superordinate status, so that they were able to control and concentrate resources. Royal cities, embodying this superordination, absorbed tribute and supported new classes of royal dependants; they were large and highly planned.[28]

More recently, H. Kulke has questioned the very concept of 'Indianization', seeing it as loaded with the presupposition of a superior and different society exercising an influence of some sort upon a more backward one. Against this, he urges that we should recognize the difference between northern India, the home of the centres of high Sanskrit culture and of the great classical empires, and the southern kingdoms which in the earliest times were actually the chief cultural partners of the states in South-East Asia and much more on a level with them; the relationship between the southern states and those of South-East Asia was one of convergence, not domination.[29]

It is clear that, at various stages in the first millennium AD, a number of coastal principalities appeared in South-East Asia with the marks of Indian court culture. It is important to recognize that these principalities were not established by large-scale migration of Indians, and lacked many of the features of

[27] B. Bronson, Exchange at the upstream and downstream ends: notes toward a functional model of the coastal state in Southeast Asia. In *Economic Exchange and Social Interaction in Southeast Asia: Perspectives from prehistory, history and ethnography*, ed. K. Hutterer, Ann Arbor, Mich.: University of Michigan, 1977, pp. 39–52.

[28] Wheatley, *Nagara and Commandery*. Wheatley's view of these states has been criticized by B. Bronson, who argues that although cities in later centuries may have conformed to this picture of them, those in the early states did not: B. Bronson, Review of *Nagara and Commandery*. *South-east Asian Studies Newsletter*, 20 (1985), pp. 1–4.

[29] H. Kulke, Indian colonies, Indianization or cultural convergence? In *Onderzoek in Zuidoost-Azie*, ed. H. Schulte Nordholt, Leiden: Rijksuniversiteit te Leiden, 1990, pp. 8–32.

Indian social organization and popular culture. Some of the terminology of caste was adopted as part of the ritual language of courts and temples, but the actual organization of the population in close-knit Indian-style caste groups simply did not appear in South-East Asia. In basic matters such as diet, some tastes and traditions remained stubbornly un-Indian. Milk never acquired importance in the kitchens of the region, and as any traveller in South-East Asia knows, dairy cattle are hard to find. Again, the use of money was well established in India by the time the 'Indianization' process was under way, but even at the height of Angkor's prosperity the Khmers were bartering or offering textiles and ingots of gold or silver in the markets.

On the other hand, we should not dismiss the Indian cultural contribution as trivial or superficial. The leisured and educated classes, without abandoning their inherited customs and traditions, no doubt considered themselves to belong to a civilization that spread across the lands on either side of the Bay of Bengal, and their literary and religious culture was closely related to that of their counterparts in India.

In some ways, the early kingdoms of South-East Asia were substantially influenced by Indian culture, and in other ways they were not. Any assessment of the influence needs to be very cautious; it is easy to be led astray by impressions based on scanty evidence. What we actually know about life in the ancient kingdoms is really teasingly slight; the information we have mostly comes from Chinese accounts, which refer to the states by Chinese names and describe them from a Chinese point of view.

This applies to the state (or perhaps the cluster of states) known as 'Fu-nan', which lay largely in Khmer territory and provided the main foundation for the development of Khmer state culture. This state therefore deserves our special attention.

6

The Beginnings of Khmer History

No one knows what the Chinese word 'Fu-nan' represents. The country to which it refers appears to have had its heartland in the Mekong delta area. The Chinese describe it as an empire, with a number of vassal states; since modern scholars doubt whether this is correct, they treat the Chinese information with suspicion, and the name 'Fu-nan' belongs in inverted commas. For convenience these will be omitted in this chapter; but it must be understood that question marks as well as inverted commas hover around Fu-nan, the first state to emerge into the light of history by courtesy of the Chinese archivists.

When the later Khmer states arose, they inherited much of the territory and culture of Fu-nan. They were not necessarily the direct descendants of the people of Fu-nan. The latter lived near the coast, engaging in seafaring, and making early contact with Indian and other traders from outside the region; the later Khmer states were inland to the north.

It has often been supposed that the people of Fu-nan were connected with the speakers of Austronesian languages of the islands rather than with the mainland Mon and Khmer; but when so little linguistic evidence survives, the pasting of such labels upon ancient communities is a speculative venture. Geography suggests that the population of Fu-nan may have been closely linked with the inhabitants of Champa, which came to occupy the coastal areas of southern and central Vietnam; their descendants today, a few thousand strong, are scattered in small communities in remoter parts of southern Vietnam and Cambodia. Coedès suggested connections with the various hill peoples around the periphery of Cambodia who speak Mon-Khmer dialects, and considered it probable that 'in the main' the inhabitants of Fu-nan belonged to the same group.[1]

What does archaeology tell us about Fu-nan? The one major site to be excavated so far tells us a great deal. At Oc Eo in

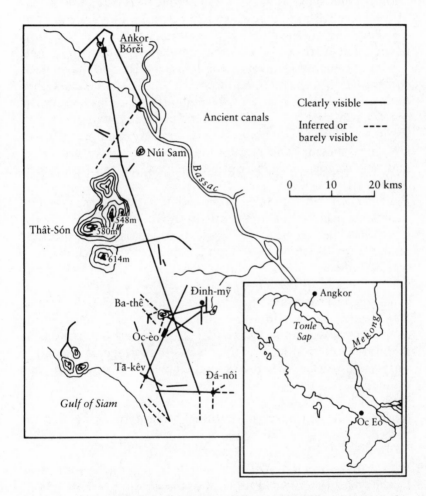

Map 5   The canal system around Oc Eo in the 'Fu-nan' period

[1]   G. Coedès, *The Making of South East Asia*, trs. H. M. Wright. London: Routledge and Kegan Paul, 1966, p. 62; translated from *Les Peuples de la péninsule indochinoise*, Paris: Dunod, 1962.

southern Vietnam, nowadays about ten miles from the sea, excavations conducted in a major operation by L. Malleret in the early 1940s revealed an urban settlement connected by trade to regions far afield. Early Buddhist art is represented. There are a bronze Buddha head in the style of Gandhara, a bronze lamp with a design suggesting an Indian mythical monster, and pieces of jewellery with Indian decoration; schist moulds for pieces of jewellery have been found, with examples of their products in pewter. There are pewter Buddhist amulets, lead medallions and decorative plaques, silver medallions thought to have been coins, silver dishes, and many stamped gold-leaf amulets. Other finds in stone, pottery and various metals include such everyday objects as a little bell, a tortoise pendant, a ring with a clasp in the image of a bull, cymbals, bowls, large cooking pots, stoves, jars, jugs, mortars and pestles, millstones, rattles, dyers' plugs and net weights. Seal inscriptions suggest the third or fourth century AD.[2]

The town site is quite large, with a geometrical layout suggesting central planning; an extensive network of canals, which has been dated to the late fifth and early sixth centuries, linked it to its rural hinterland.[3] Some canals extended seawards, indicating that the town was not on the shoreline but was connected to it.

The delta environment of Oc Eo is quite unlike the inland areas where the Khmer cities originated, and its agricultural environment was quite unlike that of the Tonle Sap region. In the marshy coastal tracts, there was no shortage of water for simple cultivation; what was needed was not irrigation, but drainage.

One Chinese source claims that the farmers of Fu-nan 'sow for one year and harvest for three'.[4] The type of agriculture

---

[2] L. Malleret, *L'Archéologie du delta du Mekong*, 4 vols. Paris: Ecole française d'Extrême-Orient 1959–63; see for example vol. ii, plates LXXXIV and XC; vol. iii, pp. 115, 304 and *passim*; artefacts found are richly illustrated in the accompanying volumes of plates.

[3] Ibid., vol. iii, p. 324, referring to 'un système de canaux de navigation eux-mêmes ramifiés en des voies secondaires de drainage'.

[4] P. Pelliot, Le Fou-nan. *Bulletin de l'Ecole française d'Extrême-Orient*, 2 (1902), pp. 248–303, at pp. 254, 274.

referred to may be a process known as ratooning – harvesting new shoots growing on a plant that has already been cropped.

At any rate, Oc Eo is generally considered to have been the main port of Fu-nan; its capital, if there was one, has not been located precisely.[5] Indeed, it is very difficult to match the fragmentary and equivocal evidence in the written sources to actual places that can be examined on the ground. Indian sources, for example, provide almost no details of the places to which traders and adventurers resorted, and Indian literature offers us mostly fable.

The Chinese, on the other hand, had from Han times (beginning in the second century BC) a tradition of state-sponsored historiography from archival sources, and these archives were nourished by the information yielded from embassies sent by feudatory states to the Chinese capitals. Early Chinese literature contains many allusions to South-East Asia. The classic study of the Chinese references to Fu-nan remains P. Pelliot's 'Le Fou-nan', published in 1903.[6]

The Chinese sources for Fu-nan are based upon various records made by travellers and officials. Parts of these records came to be preserved in fragments in the official Chinese histories, which were compilations assembled from archives during each dynasty. They present a great deal of circumstantial detail, but there are puzzling inconsistencies. Here is what one Chinese source relates:

The people of Funan are malicious and cunning . . . The character of the inhabitants is good. They do not like to fight. They are ceaselessly invaded by Lin-yi [the Cham people to the east] and have not entered into relations with Kiao-Chao [the Vietnamese in Tonkin]. That is why their embassies so seldom come . . .

Actually, the men of this country are ugly and black, with curly hair . . . In the case of mourning, the custom is to shave the beard and

---

[5] One possibility recently argued for is that it was some distance upriver at Banteay Prei Nokor: M. Vickery, Some remarks on early state formation in Cambodia. In *Southeast Asia in the 9th to 14th Centuries*, ed. D. Marr and A. Milner, Canberra and Singapore: Research School of Pacific Studies, Australian National University/Institute of Southeast Asian Studies, 1986, pp. 95–115; C. Jacques, on the other hand, situates it near Prei Veng.
[6] Pelliot, Le Fou-nan.

the hair. For the dead, there are four kinds of disposal . . . The people are of a covetous nature. They have neither rites nor propriety. Boys and girls follow their penchants without restraint.[7]

The truth about these people is tantalizingly difficult to grasp. How can its inhabitants be malicious and cunning, yet also of good character and pacific? Further, if they observe mourning with the most filial rigour and treat their deceased patriarchs to an elaborate variety of ritual farewell, how can they be said to lack rites or propriety? The Chinese accounts, it turns out, are not as trustworthy as they seem; they suffer from the contamination of observations of different places and times, and they embody Chinese perceptions which can distort the character of what is described.

The first recorded contact between China and Fu-nan occurred in about 225 AD. Two envoys, K'ang-t'ai (Kangtai) and Chu Ying (Zhu Ying), went to the court of Fu-nan. The original version of their record is lost, but substantial quotations are contained in a number of later Chinese compilations.

The difficulties in interpreting these sources are illustrated by the use which some historians have made of the foundation myth of Kauṇḍinya and Somā, the serpent spirit.

A legendary account of the founding of Fu-nan was reported by the embassy of K'ang-t'ai. According to the story, the kingdom was founded by a king or brahman from India named Kauṇḍinya. Here is the story as summarized by G. Coedès:

This king, having dreamed that his personal genie delivered a divine bow to him and directed him to embark on a large merchant junk, proceeded in the morning to the temple, where he found a bow at the foot of the genie's tree. He then boarded a ship, which the genie caused to land in Funan. The queen of the country, Liu-ye, 'Willow Leaf', wanted to pillage the ship and seize it, so Hun-t'ien [Kauṇḍinya] shot an arrow from his divine bow which pierced through Liu-ye's ship. Frightened, she gave herself up, and Hun-t'ien took her for his wife. But, unhappy to see her naked, he folded a piece of material to make a garment through which he had her pass her head. Then he governed the country and passed power on to his descendants.[8]

---

[7] Ibid., pp. 261f.
[8] G. Coedès, *The Indianized States of Southeast Asia*, tr. S. B. Cowing. Canberra: ANU Press, 1968, p. 37.

A version of what has often been taken to be the same myth is found in a third-century inscription from Mi-Son, in Cham territory. It refers to Kauṇḍinya, the founder of a new kingdom, as obtaining by magical means a spear which he took with him to the land where he encountered the princess Somā, daughter of the *Nāga* (serpent) king in his adoptive country. He stuck his spear in the ground in token of his conquest and took her to wife with the blessing of his father-in-law. The serpent princess, or *nāgī*, is an important figure of magic and power.

There are, however, various divergences between the inscription and the Chinese story. Not all versions of the latter give the founder a name which can readily be reconstructed as 'Kauṇḍinya'; he is nowhere identified as an Indian; and the indigenous queen is nowhere identified as Somā the serpent spirit.[9] It is clear that the Chinese accounts preserve an unreliable version of a type of origin myth which appears to have spread across Asia.[10] It may be wise to keep rigorously apart the Somā legend, with its parallels elsewhere, and the Chinese accounts which may have in them a reference to some historical figure.[11] The fact that a later ruler also bore the name of Kauṇḍinya (see below) may point to the existence of a genuine historical tradition, but the Chinese sources upon which we have to depend for most of what we know about these Kauṇḍinyas do not allow us to distinguish confidently between original observations and confusions between different places and times.

From the same third-century embassy comes information about Fu-nan's justice system:

---

[9]   P. Pelliot, Quelques textes chinois concernant l'Indochine hindouisée. In *Études asiatiques*, 2, Paris: Librairie Nationale d'Art et d'Histoire/Van Oest, 1925, pp. 243–63, at p. 245.

[10]   There are parallels to this myth in the Pāllava kingdom of southern India, in the story of the Thai national hero Phya Ruang, and in a Scythian legend (reported by Herodotus) telling of a river spirit (of the Dnieper) who gave birth to the first man by the king of the gods – a story which also involves a magic bow.

[11]   The Ch'in History calls this founder Huen Hui, a version of the name which cannot well be construed as representing Kauṇḍinya. C. Jacques (Histoire pré-angkorienne du pays khmer, unpublished MS) suggests the possibility that the Chinese accounts may point to a genuinely historical figure.

The law of the country is not to have prisons. The accused fasts and practises abstinence for three days. Then an axe is heated red and he is forced to carry it seven steps; or a gold ring or some eggs are thrown in boiling water and he must take them out. If he is guilty, the hand is burnt; if he is innocent, it is not. Also crocodiles are kept in the moats of the walls; and, outside of the gates, there are wild beasts in an enclosure. The accused are thrown to the wild beasts or to the crocodiles. If the wild beasts or the crocodiles do not eat them, they are considered innocent; at the end of three days, they are released.[12]

The use of ordeals is a common feature of the ancient Indian justice system; ordeals survived as a judicial procedure in the Cambodian code in the thirteenth century, when Chou Ta-kuan observed it, and as late as the eighteenth century, as reported by the nineteenth-century French scholar-official Adhémard Leclère.[13]

As for the ordinary life of the people of Fu-nan, the official history of the Southern Ch'i (Qi) dynasty (AD 479–501) tells us that

they take by force the inhabitants of the neighbouring cities who do not render them homage, and make them slaves. As merchandise, they have gold, silver, silks. The sons of the prosperous families wear sarongs of brocade. The poor wear a piece of cloth. The women pull a piece of cloth over the head. The people of Fu-nan make rings and bracelets of gold and vessels of silver. They cut down trees to build their houses. The king lives in a storeyed pavilion. They make their enclosures of wooden palisades. At the seashore grows a great bamboo, whose leaves are eight or nine feet long. The leaves are tressed to cover the houses. The people also live in houses raised from the ground . . . For amusements, the people have cock-fights and hog-fights . . . They have sugar cane, pomegranates, oranges and areca nuts in abundance.[14]

The Chinese accounts present a version of the political history of Fu-nan under 'Kauṇḍinya's' successors. At one stage

---

[12] Ibid., p. 268.
[13] Chou Ta-kuan, *Mémoires sur les coutumes du Cambodge de Tcheou Takouan*, tr. P. Pelliot. Paris: Ecole française d'Extrême-Orient, 1951, pp. 22f; A. Leclère, *Recherches sur le droit des Cambodgiens*. Paris: Challamel, 1894.
[14] Pelliot, Le Fou-nan, pp. 261f.

a general whom the Chinese called Fan Man was chosen to be king, and engaged in wars of conquest:

Once more he used troops to attack and subdue the neighbouring kingdoms, which all acknowledged themselves his vassals . . . He attacked more than ten kingdoms . . . He extended his territory for five to six thousand *li*. In Tun-sun there are five kings who all acknowledge themselves vassals of Fu-nan.[15]

This passage gives the impression of Fu-nan as an empire, but modern scholars are distrustful of such a portrayal. It is likely that the communities involved were all relatively small city-states scattered along the coast; they could conduct raids upon one another, but there were no great tracts of territory settled by agriculturalists, and it is not likely that centralized control could extend over any very large area.

Nevertheless, Fu-nan imported the Indian traditions of royal pomp. Indian royal customs were known and practised: as the Chinese tell us, 'When the King sits down, he squats on one side, raising the right knee, letting the left knee touch the earth. A piece of cotton is spread before him, on which are deposited the gold vases and incense burners.'[16] The posture described was one that was prescribed for kings, and it was later to be represented in the sculpture of Angkor and elsewhere.

Fu-nan, then, was less likely a dominant empire than the largest and most aggressive of a number of principalities. One of these, 'Tun-sun', was mentioned in the extract above. The account of it vouches for the status of Indian culture there and the rigour of its spiritual representatives' lifestyle:

In the country there are five hundred families of *hu*[17] from India, two *fo-t'u* [Buddhists], and more than a thousand Indian brahmans.

---

[15] P. Wheatley, *The Golden Khersonese*. Kuala Lumpur: Oxford University Press, 1966, pp. 15f. A *li* is a unit of measurement likely to have been (very approximately) 380 metres. This passage is preserved in the seventh-century *Liang Shu*.

[16] Pelliot, Le Fou-nan, pp. 269f.

[17] The term *hu* refers to people from the general area of Central Asia, especially Sogdians or Persians, or the kingdoms in northern India established by conquerors from there. See P. Wheatly, *Nagara and Commandery: Origins of Southeast Asian Urban Traditions*. Chicago: University of Chicago, Department of Geography Research Paper, nos 207–8, 1983, p. 353, n. 190.

The people of Tun-sun practise their doctrine and give them their daughters in marriage; consequently many of the brahmans do not go away. They do nothing but study the sacred canon, bathe themselves with scents and flowers, and practise piety ceaselessly by day and by night.[18]

There were quite a few of these little states, called into being by the Indian trade and possessed of Indian court culture. Among these, we must recognize those of the Cham people in central and southern Vietnam, while in the other direction there was a string of coastal city-states extending round the Gulf of Siam and down the Malay Peninsula. We know of these by names given them by the Chinese, but few can be precisely located on the map.

Fu-nan, like many South-East Asian states, sent tribute missions to the Chinese courts. In AD 243 a mission arrived from Fu-nan at the capital of the Wu kingdom in the south of China, sending a group of musicians as presents. There were other missions in 268, 285, 286 and 287, and in 357 an embassy was sent to the Eastern Chin dynasty (AD 317–419), which ruled southern China, with a tribute of trained elephants. The Emperor, 'considering these animals from distant lands as a source of danger to the people, ordered them returned'.[19]

Modern reconstructions of the history of Fu-nan generally attach some importance to the story of a second Kauṇḍinya who was supposed to have come from India around AD 400 by way of a place called P'an-p'an and ruled Fu-nan, re-establishing all the laws upon the Indian model.[20] However, Claude Jacques offers grounds for distrusting this Kauṇḍinya as much as the first.[21]

---

[18]   *T'ai-p'ing Yu-lan*, quoting *Nan-chou i-wu chih*, cited by Wheatley, *The Golden Khersonese*, p. 17.

[19]   Pelliot, Le Fou-nan, p. 255.

[20]   Coedès, *The Indianized States*, p. 56; cf. R. A. Stein, Le Lin-yi, sa localisation, sa contribution à la formation du Champa, et ses liens avec la Chine. *Han-hiue: Bulletin du Centre d'Etudes Sinologiques de Pékin*, 2.1–3 (1947), pp. 1–335, at p. 258.

[21]   Jacques, Histoire préangkorienne, pp. 34f: references in later Cambodian genealogies are like references to other legendary characters; stories which are legendary to begin with do not turn into historical fact by being reported in Chinese accounts. The 'Kauṇḍinya Jayavarman' who reigned late in the fifth century can be treated with much more confidence as there is inscriptional evidence of his rule.

Traders went back and forth, usually with royal sponsorship. In the latter part of the fifth century, a king of Fu-nan called Kauṇḍinya Jayavarman sent merchants to Canton; on their return, they were accompanied by the Buddhist monk Nāgasena who was on his way back to India. They were shipwrecked on the Vietnamese coast and mistreated by the Chams. When Nāgasena reached Fu-nan overland from Champa and met the king, he was given a commission to return to China taking a complaint about the Chams and presents which included two ivory stupas (models of Buddhist shrines). Nāgasena reported in China that the state religious cult was addressed to the Hindu god Śiva, and that Buddhism was also strong.

Jayavarman and his successors sent missions to the Liang dynasty in southern China (AD 502–56), and the tributes offered suggest the importance of Buddhism in Fu-nan.[22] In 539, an embassy (which, incidentally, brought a live rhinoceros) reported that Fu-nan possessed a hair relic of the Buddha.

The last part of Fu-nan's history offers us much firmer evidence than does the earlier period, because it is attested by a number of Sanskrit inscriptions recording some of the pious activities of sixth-century royalty. The references in them to various individuals have been assiduously analysed for whatever evidence they can be made to yield, but the results are equivocal. One inscription, from the province of Ta Keo, records the endowment of a brahmanical retreat by Queen Kulaprab-hāvatī, widow of the Jayavarman mentioned above; she insists upon the love he bore for her, and it has been surmised that her own son may have been passed over when Jayavarman was followed by King Rudravarman, a ruler who is mentioned in a number of inscriptions. The Queen's plaint at the fickleness of fortune may furnish a hint that she was engaged in a partisan struggle against Rudravarman.[23]

The details of political history are, however, meagre and ambiguous. We have much more solid information about the trade and tribute missions that linked Fu-nan with the outside world than about the annals of its courts. We do not know

[22] They included a coral Buddha image and leaves of the Bo tree (*Ficus religiosa*, the tree under which the Buddha was claimed to have obtained enlightenment).

[23] G. Coedès, in *Journal of the Greater India Society*, IV, no. 2 (July 1937), pp. 117–21; cf. Jacques, Histoire pré-angkorienne, pp. 47–9.

for certain whether or not Rudravarman was the last king of Fu-nan, or in exactly what circumstances his kingdom crumbled away, but we know that perspiring stevedores somehow loaded elephants and a rhinoceros upon the roughly hewn vessels that carried tribute to the courts of China.

The marine technology available to those who plied the waters of the southern seas was quite sophisticated. In these early centuries, the people who lived around the shores of South-East Asia penetrated as far as Madagascar long before Europeans were able to sail out of sight of their coasts.

Horses too came to Fu-nan by sea, ultimately from the Yueh-chih (Yuezhi) country in Central Asia. Iron came from Tan-tan (Dandan), a state to the south-west. Less bulky commodities traded around the coast included precious metals, tin, ivory, glass, coral carved into images, and pearls.[24]

Fu-nan was a thriving market, drawing Indian and other traders in quest of profit; it is only natural that, in the course of time, the Khmer chieftaincies in the interior should have been drawn into the network of exchange, acquiring the trappings of Indian culture and seeking to extend the sphere of their authority towards the favoured coast.

The process began with the intensification of overseas trade. The foreigners came seeking gold and forest products such as resins and aromatic wood. They brought with them carnelian, used for many inscribed seals found in many parts of South-East Asia, as well as agate, glassware and Buddhist or Hindu icons. Thus the initial contact with foreigners on the coasts produced a chain reaction of social and cultural readjustment that passed along the Mekong, as well as round the Vietnamese coast and the Gulf of Siam. The inland Khmers, who lived on the fringes of the forest or in clearings within it, were seasoned in its ways; inevitably they were drawn into the ambit of the new commercially orientated culture with its demand for forest products.

---

[24] One commodity traded was described as a kind of diamond found in the sea; it was said to become so hard when exposed to the light that it could not be broken even with an iron hammer, though, mysteriously the task could be accomplished with the horn of a ram. Ma Tuan-lin, *Ethnographie des peuples étrangers à la Chine*, 2 vols, tr. Marquis d'Hervey de Saint-Denys. Geneva: Georg, 1883, vol. 2, p. 438 and ibid., n. 12.

Their chieftains became pre-eminent in wealth and authority, and their successors were the rulers of the Indian-style principalities which eventually were to incorporate the whole Khmer territory. This at least is a plausible reconstruction of the alchemy of state formation in this part of South-East Asia. It is almost literally alchemy, considering the operation within it of the Indian quest for gold. By the end of the sixth century, with the decline of the coastal trading centres, inland Khmer principalities came into their own.

7

The Early Khmer Kingdoms and the Rise of Angkor

Late in the sixth century, 'Fu-nan' disappears from the Chinese record, and its place is taken by the Khmer city-states further north where minor *rajas* competed for hegemony. This formative stage lasted to the rise of Angkor in the ninth century, and here we shall be looking at what little is known of Khmer history in this period.

Some historians are inclined to place the ancestral home of Khmer statehood at the site of Vat Ph'u in Laos, near Bassac and not far from the confluence of the Mun and the Mekong rivers. Recent excavations in the area have yielded evidence of constructions thought by some to be Cham, but at present firm conclusions cannot be drawn. Nevertheless, it is often thought that Khmer dominion was asserted over formerly Cham territory, and Khmer nationhood first conceived, in the area of Vat Ph'u.

One historian, L. P. Briggs, responds to the charm of an ancient landscape, heavy with history: 'The scene from the esplanade is magnificent. In contrast to Preah Vihear, the mountains are wooded and the fields and marshes are green. The view leads down to the river and across the valley to the plateau of Boloven.'[1] He goes on to quote L. Finot, the first director of the *Ecole française d'Extrême-Orient*: 'I do not know that the Cambodian architects have ever shown more taste in the choice of a site, more art in its planning, more skill in combining the

[1] L. P. Briggs, *The Ancient Khmer Empire*. Philadelphia, Pa: American Philosophical Society, 1951, p. 163.

accidents of its terrain and the arrangement of buildings upon it, in such a way as to produce a striking impression of nobility and majesty.'[2] An inscription thought to date back to the later fifth century records the pious activity of a king Devānīka, entitled a 'great king of kings' (*mahārājādhirāja*), who had come from far away. It has been speculated that he may have come from Champa.

However, there is no real indication where his origin might have been. The origins of the Khmer principalities that succeeded 'Fu-nan' are teasingly obscure. Although Vat Ph'u may mark an ancient sacred site, nearly all the activities of Khmer rulers solidly attested in the period following 'Fu-nan' took place further south, within the area of modern Cambodia. The ancient settlement at Vat Ph'u was not at the heart of an empire; nor was it the centre of coalescence where larger kingdoms began to appear in the period after 'Fu-nan'.

It was in the seventh and eighth centuries that these kingdoms appeared; we know something about them from the inscriptions of their rulers. The first inscription in the Khmer language, heavily influenced by Sanskrit vocabulary, is dated AD 612 and comes from Angkor Borei; in the following century there were many more. But the details of political geography in each generation are obscure. For some of what we know, we are again indebted to Chinese sources, which speak of a Khmer state called 'Chen-la' (Zhenla). It is not clear what this name represents, but it is clearly an attempt to represent a foreign name with Chinese syllables.

Just as with 'Fu-nan', we are confronted with a peculiarly Chinese perception of other parts of the world. Many historians believe that for virtually all the 'Chen-la' period there was no one major kingdom of the Khmers but an arena of principalities in competition. Thus, at one extreme we have before us the suggestion in the Chinese sources that the Khmers were subjects of a single unitary state, Chen-la, which split into two for a period in the eighth century, and at the other we have the view of 'Chen-la' as an arena of competing transient chiefdoms. It is clear at least that certain kings were able to assert their

---

[2] L. Finot, Vat phou. *Bulletin de l'Ecole française d'Extrême-Orient*, 2 (1902), pp. 241–5, at p. 241.

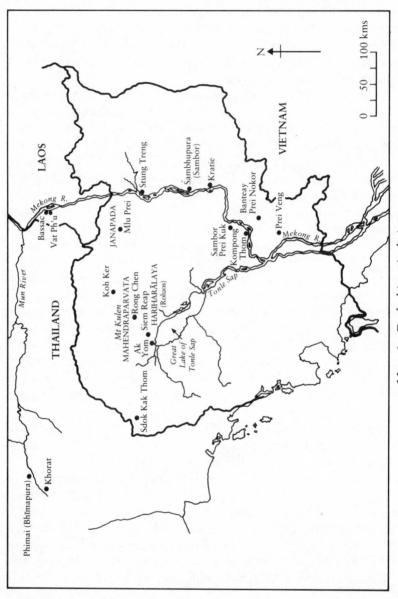

Map 6   Early historical sites

authority over a great part of the Khmer territory, and it has recently been suggested by Michael Vickery that there was indeed for most of the seventh and eighth centuries just one main centre of power. On his view, the competition was not so much between separate states as between different cliques clustering around members of the Khmer royalty.[3]

The record begins with King Bhavavarman, who is known from Chinese sources and from a couple of inscriptions. He flourished late in the sixth century, and the site of his capital Bhavapura has been debated; most recently it has been argued that it was in the vicinity of Sambor Prei Kuk (near Kompong Thom), a site famous for the monuments of a later ruler.[4]

The most influential pioneering work on the period of transition from Fu-nan to Chen-la was carried out by Coedès, who saw Bhavavarman as a descendant of Fu-nan royalty who married into Khmer royalty, became a Khmer ruler in the north and conquered Fu-nan. The assumptions behind this reconstruction are now widely questioned; the suggestions that have been made on the basis of more recent research do not accept the Chinese picture of a major political discontinuity between separate and successive kingdoms, Fu-nan and Chen-la. There was a geographical discontinuity – Fu-nan was in decline during the sixth century, and in the seventh centres of power appeared further north – but this does not mean that one political block displaced another.

We learn from the inscriptions that Bhavavarman was the grandson of a 'Sārvabhauma', which as a title means 'Lord of all the Earth'; there is no overwhelming reason for identifying this individual with any known ruler, but it may be that he was the Great King of Kings, the Devānīka of the Vat Ph'u inscription; or he may have been Rudravarman of Fu-nan. Bhavavarman's father was Vīravarman; there is no persuasive evidence either for asserting or for denying that Vīravarman was a king, whether of Fu-nan or of Chen-la.

Bhavavarman's kingdom was probably confined to the area around the Great Lake, extending towards the Mekong on the

---

[3] Michael Vickery, Where and what was Chenla? Unpublished MS.
[4] See C. Jacques, Histoire préangkorienne du pays khmer. Unpublished MS.

east. His kinsman[5] and eventual successor was Citrasena, who took the regal name Mahendravarman and followed a career of conquest that took him into what is now north-eastern Thailand. In about 600, after the death of Bhavavarman, Citrasena-Mahendravarman returned to Bhavapura; he was responsible for the endowment of a number of shrines containing *lingas* (phallic emblem of the god Śiva) along the Mekong. The kingdom was probably extended into part of the former territory of 'Fu-nan'. An embassy was sent to Champa.[6]

Īśānavarman, probably descended from Citrasena, appears to have extended his influence over a great part of Cambodia; his dominion extended westward as far as Chanthaburi on the Thai coast, and perhaps in the opposite direction to the coastal area near the modern Vietnamese border, where an inscription refers to him as overlord. However, none of his inscriptions has been found north of the Dangreks, and the excursion of Citrasena-Mahendravarman into north-eastern Thailand should be seen as an episode in imperial history rather than evidence of any permanent establishment of the dominant Khmer power so far north. In some later centuries, though, the whole area around Phimai, north of the Dangreks in Thailand, was to be controlled and settled by the Khmers.

Īśānavarman was flourishing during the 620s. His reign is attested by fourteen inscriptions. By 628 he was dead (or else his dominions were falling apart).

The cult of Śiva was patronized by the early rulers of Chenla, as the foundation of *linga* shrines by Mahendravarman clearly illustrates. The seventh-century traveller I-ching (Yijing) was possibly referring to Mahendravarman when he wrote that 'the way of the Buddha prospered and spread, but nowadays a wicked king has expelled and exterminated all the monks'.[7]

---

[5] His brother, according to Claude Jacques, 'Funan', 'Zhenla': the reality concealed by these Chinese views of Indochina. In R. B. Smith and W. Watson (eds), *Early South East Asia: Essays in archaeology, history and historical geography*, New York: Oxford University Press, 1979, pp. 371–9, *contra* Georges Coedès, who finally opted for the identification as cousin.

[6] G. Coedès, *The Indianized States of Southeast Asia*, tr. S. Cowing. Canberra: Australian National University Press, 1968, p. 69.

[7] I-ching, *A Record of the Buddhist Religion as Practised in India and the Malay Archipelago*, tr. J. Takakusu. Oxford: Clarendon Press, 1896, p. 12.

Another ruler, Jayavarman I, came from the area north-east of the Great Lake; he is known to have been ruling in the period AD 657–91. He was the son of an independent prince, Candravarman, and his mother was connected through a mysterious '*Yuvarāja*' (or 'Crown Prince') to Īśānavarman. He established his capital Purandarapura at a site which Claude Jacques has identified with Ak Yum (west of the Phnom Bakheng at the centre of Angkor).

These three men are the most famous kings of seventh-century Cambodia. The epigraphy of the Chen-la period would allow us to include a great deal of genealogical history in the record, but in most cases it is not clear how much power the 'kings' cited in the genealogies had, or where they reigned. The picture given by the Chinese sources is certainly too simple; it portrays for us an undivided kingdom, called Chen-la, in the seventh century, and in the eighth this kingdom is represented as having split into two – a Land Chen-la to the north and a Water Chen-la to the south. This division was said to have occurred in AD 706, and it remained in effect according to Chinese sources until 838, when steps had already been taken towards the unification of the Khmers under one ruler.

Even during the lifetime of Land Chen-la, in the seventh century, different principalities were sending their own embassies to China; in the year 638 four embassies came from the north-west of the Khmer territory. Various kings are named in the inscriptions. An Īśvarakumāra ruled at Jyeṣṭhapura in the north-west. A Bhavavarman II may have to be recognized in the eighth century, possibly from a separate line. Pierre Dupont recognized five distinct dynasties sharing central and eastern Cambodia in about the middle of the eighth century.[8] During the Water Chen-la period, it was said in the *History of the Former T'ang* that there were various little towns to the east, 'all of which are called kingdoms'.[9] Claude Jacques identifies

---

[8] P. Dupont, La dislocation du Tchen-la et la formation du Cambodge angkorien (V^e–IXe siècles). *Bulletin de l'Ecole française d'Extrême-Orient*, 43 (1943–6), pp. 17–55, at p. 54.

[9] O. W. Wolters, North-western Cambodia in the seventh century. *Bulletin of the School of Oriental and African Studies*, 37 (1974), pp. 355–84, at p. 370.

a series of thirteen cities likely to have been independent principalities at times.[10]

Recent work by Michael Vickery seeks to map the relationships between the various kings and princes (and their wives) and to make reliable inferences about the location and extent of their domains. One broad conclusion he makes is that it is possible to trace the gradual evolution of political institutions from the early local masters (called *poñ*) of small communities clustered around, and identified in part by, the ponds which sustained their agricultural efforts. These 'ponds' seem to have been the artificial tanks or other water sources which were necessary to sustain the occupation of land, and around which hamlets or divisions of larger settlements were grouped. Vickery has sought to trace from the evidence of inscriptions the history of the status of these *poñ* and the evolution of larger units of power.[11] On the other hand, Jacques has argued against the identification of *poñ* with minor local chiefs, noting that it was possible for a prince, the son of the lord of Jyeṣṭhapura, to have the title of *poñ*.[12] At all events, this title died out after the seventh century; it was superseded by the title *mratāñ*, which appeared in the later seventh century in the north and became frequent as an important title from the eighth century through into the Angkor period.

The tendency in recent research has been to diminish the size, political centralization and power of the early Khmer states, although Vickery's work suggests that this tendency may be going too far. There may have been a measure of division in the eighth century (as the Chinese reference to a split between Land and Water Chen-la asserts), but the epigraphy of the Angkor

[10] Jacques, 'Funan', 'Zhenla', p. 378. The cities are Aninditapura, Bhavapura, Vyādhapura, Śreṣṭhapura, Amoghapura, Cakrāṅkapura, Bhīmapura, Tāmrapura, Dhānvīpura, Purandarapura, Liṅgapura, Ugrapura, and Dhruvapura.

[11] M. Vickery, Some remarks on early state formation in Cambodia. In D. Marr and A. Milner (eds), *Southeast Asia in the 9th to 14th Centuries*, Canberra and Singapore: Research School of Pacific Studies, Australian National University/Institute of Southeast Asian Studies, 1986, pp. 95–115.

[12] C. Jacques, Le pays khmer avant Angkor. *Dossiers histoire et archéologie*, 25 (March 1988), p. 88. He is not convinced of the close link between *poñ* and water sources.

period, he suggests, provides evidence of a clustering of lines of royal descent around the royal women of Śambhupura in the eighth century. This clustering may reflect the continuing integrity of a main centre of power, however many princes were competing for it.[13]

Whether the Khmer states were few or many, they were sophisticated and cosmopolitan; their masters could afford to live in style, and their wise men could plumb the secrets of Sanskrit religious texts. The Cambodians believed in splendid royal ceremonial:

Every three days the King goes solemnly to the audience-hall and sits on a bed made of five pieces of sandalwood and ornamented with seven kinds of precious stones. Above this bed is a pavilion of magnificent cloth, whose columns are of inlaid wood. The walls are ivory, mixed with flowers of gold. The ensemble of this bed and the pavilion form a sort of little palace, at the background of which is suspended . . . a disc with rays of gold in the form of flames. A golden incense burner, which two men handle, is placed in front . . . More than a thousand guards dressed with cuirasses and armed with lances are ranged at the foot of the steps of the throne, in the halls of the palace, at the doors and peristyle.[14]

This then is the patchy record of the principalities of Chen-la. It was not until the reign of Jayavarman II that a foundation for durable Khmer political unity was laid. The circumstances of the rise of this monarch are obscure. He left no inscriptions of his own but is frequently referred to in the inscriptions of later kings, who regarded him, officially at least, as the founder of the kingdom. He was said to have come from 'Java', though this name is perhaps more likely to refer to somewhere on the Malayan coast. In asserting Khmer unity and independence, he was rebutting the claims to overlordship of 'Java', but we do not otherwise know of the historical circumstances in which such overlordship might be recognized.

Arab sources offer an intriguing story of eighth-century derring-do in which it is tempting to seek an explanation of these circumstances; however the story, though a good one, is

---

[13] Vickery, Where and what was Chenla?
[14] Ma Tuan-lin, *Ethnographie des peuples étrangers à la Chine*, 2 vols, tr. Marquis d'Hervey de Saint-Denys. Geneva: Georg, 1883, vol. 2, p. 461.

likely to owe much to the contamination of legend. It is attributed to a merchant called Sulayman, who passed through South-East Asia in 851, half a century after the events which he related. These credentials might carry some weight, but in fact it is likely that the story attributed to Sulayman originated from a later source. For what it is worth, the surviving account tells of the Mahārāja of Zabag, a maritime confederacy in the South-East Asian archipelago, possibly a name for a confederacy of the Malays (referred to as 'Javanese') who were conducting raids around the coasts, pillaging as far north as Champa.

The Mahārāja of Zabag came to hear of idle words that had been uttered in public by the King of the Khmers:

> 'I have one desire,' said the King, 'which I would like to satisfy.' The minister, who was sincerely devoted to his sovereign and who knew his rashness in making decisions, asked him: 'What is that desire, O King?' The latter replied: 'I wish to see before me, on a plate, the head of the Mahārāja, King of Zabag.'

The minister sought to dissuade his master from entertaining any such fancies, and especially from voicing them in public. But the damage was done. The Mahārāja learned of the episode, and determined to punish the Khmer King for his vanity.

The Mahārāja assembled a well-equipped fleet of a thousand vessels and sailed up the river leading to the Khmer ruler's capital to take it by surprise. The palace was captured and the errant King brought before the emperor, who declared to the captive that he was about to do to the Khmers exactly what their King had wished to do to Zabag – not to plunder and annex the kingdom, but to see the ruler's head on a plate. The execution was performed, and the conqueror went home without doing any harm to any of the Khmers:

> The Mahārāja then had the head of the King of Khmer washed and embalmed. It was put in a vase and sent to the King who had replaced the decapitated King of Khmer on the throne ... After this moment, the Kings of the Khmer, every morning, on rising, turn the face in the direction of Zabag, incline themselves to the earth and humiliate themselves before the Mahārāja to render him homage.[15]

---

[15] Briggs, *The Ancient Khmer Empire*, p. 68.

We cannot accept this story as historical, but it may be based, with some embroidery, upon events that actually took place. At all events, even if we ignore the story, it is reasonable to suppose that in the latter part of the eighth century Chen-la was in disarray, and that (as an eleventh-century inscription tells us) the task of Jayavarman II was not only to unite the Khmers but also to rebut the claims over them made by the 'Javanese'. With his career, important steps were taken towards the unification of the Khmers beneath the authority of one throne.

The ninth century saw the establishment of a Khmer kingdom near the northern shore of the Great Lake floodwaters, well placed to benefit from the quarries of the Kulens to the north, the cornucopia of fish offered by the Lake, and the routes to Cham and Mon territory to east and west respectively. The ruler who laid the foundations for this larger state was Jayavarman II.

Kings in Cambodia were officially known after their deaths by posthumous titles. Jayavarman II, when he died in about AD 834, went to his own special heaven and was thereafter known by his posthumous name, Parameśvara, which declared his destiny in the abode of the supreme lord Śiva.

The great days of the Khmer people had begun, though they might not all have known it yet. A multitude of fiefs run by families of warrior barons was not to acquire a sense of communal identity overnight. But they had plenty of time to become accustomed to greatness. The awesomeness that was Angkor lasted for several hundred years.

How important was the reign of Jayavarman II really? The tendency of much recent research has been to dismantle the images of proud monolithic monarchical states set up for us by the eulogistic inscriptions; in their place, we are offered a kaleidoscope. The graven images portray a series of great kings ruling great kingdoms. The kaleidoscope presents a constantly shifting pattern of power relationships, made of fragments.

The image of Jayavarman II as founder of an empire is the work of later rulers, who looked back to his achievements as a source of legitimacy. He did not leave any personal record of great deeds or any impressive monuments, however; his achievements are likely to be exaggerated by those who recounted them much later for their own purposes. It could be argued that his reign did not mark a decisive new departure; it was just a stage along the way.

Symbolic of this continuity with the past is the (adventitious) fact that he was not the *first*. Jayavarman II is so numbered in conformity to the conventions of modern historians. These conventions are based upon the work of French scholars, who have established the standard lists of rulers, including all the Jayavarmans, Sūryavarmans and so forth, in the region. Where the Khmers are concerned, the numbering of kings begins in the period of 'Chen-la'. This is a reminder that, whether Jayavarman regarded himself as first or second, his kingdom was continuous with the earlier monarchies, and Jayavarman I had already been and gone.

Nevertheless, it would be a mistake to divest the reign of Jayavarman II of all special significance. The very fact that it was later looked back upon as the beginning of a pan-Khmer regime indicates that there was, however gradually it was consolidated, a real discontinuity between the jostling principalities of 'Chen-la' and the empire that came into being during the ninth and tenth centuries.

Any modern historical analysis of the changes which were taking place in the Khmer sense of political identity must consider practical, mundane factors such as economic and demographic expansion, the ability to acquire booty for the gratification of warriors and the manipulation of patron–client networks. However, people who live through changes do not see them in the same way as historians centuries later. Whatever the economic or social factors responsible for unification might have been, the process was a stressful one that demanded a redefinition of loyalties, and the Cambodians needed a way of representing such a redefinition to themselves.

Loyalties were defined in ritual terms. The *devarāja* cult, instituted by Jayavarman, is a ritual statement, and it is possible to regard it as an expression of a Khmer ideal of political unity, even though this ideal was not realized immediately or for some time thereafter.

Its importance as a symbol can be acknowledged. What we need to recognize, though, is that there is no compelling evidence that Jayavarman II and his contemporaries already had this sense of political identity, fully fledged. The Khmers of later centuries, who saw themselves as legatees of the unitary state that came into existence only fitfully and by degrees, were able to project their sense of identity back upon it.

At all events, according to an eleventh-century inscription, the cult was established by the king and known as the *kamraten jagat ta rāja* (in Khmer), or *devarāja* (in Sanskrit).

Then His Majesty Parameśvara ['Supreme Lord', an epithet of the god Śiva and the posthumous name of Jayavarman II] went as lord (*kurun*) over Mahendraparvata ... Then a brahman called Hiraṇyadāma, expert in magic science, came from Janapada, because His Majesty Parameśvara had invited him to perform a ceremony such as to make it impossible for this land of the Kambujas to offer any allegiance to Java, and such as to make possible the existence of a lord over the earth who was absolutely unique, who should be *cakravartin* (lord of the whole world).[16]

The cult had attached to it a line of hereditary priests; the long inscription from Sdok Kak Thom (dating from the eleventh century), from which the passage above is taken, was inscribed on behalf of this line, in order to record the grants and privileges to which the family was entitled by virtue of the office accorded it by Jayavarman II and the bounty of some later kings. The founder of the line, Śivakaivalya, was taught the liturgy by the Hiraṇyadāma named above, and passed it on; the office of chief priest was transmitted in the maternal line.

The cult, then, was important to a family of priests in the eleventh century; this does not mean that it was important as a decisive statement of sovereign power at the time of its institution by Jayavarman II. Its significance is devalued somewhat by evidence that it was not unique after all. An inscription from near Ba Phnom says that the 'Lord of the Earth' (*prthivīnarendra*) had a ritual conducted which was to make it impossible for 'Java' to press claims upon the Khmers;[17] it is likely that the Lord of the Earth was in fact Jayavarman, and

[16] Sdok Kak Thom stele inscription, lines 70ff: G. Coedès and P. Dupont, *L'inscription de Sdok Kak Thom. Bulletin de l'Ecole française d'Extrême-Orient,* 43 (1943–6), pp. 57–134.
[17] C. Jacques, La carrière de Jayavarman II. *Bulletin de l'Ecole française d'Extrême-Orient,* 59 (1972), pp. 205–20, at pp. 212f.

this ritual is of course very similar to the later, and more famous, *devarāja*; when we consider that, in principle, there might have been any number of such rituals conducted without any obvious major political consequences it becomes clearer that we should not jump to conclusions about the immediate political import-ance of the *devarāja*.

What, precisely, did the cult involve? G. Coedès, pioneer and grand master of Angkorian studies, identified it with the cult of kings at state shrines, but more recent research has discarded this identification. J. Filliozat regarded it as a cult of Śiva under the name of Devarāja, which this god bore in South India; he emphasized the purity of its Indian descent.[18] H. Kulke took the important step of dissociating it decisively from the cult of royal shrines, and suggested that it was a bronze image of Śiva.[19] More recently, C. Jacques has suggested that, instead of seeing the Khmer version of the name as a translation of the Sanskrit (*devarāja* = 'king of the gods', or, as some took it, 'god-king'), the latter was in fact a translation of an originally Khmer name for a local Khmer god – the 'god who is the king', *kamraten jagat ta raja*.[20] Michael Vickery accepts the *devarāja* as a type of Khmer cult, but denies that the evidence allows us to recognize its operation before the tenth century.[21] Whatever the origin and meaning of the term, it must be recognized that the cult had to take its place within the universe of Khmer religious thought, as a patron spirit with protective power, like the *nak ta*.

The cult, then, may well serve for us as an important symbol of the Khmer sense of identity, but it is unlikely that such success as Jayavarman achieved is to be attributed essentially to any declaration of his divinity. To appreciate the achievements of his reign we need to look at his political career.

---

[18] See particularly G. Coedès, *Angkor: An introduction*, tr. E. Gardiner. Hong Kong: Oxford University Press, 1963.
[19] H. Kulke, *The Devarāja Cult*, tr. I. W. Mabbett, Cornell University Southeast Asia Program, Data Paper no. 108. Ithaca, N.Y.: Cornell University, 1978.
[20] C. Jacques, The Kamraten Jagat in ancient Cambodia. In *Indus Valley to Mekong Delta: Explorations in epigraphy*, ed. Karashima Norbu, Madras: New Era Publications, 1985, pp. 269–86.
[21] M. Vickery, The reign of Sūryavarman I and royal factionalism at Angkor. *Journal of Southeast Asian Studies*, 16, no. 2 (1985), pp. 226–44, at p. 235.

This involved a great deal of travel. Originating from the principality of Aninditapura, he spent time in 'Java', possibly (as we have seen) somewhere on the Malay Peninsula. Part of his early career may have been spent as a prisoner or hostage among these 'Javanese'. His first power base among the Khmers was probably in the vicinity of Prei Veng; this served as a home base for his campaigns. Jayavarman subsequently made himself master of Śambhupura (Sambor, on the Mekong above Kratie), probably by marriage to a princess there. For a time he ruled at Indrapura. His later peregrinations took him to the region north of the Great Lake, the later heartland of Angkor and the territory of Aninditapura. He establishd capitals at Hariharālaya (a few miles south-east of Siemreap), Mahendraparvata (in the Kulen hills to the north of Siemreap and the site of his declaration of Khmer independence), and Amarendrapura (somewhere to the west of the Angkor district). Several inscriptions suggest that Jayavarman had groups of settlers sent from Vyādhapura to colonize districts at Amarendrapura. Finally he settled again at Hariharālaya, which remained the Khmer capital district for most of the ninth century.

There has been doubt about Jayavarman's dates. It has long been conventional to date his accession from the consecration on Mount Mahendra in 802, but it appears that his career as monarch had then already lasted some time. Jacques has pointed out that there was a Jayavarman at Indrapura[22] as early as AD 770; if this was Jayavarman II, obviously his reign began much earlier than has normally been thought. Jacques has argued that his rule began in 790 and lasted to about 835, when he was eighty-four.[23]

Despite the length of his reign, we have little evidence of any

[22]   A city which is to be identified with Banteay Prei Nokor, according to Jacques, although Vickery has argued for an identification with the site of Sambor Prei Kuk. See M. Vickery, Some remarks on early state formation in Cambodia. In Marr and Milner, *Southeast Asia in the 9th to 14th Centuries*, pp. 95–115.
[23]   Inscription K583 at the Baphuon refers to a Parameśvara (Jayavarman's posthumous name) reigning in 790, which supports the earlier dating of Jayavarman's accession. There is doubt about the location of Vyādhapura and Indrapura, both of them cities said to have been controlled by Jayavarman. See Jacques, La carrière de Jayavarman II.

constructive activities. There is an inscription referring to his digging a reservoir in Indrapura, probably in the early part of his reign. Also, the three-tiered pyramid of Rong Chen on a high point of the Kulen hills may date from his residence at Mahendraparvata.

The assessment of his empire-building activity is problematic. Somehow, in the course of a series of manoeuvres that are nowhere recorded in any detail, he made himself master of a substantial part of the land of the Khmers. The Prasat Ben inscription refers to a ruler whose empire extends in the four cardinal directions to China, the ocean, Champa and 'Sūkṣma-kamrātaka' – possibly the Cardamom Hills – and it has been thought that the ruler here identified is in fact Jayavarman II.[24] If so, the implication is that his dominion extended, at its greatest, as far as that of the founder of the city of Angkor proper, Yaśovarman.

However, we should not be misled by hindsight into imagining that, because he wanted to unify the Khmers, and because we know that ultimately the Khmers were unified, the job was done effectively and for good by Jayavarman. What his frequent changes of capital suggest is that he was engaged in constant struggle against the barons of the principalities that made up 'Water Chen-la'. His move from Amarendrapura to Mahendraparvata may represent a retreat rather than a triumphal progress; Mahendrapura was established at an in-convenient site and was never used as a model for the design of capitals in later reigns. The establishment of Hariharālaya as his last capital does not mark the end of the process of pacification; it marks one stage, which was to be followed by others under his successors.

Unification was an irregular and fitful process, not a once-for-all achievement; but in the end it came to be embodied in the Khmer state that survives today. Unity was not eternally predestined; after all, the Mon communities did not turn into a comparable nation. Unity was the product of particular historical conditions.

---

[24] G. Coedès, *Inscriptions du Cambodge*. Paris and Hanoi: Ecole française d'Extrême-Orient, 1937–66, vol. 7, p. 164; Jacques, La carrière de Jayavarman II.

The natural advantages of the region must be a part of the explanation of Angkor's history of glory; but there must also be a great deal else. The Khmer realm was itself an artefact. It was a constellation of communities sustained by stretches of water; it was contained within a larger community of people who spoke Mon-Khmer dialects. We may hope to uncover some of the geographic, economic or demographic facts that brought these principalities together and gave to the larger Khmer realm an independent reality; we must remember, though, that for the Khmers themselves it was the powerful spiritual energies of the great gods that made them, in any practical sense, one; and upon these gods depended the careers of a succession of kings.

8

The Kings of Angkor

In dealing with Angkor, the historian has to choose between a chronological account and a thematic one. The disadvantage of the first is that it arbitrarily dismembers thematic topics (such as architecture or agriculture or society) into fragments that are separated from each other in order to be placed in their respective reigns or sub-periods. The disadvantage of the second is that it masks the important changes that took place, and which are necessary to the understanding of the dynamics of Khmer history in its various aspects.

Here, both approaches need to be combined. So far, we have been following the evolution of Khmer culture from prehistoric times to the rise of Angkor. In the present chapter, we shall survey the political history of Angkor, one of the most spectacular empires of early South-East Asia. In the following seven chapters, some of the major aspects of traditional Khmer history and culture (primarily in the period of Angkor) will be explored thematically before we move on to more recent history in the final two chapters.

The rise of Angkor did not all at once mark a quantum leap into a new type of society, but a programme was articulated, an aspiration declared: the Khmers were to be brought under a single independent regime, free of the claims of any foreign power. The rituals instituted by Jayavarman in consecration of this declaration were accompanied by conquests that brought the Khmers further towards unity.

The name 'Angkor' is applied either to the empire ruled by

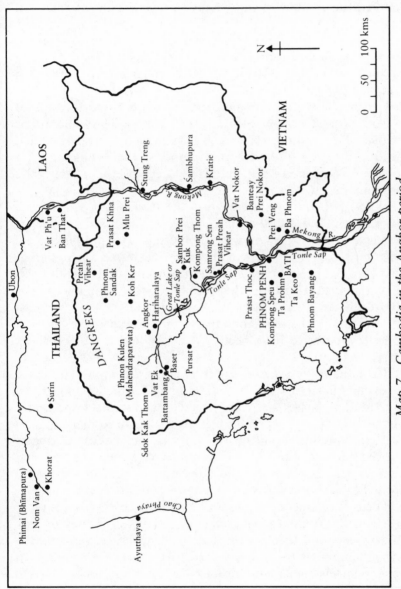

Map 7 *Cambodia in the Angkor period*

Jayavarman's successors or to the complex of monumental buildings (of which Angkor Wat is the most famous) that marked the capitals of most later rulers. During the reigns of Jayavarman II and his immediate successors, this complex had not begun to take shape. Roluos (Hariharālaya), the site of Jayavarman's final capital, is about eight miles to the south-east of the present-day provincial capital of Siemreap. The main complex of monuments is a few miles north of it.

For much of the remainder of the ninth century, the successors of Jayavarman ruled at Hariharālaya. The foundations of one of these successors, Indravarman I (*c*.877–889/890 AD) deserve attention, because they stand at the beginning of a long record of monuments built by kings to fulfil a systematic programme.

His first major foundation was the Preah Koh, a group of tower shrines dedicated to his parents, his maternal grandparents, and to Jayavarman II and his queen; the second was the Bakong, the first of the state shrines set on pyramids that became the hallmark of the Angkor kingdom. It is thought that the central shrine that crowned this monument was destroyed during the fighting that attended the succession to Indravarman. The sandstone tower that now occupies the top terrace appears to have been added two and a half centuries later.

The modern-day visitor may still admire these foundations on an excursion from Siemreap, a short trip across flat country by a road that passes between ricefields and crosses the water channels by humpbacked bridges. At the Preah Koh, a statue of the bull Nandin, mount of the god Śiva, sits forever staring at the crumbling towers. The Bakong may be approached along a causeway guarded by a great *nāga* serpent that lifts its seven stone heads to the sky.

These monuments represent a pattern that was to recur often in the quest for legitimacy: a group of shrines to previous rulers and their wives, and then a pyramid representing the mountain of the gods, destined to receive the king's own relics – jewels, gold leaf, hair locks, nail parings, and so forth – after his death. Indravarman was a prototypical emperor, a fact proclaimed (though we do not have to take the details literally) by the inscription which says: 'His rule was like a crown of jasmine on the lofty heads of the kings of China, Champa and Java.'[1]

Inscriptions like this, and those of the temples endowed in the first two centuries of Angkor, are continuous with those of the 'Chen-la' period in attesting merit-earning activity by endowing religious foundations; they list large numbers of temple servants attached to these foundations, and many of them have sections composed in sophisticated Sanskrit verse. One innovation that has been observed on the evidence of such inscriptions is a new tendency to found villages by the deliberate transplanting of groups of people. Another important development in the ninth century was the building of tomb-shrines that constituted the ritual centre of the kingdom; in later centuries such structures were to surpass in importance the royal shrines which, in the earlier periods of Khmer history, had been built to mark holy sites on mountains.

The centring of Angkor upon an artificial mountain of the gods was more grandly performed by King Yaśovarman (c.889/890–910/912), after a period of fratricidal strife. The battles that attended this competition involved a great naval conflict on the Great Lake and may have seen the destruction of most of the royal city, so that the move north was expedient.[2] Possibly he had been viceroy at the eventual site of Yaśodharapura before his accession.

The capital site chosen by Yaśovarman enabled him to place a real hill, the Phnom Bakheng, at its centre. Symbolically it was the mountain of the gods, Mount Meru at the centre of the cosmos, and the kingdom was the centre of the world. From the steeply pitched terraces of the Bakheng monument, nowadays surrounded by scrubby woodland, one could command a king's-eye view of the great city of Yaśodharapura, which for centuries was to mark the home territory of Khmer kings. In the 1960s it was still possible for tourists to ascend the Bakheng hill on the back of an elephant, and no doubt Yaśovarman did the same. The sense of rising above it all must have been

[1] G. Coedès, *Inscriptions du Cambodge*, 8 vols. Paris and Hanoi: Ecole française d'Extrême-Orient, 1937–66, vol. 1, p. 43.
[2] C. Jacques, Sur les données de la stèle de Tuol Ta Pec, K.834. *Bulletin de l'Ecole française d'Extrême-Orient*, 58 (1971), pp. 163–75.

exhilarating for him as he peered down almost vertically from his gently swaying mount at the gleaming temple towers and tiled roofs far below, feeling the caress of a softly cooling breeze.

The extent of his empire is attested by his inscriptions, which have been found in the south of present-day Cambodia, in Laos, and west into Thailand, near Chantaburi. There is no evidence of his dominion at Sambor Prei Kuk, regarded by some historians as the old Bhavapura of 'Chen-la' times.

Yaśovarman's constructions are impressive. Not only was he responsible for the building of the Eastern Baray, eight times the size of Indravarman's reservoir, but his capital city Yaśodharapura was enclosed by a fortifying embankment marking a square 4 kilometres long on each side. At its centre was the Bakheng, with its five tower sanctuaries on the topmost of its five tiers.

The king also constructed a causeway connecting the capital with the older city site at Roluos. Satellite photography helps us to identify parts of this route, which runs north-westwards from Roluos along a line that meets the eastern wall of Yaśodharapura a little north of its mid-point. Now, a number of later kings built their palaces just to the north of their state shrines in the centre of their capitals. In such a case, a ceremonial approach road running eastwards (the auspicious direction) from the palace to the city wall would meet it at a point a little to the north of the mid-point of the east wall; this precisely describes, for example, Jayavarman VII's city of Angkor Thom, with axial roads bisecting the four walls, and a fifth gateway opposite the palace. The fact that a highway ran to meet the east wall of Yaśodharapura at the appropriate point is therefore evidence that the palace, made of wood and now vanished without trace above the ground, was to the north of the Bakheng. Archaeology may uncover evidence of the palace in the future.[3]

Twenty stele inscriptions in different places commemorate the founding of religious foundations (some along the side of the Eastern Baray), and set out rules for the conduct of their denizens. They should wear only white; they should not deck themselves with parasols or ornaments. A scale of fines is set out

[3]   C. Jacques, personal communication.

for infringement of the rules: where a prince pays 20 *pala* of gold, a commoner pays only three-quarters of a *pala* or receives a hundred blows of the rattan.

Yaśovarman was, according to inscriptions, a formidable foe – it was said that he shattered a solid block of copper into three with a single blow of his sword.

His capital site remained until the fourteenth century at the heart of the empire; later rulers built new great shrines to represent the centre of the world, new palaces, new complexes of religious and administrative buildings, but they clustered around or overlapped Yaśodharapura, their gilt towers reflected in the waterways that progressively extended the system founded upon the reservoir of Yaśovarman's Eastern Baray.

In a sense, he was Angkor's founder, but it would be a mistake to suppose that the foundation of the Khmer empire was now secure. On the contrary, there were to be many serious reverses, and a constant threat of fragmentation into numerous prin-cipalities. Indeed, it is possible that, after Yaśovarman, the empire fell apart, to be put together nearly half a century later by Rājendravarman (*r.*944–*c.*968). This is suggested by the absence of inscriptions or other material remains attesting the dominion of successor rulers over the outer provinces. It has been argued that the kings who followed Yaśovarman failed to control a large area.[4]

In any case, an era of renovation and consolidation began with the accession of Rājendravarman, who claimed descent from the rulers of Bhavapura. He also had links with the old 'Chen-la' royalty. It has been speculated that, from the point of view of some Cambodian lords, he was the restorer of an old legitimacy while Jayavarman II and his successors were upstarts.[5]

When he began his reign as ruler of Angkor, he restored Yaśodharapura as his capital and built many temples, of which two pyramidal *liṅga* shrines, the Pre Rup beside the Eastern Baray and the East Mebon on an artificial island in the middle

---

4 Jacques, Sur les données.
5 This was argued by P. Dupont, La dislocation du Tchen-la et la formation du Cambodge angkorien (VIIᵉ–IXᵉ siècles). *Bulletin de l'Ecole française d'Extrême-Orient*, 43 (1943–6), pp. 17–55.

of it, deserve particularly to be mentioned as ritual statements of royal power. He claimed an empire extending to southern Vietnam, Laos, much of Thailand, and even into central Vietnam, China and Burma. An expedition to Champa in 950 enabled him to seize as booty a gold statue at the temple of Po Nagar.

With the reign of Rājendravarman, we encounter one of the major discontinuities that mark the history of the Khmers. Perhaps, in the long run, it is more significant than those marked by the consecration of the ideal of Khmer unity by Jayavarman II or the establishment of the long-lived capital Yaśodharapura by Yaśovarman.

This is because it appears to be Rājendravarman who inaugurated the institutions of centralized government and entrenched the power of Angkor in the provinces through the agency of teams of officials. Ancient principalities, with the scions of their lineages still eager for autonomy, began to be absorbed within the apparatus of a national monarchy. Administrative divisions were standardized. The great palace designed by Rājendravarman's minister Kavīndrārimathana was the hub of a bureaucracy that extended its control into the further reaches of the empire; and the five proud towers of the Eastern Mebon stood for the authority of the royal icon, Śiva Rājendreśvara, over the world. Such claims, of course, could not be made good all at once, and the centrifugal forces within the empire could not be altogether reversed. Nevertheless, the old ideal of a single independent Khmer kingdom was beginning to take on political reality.

The eleventh century opened with a conflict between rival claimants. At Angkor, Udayādityavarman I reigned only from 1001 to 1002, when the throne was seized by his rival Jayavīravarman. Meanwhile, the third contestant, a prince who was to be known to history as Sūryavarman I, fought his way to the capital. First he moved northward up the Mekong from a power base at Sambor, then west across the Dangreks and finally south to Angkor in about 1010. He dated the beginning of his reign back to 1002.

Once in power at Angkor, he took steps to have the loyalty of his officials graven in stone, quite literally: the oath of allegiance, dated 1011, was inscribed in duplicate inscriptions on stone piers and subscribed by the names of about 400 officials (tāmṛvāc) who swore to be loyal:

This is the oath which we, belonging to the body of tāmṛvāc of the first category [in other versions, the second, third or fourth], swear all, without exception, cutting our hands, offering our lives and our devotion gratefully, without fault, to His Majesty Śrī Sūryavarmadeva, who has been in complete enjoyment of sovereignty since 942 Śaka [AD: 1002], in the presence of the sacred fire, of the holy jewel, the brahmans and the ācāryas. We will not revere another king, we shall never be hostile, and will not be accomplices of any enemy, we will not try to harm him in any way.[6]

His monuments include four important liṅga shrines in the provinces, situated in the four cardinal directions to symbolize his dominion over the four quarters of universal space.[7] His empire was evidently as great as those of his predecessors, though its precise extent is not clear; whether or not his administrative control extended as far as the area of Lopburi on the Chao Phraya, there is no doubt of the presence of a strong Khmer cultural influence there.[8]

Conspicuous among his public works was the Western Baray, which measured 8 × 2 kilometres and might have had a capacity as great as seventy million cubic litres. This was the greatest of the reservoirs that adorned the centre of empire, mirroring the heavens, and its construction added an enormous increment to the supplies of water furnished by the state hydraulic system, whether for domestic or agricultural use; Claude Jacques thinks that when the Western Baray was built, the Eastern still held water.[9]

This extension of the water resources of the capital reflects an expansion likely to have been typical of the empire as a

[6] G. Coedès, Etudes Cambodgiennes, IX: Le serment des fonctionnaires de Sūryavarman I. Bulletin de l'Ecole française d'Extrême-Orient, 13 (1913), pp. 11–17.
[7] These were the temples of Śikhareśvara in the Dangreks to the north, Īśānatīrthi to the east, Sūryādri to the south (Phnom Chisor), and Jayakṣetra to the west near Battambang (Vat Baset).
[8] An inscription of Sūryavarman was found at Lopburi. However, this may have been moved there subsequently and does not prove his authority to have been accepted in that region.
[9] C. Jacques, Angkor. Paris: Bordas, 1990, p. 99.

whole – an increase in economic activity, an elaboration of the landowning system, and an increase in population. The eleventh century saw the empire become more populous and the economy more complex. The emperor brought the religious foundations dotted about the realm into an integrated, government-supervised system dominated by a group of state temples endowed by the king; we must remember that these temples had a vital importance to the economy of the state, as repositories of the considerable wealth with which they were endowed, as sometimes very large controllers of manpower, and as the likely chief providers of education. Monks and priests, often from the great families, were the only experts in the literature of high culture, and their status gave them influence as advisors of kings and consultants or officials at all levels of government.

Indeed, the Sdok Kak Thom inscription, composed in about 1052, reveals a system that can be called ecclesiastical colonization. The history of the priestly family there recounted is a record of endowments of temples in new territories. First, a district is granted by the king's order; then, one by one, settlements are created within it by the establishment of temples in particular spots, each with a stone *linga* marking its sacred shrine and a community of incumbents, artificers, servants and bonded labour granted by benefactors to supply its needs. The process shows how a growing population expanded into new areas as part of a state-sponsored system.

The reign of Sūryavarman is marked also by a considerable increase in the number of inscriptions. These record endowments of temples, and they refer to numerous cases of contested land-ownership, where rival families claimed rights over land. Perhaps the apparently greater importance of land-ownership reflects the increasing competition as population grew. Everything is relative, though; we must remember that cultivable land in Cambodia remained until modern times much more readily available than in the thickly populated parts of Asia such as northern Vietnam, China or central Java.

A noteworthy feature of the eleventh century at Angkor is the importance of dynasties of priest-ministers who had considerable influence upon policy. Udayādityavarman II, for example, was served by the priest-minister Divākarapaṇḍita, who appears in the record also as a servant of Udayādityavarman's successor Harṣavarman III and then as officiant at the coronation of Jayavarman VI in 1080. This king appears to have initiated a new line of rulers, the Mahīdhara line.

The rulers from Jayavarman VI's family had territory in Thailand. The pattern of demographic spread suggests a westward thrust. The many Khmer remains in north-eastern Thailand, particularly at Phimai, represent an important phase in Cambodian cultural expansion; every account of Thai cultural and artistic history finds room for a 'Khmer period', reflecting the extension of Angkor's presence to the west, in the tenth and eleventh centuries. Eventually there were groups of Khmers not only in the north-east of Thailand but in the Chao Phraya valley, a region whose gradually increasing population and access to the sea was eventually to make it a rival economic area to the Lakes environment which furnished the resources of Angkor.

From the eleventh century on, Angkor was a major empire. Sūryavarman II (consecrated in 1113; his reign ended about 1145–50) was the builder of Angkor Wat, the most spectacular of all the monuments that remain to attest the empire's glory. He was related to a sister of the last two kings, but he had to fight his way to the throne, where he was ceremonially installed by Divākarapaṇḍita. This dignitary had served Udayādityavarman over sixty years earlier; now aged and venerable, he was made the recipient of the highest titles the king could give.

Sūryavarman's national shrine, Angkor Wat, is the most famous monument of all. Its outer enclosure measures about 815 × 1,000 metres, making it large enough to have contained the palace and government buildings. Its name ('city-monastery') is modern, but the original foundation was in honour of Viṣṇu, and had its ceremonial approach from the west, probably because of the association of the west with Viṣṇu.

In a later chapter we shall be taking stock of this monument as an achievement of Khmer imagination, but its importance as a political statement demands that we should consider it here too. For the scale of it, with its moats and linked waterways making a significant contribution to the hydraulic resources of the capital district, made it an expression of royal power that most Khmers had to respond to; it exacted their labour in its

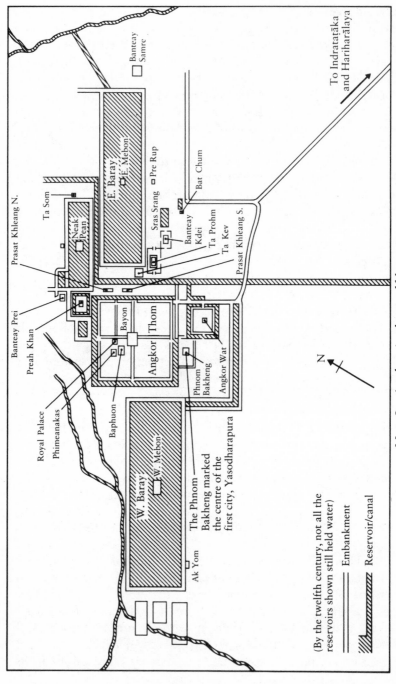

Banteay Samre

Ta Som

Prasat Khleang N.

E. Baray

E. Mebon

Neak Pean

Pre Rup

Sras Srang

Bat Chum

Banteay Kdei

Ta Prohm

Ta Kev

Prasat Khleang S.

Banteay Prei

Preah Khan

Royal Palace

Phimeanakas

Baphuon

Bayon

Angkor Thom

Phnom Bakheng

Angkor Wat

W. Baray

W. Mebon

Ak Yom

The Phnom Bakheng marked the centre of the first city, Yasodharapura

N

To Indratatāka and Hariharālaya

(By the twelfth century, not all the reservoirs shown still held water)

———— Embankment

〰〰〰 Reservoir/canal

Map 8   Angkor in the twelfth century

construction, it promised divine favours for the kingdom as a result of the ruler's piety, and it commanded their admiration, however grudging, whenever they passed within sight of its proud towers.

The sculpture of Angkor Wat is particularly lavish, providing us with a tangible image of the aspirations and values of the culture which created it. Particularly eloquent are the high panels that stretch for hundreds of metres around the gallery surrounding the central pyramid. These carvings bear witness to the visions of divine power and infernal punishment which gave dynamism to the mental world of the Khmer élite. The scenes portrayed include themes from myth as well as a few stylized representations of real life; their content will be summarized later, but let us note here that one of them, the western part of the south wing, shows a grand march-past reviewed by King Sūryavarman; the panel is about a hundred metres long. Inscriptions help us to identify some of the generals and contingents. Thus, units from Lavo are commanded by Prince Śrī Jayasiṃhavarman, and at the right-hand end of the parade we see a Thai contingent. Significantly, they are represented as a motley, ill-drilled bunch, marching out of step in contrast to the nearby Khmers. To the Khmers, these Thai people were uncouth provincials; with hindsight, we can recognize the irony, for within the next two or three centuries Thai feet, in step or not, were to trample over the débris of Angkor.

Sūryavarman's reign was disturbed by wars with the Chams, who were perennial rivals and frequent enemies throughout Angkorian history; following a victory, Sūryavarman was able to put his own man (a brother-in-law) on the throne at the Cham capital of Vijayapura. It was a period of greater involvement in the outside world: embassies were sent to China, and honours were bestowed upon the king by the Chinese emperor Kao-tsung.[10]

Angkor under Sūryavarman was at the peak of its glory. The institutional reforms of Rājendravarman were secure, giving a

[10] The Chinese interest in southern vassals stemmed rather from desperation than from benevolence: this was the crisis of the Sung dynasty, when Jürchen invaders deprived the rulers of the northern half of their empire and threatened to wipe them out altogether.

measure of centralization to the administration of the empire. A large hydraulic system had been created; it was unlike anything else in the region and it bestowed a powerful increment of prestige upon its masters (quite apart from whatever contribution it made to agriculture). Gilded temples everywhere testified to an impressive nexus between the wealth and the piety of benefactors past and present. Luxuries and curiosities from the whole of the known world converged upon the capital by barge and by cart. There was no rival power close enough to be a serious threat except the Chams, and for the time being the Khmers had the upper hand. There were good relations with the Chinese. Lit by the auspicious radiance of a sun king such as Sūryavarman, it must have seemed to many that the empire would never know a twilight.

However, in politics no equilibrium remains undisturbed for very long. Champa's fortunes revived. By the 1170s, the Chams were able once more to mount a successful attack upon Angkor. This was partly due to a surprise naval attack; their fleet stole up the Tonle Sap and across the Great Lake before the Khmers could muster their defences. (Naval conflict with the Chams is illustrated in the bas-relief carvings on the walls of the Bayon temple.) For a while, Angkor was humbled.

As always happened in the centuries-long conflict between the Khmers and the Chams, the submission was only temporary. Supply lines for a conquering army were not quite short enough for victory to be turned into permanent annexation, and the differences between the two people – historical, linguistic and cultural – were insuperable barriers to assimilation. The dominion of the Cham king Jaya Indravarman IV was soon brought to an end, and a Khmer prince fought his way to power. This prince was Jayavarman VII, the last of the great kings and the most spectacular in achievement.

9

The Immortals

On all sides are great tree-trunks, their roots penetrating to unfathomable depths, supporting a vault of foliage lost in shadow; branches stoop down to the earth and take root; seemingly endless creepers run from tree to tree, their origins undiscoverable; there are inextricable thorns, and fronds of surpassing elegance and delicacy; expansive flowers of outlandish appearance bestrew the ground, or deck a tree-top with a fiery dome, or ensconce themselves in the fork between two boughs; the bark of the trees is black, or gnarled, or slimy, and one cannot touch it without a shudder; there are dead branches upon a thick carpet of mould and decay; on all sides sap thrusts up and life abounds in overwhelming profusion.

In the same way . . . religious feeling makes itself powerfully manifest and dominates the whole of life; it encompasses the activities of every day, the most consequential as well as the most lowly, that form the close mesh of its observances.[1]

The Jesuit missionary Léopold Cadière wrote these words as a metaphor for the *real* religion of the Vietnamese. Not the book-religion of the imperial court with its Confucian ceremonial, or of the Buddhist temple library with its yellowing scriptures, but of the ordinary Vietnamese villagers among whom he worked.

He likened their religion to the life of the forest upon the slopes of the Vietnamese Cordillera, teeming with a thousand

---

[1] L. Cadière, *Religious Beliefs and Practices of the Vietnamese*, a translation of chapter 1 of *Croyances et pratiques des vietnamiens*, first published Hanoi, 1944; reprinted – *Bulletin de la Société des Etudes Indochinoises*, XXXIII (1958) Clayton, Victoria: Monash University, Centre of Southeast Asian Studies, 1989, p. 1.

species of tree, creeper, wildflower, lichen and fungus, full of contrasts, always growing and changing. As a keen amateur botanist, he had an eye sensitized to the inexhaustible varieties of nature. In this universe of growth and vitality he recognized an apt metaphor for the profusion of spirits, genies and gods that peered at the Vietnamese from every dark corner of their collective imagination. The image is also appropriate for the Khmers.

They came from the forest; the forest remained, never very far away, as paradigm and symbol of the dark, chaotic and dangerous world of nature from which civilization was born. No Khmer could ever be completely at ease alone in the dark forest. Practical fears of physical dangers certainly contributed to their unease, but there was more. The invisible beings that dwell in the wild inspire dread, even in those who might be expected not to care: there is no greater challenge to the cultivated serenity of a Buddhist monk than the requirement that he should spend a period of solitary meditation, alone in the wild woodland, watched from all around by the unseen spirits.

Religion explains things. As a botanist classifies the plants of the forest and relates them to a rational biological theory, so the Khmer villager seeks to domesticate the unknown. He has acquired a whole catalogue of spirit and magic lore to guide him through his dealings with the invisible powers that surround him, and to guide his everyday life in a world where the invisible powers also played a part.

What sorts of spirits do we find in the Khmer religion? A large embracing class is that of the *nak ta*, ancestral spirits of the neighbourhood. They are village familiars, associated with hills or mounds or various types of tree, where they take up residence. Their icons, rough images of wood or stone, are always simple, even crude, for the spirits they embody belong to untamed nature. Typically, the energy of one of these *nak ta* is concentrated in a rough stone taken from near the foot of the tree where the spirit dwells and enshrined within the *khtom*, a miniature house on piles beside the tree-trunk, with its opening facing the tree.

The stories that tell of their past life in human form generally attribute to them a violent premature death, a common feature of local cult spirits in the region (compare the Burmese *nat*), for

Plate 14 Nak ta *spirit shrine, Siemreap, showing how an Angkorian image can be appropriated as the icon of a local cult*

such a death feeds a powerful will to haunt the scenes of a spirit's earthly existence. The *nak ta* are propitiated especially in times of dearth or other disaster.[2]

Earth spirits play an important part, as throughout South-East Asia, where the *nāga* (serpent) spirits often figure as guardians and owners of the soil. One ancient Khmer belief held that all the land belonged to the subterranean serpent demon Krong Peali. Mountains, indeed elevations of any height, were com-

---

[2] On the spirits of the locality, see particularly Ang Chouléan, *Les Etres surnaturels dans la religion populaire khmère*. Paris: Cedoreck, 1986.

monly believed to be the visible form of powerful territorial spirits, and we have the authority of Chau Ju-kua for the claim that every year the king went to a temple on the summit of Mount Ling-kie-po-p'o and made human sacrifices at night to the spirit P'o-to-li.[3] Ancestral spirits have merged with the very contours of the land; their energies are most accessible on the summits of hills, and the shrines of spirit cults have been erected in high places throughout Khmer history.[4]

There are many other categories of spirit: zombies, shades of individual ancestors, dangerous female tree spirits, souls damned to hell, ghouls, ogres with magic powers, the omnipresent *nāga* serpents which dwell in the earth, and female bird spirits. Many of these (*preta, yakṣa, nāga, kinnara*) are known by names which come from Sanskrit and can easily be recognized as borrowings from the vocabulary of Hindu or Buddhist myth. In origin, though, the spirits recognized by the Khmers are local. A study by Ang Choulean cites a wide assortment of spirits, each with its special characteristics: the so-called 'protector' spirits who are often dangerous forest demons but sometimes appear as guardian angels of lineages; the fearsome spirits of violent death, sometimes visible as balls of fire yet capable of becoming benign guardians in Buddhist monastery precincts; the spirits of stillborn babies, mummified and placed in tiny coffins which serve as amulets; the spirits whose powers are confined to the lives of small children.[5]

There are many others besides: 'dwarf herdsmen', usually in the form of children, who carry catapults and look after wild animals, particularly elephants; 'men of truth', who are regarded as human hermits seeking the truth in the forest, transformed into immortals who delight in perfume and flowers and are nourished by pure thought; ghosts of naughty monastery acolytes who, as big, ugly and dirty spirits, hover around the monastery precincts to annoy the living; family ancestors

---

[3] Chau Ju-kua, *Chau Ju-kua: His work on the Chinese and Arab trade in the 12th and 13th centuries*, tr. F. Hirth and W. W. Rockhill. St Petersburg: Imperial Academy of Sciences, 1911, p. 53.
[4] O. W. Wolters discusses this, giving the example of Vat Baset in the north-west: North-western Cambodia in the seventh century, *Bulletin of the School of Oriental and African Studies*, 37 (1974), pp. 355–84, at p. 368.
[5] Ang, *Les Etres Surnaturels*.

who are roused to anger by the misdemeanours of their living descendants (especially a girl showing even the slightest signs of taking or wanting a lover); sorcerers who can torment people by magically shrinking and expanding things they eat; witches who delight in causing harm to babies at childbirth; house guardians who are usually frail, timorous female spirits often capable only of disturbing the sleep of those within the house to warn of danger.[6]

There is a sense in which this religion of local, immanent powers in the environment was and is the *real* religion of the Khmers. It plays a part in the villager's hopes and fears that is much more lively than the myths and rituals of imported Hinduism, or even of the much more popular Buddhism with which the Khmers identify themselves in modern times.

This is illustrated by a telling incident from the 1960s. A witness at court was strongly suspected of telling lies. He persisted with his version of the case, even after swearing on a pile of volumes of Buddhist texts. In order to test whether a more plausible version could be extracted by other means, the magistrate asked him to swear by the spirit of a nearby sacred tree, which should kill him if he did not tell the truth. He promptly changed his tune.[7]

In a sense, the spirits around ordinary people represented the supernatural forces which can be active and palpable in their lives. Yoshiaki Ishizawa says: 'The *neak ta* [= *nak ta*] were the divinities of the very life of the peasants.'[8] On the other hand, a world faith such as Buddhism or Hinduism stood for abstract truths and moral laws, which are impersonal and remote.

It is tempting to draw a line between folk cults, bundled together and labelled 'popular', and the supposedly more sophisticated practices and philosophies of the Hinduism and Buddhism that came from outside and acquired an apparatus of ceremony and scholarship at the royal courts and in the big monastic foundations.

---

[6] Ibid., pp. 115–296.

[7] C. Jacques, personal communication.

[8] Yoshiaki Ishizawa, A la recherche des fondements de la culture en Asie du Sud-est et au Japon. . . . In *Cultes populaires et sociétés asiatiques: appareils cultuels et appareils de pouvoir*, ed. A. Forest, Paris: Harmattan, 1991, pp. 169–83, at p. 176.

Such a line may drawn; but the mistake would be to imagine that it is a line between two different sorts of religion, each essentially self-contained and operating without reference to the other. What the line represents is, rather, a discontinuity within the structure of indigenous Khmer religious thought. This structure accommodates distinct ritual spheres: that of the village community and that of the great lord. Each sphere is in a sense self-contained and autonomous, but they are parts of a single world view and obey basically the same rules.

Within each sphere there is a close, more or less exclusive relationship between the human client and a protecting patron spirit. Each village community has its *nak ta*, an ancestral spirit or a number of them, domesticated by ritual to the protection of the place. The rulers of Angkor, correspondingly, established cults of grand divinities to guard the kingdom. In doing so they employed the ingredients and vocabulary of imported religion; but their patrons were *nak ta* nevertheless. In Angkor, it was normal for kings to set up *liṅga* shrines at the ritual centres of their kingdoms. Other shrines marked the boundaries or outlying provinces. Sūryavarman I, for example, set up four great *liṅga* shrines to north, south, east and west of the capital, representing Śiva's protection of the empire as a totality.

In his valuable study of the *nak ta*, Alain Forest has argued against the notion that these patron spirits were essentially supernatural doubles of a hierarchy of territorial officials.[9] Lower spirits might on occasion be represented as giving homage to higher, but basically the patron spirits of the community belonged with the community, while the patron spirits of rulers belonged with the rulers. By slotting into such a pattern, with its two levels, the Indian gods were in effect validating the autonomy of the communities that made up the kingdom, each with its own ritual sphere.

Imported religion could play a functional part in a variety of ways that affected the belief and practice of the villager. Forest suggests that Theravāda Buddhism, when it came to dominate in the post-Angkorian period, had a special role in village religion as a token of ordered relationships and harmony between

9   A. Forest, *Cambodge: pouvoir du roi et puissance de génie.* In Forest (ed.), *Cultes populaires,* pp. 185–223.

senior and junior, male and female, officials and subjects; gifts given to monks were tokens of the givers' rank and at the same time were covenants of conformity to the limits and responsibilities of rank. Implicitly the Buddhist order stood for a

Plate 15   The Buddha, sheltered by the serpent Mucilinda as he meditates

social stability secure from excessive interference by the magic powers of spirits.[10]

At many points, Indian religion latched on to the pre-existing beliefs, so that, for example, Buddhist monks might sometimes be asked to play a part at rituals propitiating the *nak ta*. Local spirits might be redescribed as forms of Śiva; local tree cults might be incorporated into the lore of transmigrating Buddhist 'stream-winner' spirits destined for enlightenment; Buddhist texts might be intoned to placate the serpent spirits that own the piece of land one profanes by clearing or building; Hindu ritual might garb the ceremony of a local mountain goddess who demands a sacrifice: elements from different spheres are mingled.[11]

So the Indian religions were not irrelevant to Khmer society. On the contrary; no gulf was fixed between powerful local spirits and abstract Hindu–Buddhist images. One took over where the other left off. As Ishizawa goes on to say:

From the point of view of the Cambodians themselves, who consider themselves pious Buddhists, there is certainly no separation or disparity between the Buddha and the *neak* [=*nak*]*ta*. The first is superimposed upon the second, just as a positive image may be superimposed upon a negative. Belief in the Buddha was originally incarnated in belief in the *neak ta*.[12]

---

[10]   Ibid., pp. 221f.

[11]   This point has been made by Solange Thierry: 'The Buddhist monks are in attendance even at rites concerning the agricultural cycle; either the god Indra or some *nak ta* watch over the foundation of a Buddhist monastery; and the Worshipful Earth Spirit, Brah Bhum, is invoked at the ceremony of the Fifteenth Day in honour of the dead. This syncretism is powerful, being deeply embedded in the conduct of ceremony; it is also flexible and diffuse, lending itself to local variations and diverse interpretations. The Cambodian is not bothered by the contradictions: he knows, if he has acquired some Buddhist ideas, that the individual soul has no existence (the doctrine of *anatta*), but he knows also that he has nineteen souls, nineteen 'vital spirits', *brah lin*, which make up his individuality, and that if one or another of them is lost, he will fall ill. His various beliefs, making up his spiritual and religious 'culture', are all on an equal footing.' S. Thierry, *Etude d'un corpus de contes cambodgiens*, Paris and Lille: Librairie Honoré Champion, 1978, p. 76.

[12]   Ishizawa, *A la recherche*, p. 176.

Of course, the Sanskrit tradition of Hinduism and Buddhism was at its purest in the great religious foundations that were endowed by the great men and women of the land. There was spiritual merit in bestowing revenues or war booty upon one of the temples that dotted the landscape, reassuring symbols of permanence and order with their graceful stone towers. The bestowal upon them of usufruct could bring tax benefits to a landowner; the orders of scholar-priests dwelling within them offered careers to the sons of great families; the sacramental power of their holy offices ensured rewards in lives to come for their pious benefactors.

Inscriptions tell us about the lavish prestations that were required to maintain their spiritual routine. Each temple needed rice for the ritual offerings each morning, at midday and in the evening. There were special rites to mark the great festivals, especially at New Year. Gifts made to temples included all that was needed to support the cycle of rituals and its attendant priesthood: beans, sesame, beeswax, ginger, honey, syrup, clarified butter made from the milk of specially maintained herds, perfume specially ground for temple use.[13] Armies of temple servants were required for the upkeep of temple establishments. The largest foundations, employing thousands of people, were veritable cities in their own right.

The temples, so richly endowed by the great, were usually Hindu. Some were at least partly Buddhist. Of these, the most famous is the Bayon, build by Jayavarman VII (c.1181–c.1218). The precise sectarian affiliation of particular foundations is rarely attested, and the only Buddhist sect clearly identified by the historical record is the Vijñānavādin school of Mahāyāna Buddhism, which cleaves to the doctrine that the world is essentially nothing but mind-stuff (*cittamātra*). It is evidenced around the end of the tenth century, and some of the inscriptions of the reign of Jayavarman VII appear to reflect the teachings of this school.[14] However, sects were not exclusive; even where the central shrine of a temple was dedicated to a

[13] J. M. Jacob, The ecology of Angkor: evidence from the inscriptions. In *Nature and Man in South East Asia*, ed. P. A. Stott, London: School of Oriental and African Studies, 1978, p. 111.
[14] J. Boisselier, *Le Cambodge*. Paris: Picard, 1966, p. 301.

particular deity or *bodhisattva*, the surrounding galleries and subordinate shrines were commonly graced by images of the divinities of other sects.

Theravāda Buddhism, dominant after Angkor, emerged as a distinct cohesive tradition only late; Chou Ta-kuan, late in the thirteenth century, offers us the first detailed evidence of the religious persuasion that was soon to displace nearly everything else. He tells us that the bonzes would shave their heads, wear yellow robes and bare their right shoulders; they would knot a strip of yellow cloth around their bodies and go barefoot. They would all eat fish and meat (although they drank no wine), and they would make offerings of meat and fish to the Buddha. They ate just one meal a day (as in modern times), taken in the house of a donor. There were no nuns. The king would consult them on serious matters.[15]

Most of the monks were ordinary men, susceptible to the influence of the surroundings in which they were brought up. The population was overwhelmingly rural, and so even the monks and priests who came from aristocratic families cannot have been far removed from their ancestral culture of local spirits. Inevitably, they interpreted their Indian religion in ways that made it cohere with the religious culture they knew.

The accommodation of Indian religion to local belief can easily be illustrated from the popular stories that make up a rich oral tradition. Let us notice just one. It tells of a man who returns to his village to find that his wife and children are dead, and a demoness has taken his wife's form. He flees; the fell spirit pursues him; he rushes into a Buddhist monastery where the fortnightly ritual of confession and reciting of the discipline is in progress; the head teacher conducts the fugitive into a meditation hut, recites Buddhist scriptures, and draws a magic circle around the man – a *sīmā* or boundary, delimiting sacred space. The demoness is kept at bay by this powerful magic.[16]

Buddhism in South-East Asia (or in any place where it is part of the culture of a whole society) consists of many things, and the peculiarly rational teaching with which westerners often

[15] Chou Ta-kuan, *Mémoires sur les coutumes du Cambodge de Tcheou Takouan*, tr. P. Pelliot. Paris: Ecole française d'Extrême-Orient, 1951, pp. 14f.
[16] Thierry, *Contes Cambodgiens*, p. 294.

Plate 16   Modern Theravada Buddhist monk

identify it is only one. Few South-East Asians would recognize the intellectual version of the religion as part of their own practice. Anybody who has observed Theravāda Buddhism in a twentieth-century village will appreciate that the Buddha is treated by his devotees as a benevolent deity, and the precincts and the personnel of his monastic communities are seen as vessels of his undoubted spiritual power.

Before the decline of Angkor it was the brahmanical rituals and cults of Hinduism that were more lavishly patronized. They belonged in a single religious universe with the whole pantheon of local spirits. These spirit beliefs are wholly continuous with those that can be observed among Khmers of modern times. Writing about the cult of the *devarāja* instituted by Jayavarman II, for example, Nidhi Aeusrivongse emphasizes the continuity between such cults and the world of local spirits; an invisible force, 'life-power', was felt to flow between the spirit and the profane worlds, and the person of the king could act as a conduit for this power.[17]

The continuity of this lore of local spirits with the imported Hinduism and Buddhism can be seen clearly when we observe the uses to which both sorts of religion are put.

A fundamental principle of cosmological thought is mimesis or imitation. Actions or objects in the profane, physical world are thought to influence the invisible, transcendent world when they imitate its structure. Thus, when certain sorts of spirits, which manifest themselves as fireballs, are to be exorcised, the procedure involves setting light to specially made firebrands and beating them with sticks, thus imitating in a ritual action the process which is to be projected into the world of the spirits.

Again, when one makes offerings of rice balls to the spirits of the dead, there must be nineteen balls to match the nineteen *brah lin*, the spirits which make up each individual. Four pots of rice are cooked on the corners of a funeral pyre and grain is thrown on the cinders. Death is the birth of a new life for the

---

[17] Nidhi Aeusrivongse, Devarāja cult and Khmer kingship at Angkor. In *Explorations in Early Southeast Asian History: The origins of Southeast Asian statecraft*, ed. K. R. Hall and J. K. Whitmore, Ann Arbor, Mich.: University of Michigan, Center for South and Southeast Asian Studies, 1976, pp. 107–48.

Plate 17   Buddhist stupa at Wat Phnom, Phnom Penh

transmigrating soul; rice grains, similarly, produce new plants, and the ritual action can be expected to hasten a good rebirth for the deceased.

Modern popular beliefs about the significance of the monuments of Angkor absorb them wholly into this same world view, making them part of the apparatus employed to imitate the invisible in the forms of the visible. A legend current in recent times integrates the architecture of Angkor into a widely shared perception of the universe. It tells of Preah Ket Mealea, son of the god Indra by a human wife. This prince, as a boy, was taken up to heaven by his father and given a guided tour of the glittering palaces of the celestial realm. When he had seen them all, Indra told him that he was to be given the kingdom of Cambodia, and he could choose any building he had seen as the model for a monument which the divine architect would reproduce for him in his earthly kingdom. Amazed, he hesitated to answer, unwilling to set himself up alongside the gods by appropriating the design of a heavenly palace. But then he declared that he would choose the least grand of all the buildings in Indra's royal precinct, the heavenly stables.

And so it was. An embodiment in stone of what the prince had seen in heaven, an exact duplicate of Indra's stables, was built at Angkor. It was Angkor Wat, the grandest and most famous of all the monuments of Angkor, which until recently figured on every Cambodian national flag.

No doubt Angkor was made of ordinary materials supplied by nature, and designed by all-too-fallible mortals; nevertheless, as we can see from the evidence that they have left us, the architects employed by mortal kings were seeking to make the city a mirror of the celestial realms. The same principle of mimesis that informs 'folk' religion dominated the aspirations of the architects.

We shall be looking later at the work of these architects. Here, though, it is important to note that the great stone shrines that dot the landscape of Angkor were intended as replicas of the furniture of the heavens. Perhaps 'replica' is not quite the right word; by imitating the divine forms, they made them real and present. Thus, the pyramidal monuments topped by tower sanctuaries imitated and made real the mountain of the gods, Meru, which lies, immovably, at the exact centre of the

Plate 18   Indra, mounted on the divine elephant Airāvata

universe. Yaśovarman laid his capital Yaśodharapura sym-
metrically around the Bakheng monument; thus his version of
Mount Meru *was* the centre of the world. The Bakheng terraces
are studded with subordinate shrine towers, 108 altogether.
This represents the twenty-seven constellations recognized by
Indian astrology multiplied by the four phases of the moon.
J. Filliozat has argued that this makes the Bakheng a pivot
of celestial time and space. Further, the pyramid is, like all
the other Mount Meru monuments at Angkor, square in plan.
From any one side one can see thirty-three tower shrines, including the topmost sanctum. These are the thirty-three gods
who supposedly inhabit Mount Meru.[18]

The ordinary inhabitants of Yaśodharapura walked with
the gods. Every shrine was a myth in stone, making real the
transcendent order that informed, permeated, ordered and explained the union of a multitude of local communities, with
their separate cults and traditions. Every piece of statuary was
a reminder of that order. Every ambitious king renewed the
covenant with the gods by shifting the ceremonial centre to a
new site with a new Mount Meru dedicated to his own favoured
god. Most kings were devotees of Śiva. Sūryavarman II, builder
of the great Angkor Wat, dedicated his temple-mountain to the
god Viṣṇu, who presides over the beginning and end of each
world-cycle; Jayavarman VII likewise placed a Buddhist image
at the centre of the Bayon.

Cambodian statues represent gods, and sometimes real
people, kings or great men and women. Famous are the smiling
faces of the *bodhisattva* (future Buddha) Avalokiteśvara, whose
head is sculpted with four faces gazing north, south, east and
west from the many towers of Jayavarman VII's Bayon shrine
dating from the beginning of the thirteenth century; his
smile, which has been variously seen as enigmatic, com-
passionate, all-knowing or complacent, shines over the tumbled
stones, projecting multiple images of himself to fill the space
of the kingdom.

The Śiva *liṅga*, a stone phallic emblem upright in a shallow
trough within its sanctuary, is an emblem of this god but also,

---

[18] J. Filliozat, Le symbolisme du monument de Phnom Bakheng. *Bulletin de
l'Ecole française d'Extrême-Orient*, 49, no. 2 (1954), pp. 527–54.

clearly, apt as the focus for a fertility cult. The containing *yoni* stone upon which it is set in its trough represents the matrix or womb of life. A gutter (*somasūtra*) leads from the trough through the wall, carrying away the sacral fluids poured upon the *liṅga*. In the same way, waters fall on the earth, and life comes forth. Superimposing different layers of symbolism and employing the familiar principle of mimesis, this ritual captures the procreative power of Śiva for the prosperity of the community.[19] In India, it first spoke to the needs of simple communities living close to the land. In Cambodia, even when decked in the grandeur of imperial pomp, such a ritual was still addressed to the interests of an agricultural people as a whole, whether the mass of the population was grateful or not. With the decline of Angkor, rituals that had been addressed to the great gods retreated into their original matrix of folk culture, merging with cults of rough stone icons and cave shrines. Such cults have persisted through the years of civil war to the present day; sites of some were studied in 1989 and 1990 by Chouléan Ang.[20]

Religious values, preached by the respected Indian schools, surrounded kingship. The sect of the Pāśupatas, for example, is mentioned by some inscriptions; its leaders were in the confidence of rulers in Angkor as elsewhere in the world of Indian culture. Kings were portrayed in art and epigraphy as ascetics, as devotees of Śiva, possessing magic power, and the gifts offered by such rulers to favoured subjects were, O. W. Wolters has argued, seen as transmissions of supernatural power capable of benefiting the recipients in the beyond.[21] These attitudes to kings were continuous with pre-Hindu indigenous ideas of supernatural prowess or *mana* wielded by great men.

---

[19] On the *liṅga* ritual in South-East Asia, see particularly P. Mus, *India Seen from the East: Indian and indigenous cults in Champa*, ed. and tr. I. W. Mabbett and D. P. Chandler. Clayton, Victoria: Monash University Centre of Southeast Asian Studies, 1975, esp. pp. 28–33.
[20] Ang Chouléan, Recherches récentes sur le culte des megalithes et des grottes au Cambodge. *Journal Asiatique*, 281, nos 1–2 (1993), pp. 185–210.
[21] O. W. Wolters, Khmer 'Hinduism' in the seventh century. In R. B. Smith and W. Watson (eds), *Early South East Asia: Essays in archaeology, history and historical geography*, New York: Oxford University Press, 1979, pp. 427–42.

The Indian religions were not falsified, but they were domesticated. They provided a language that could be used for the articulation and refinement of Khmer religious thought. This language could not be used by everybody, but, for those who could respond to its messages, it created a framework of order that was carved upon the face of the forest's primeval chaos.

10

Daily Life

One means of recording words employed by the ancient Khmers was to indite their thoughts with chalk on blackened deerskin. We can never know what literature was created in this way, for deerskin is perishable and what is written upon it will not survive for posterity unless it is preserved by a tradition of recopying. The ancient Khmers had archives, and scribes did copy manuscripts, but the tradition was not preserved after about 1400 (perhaps because of destruction wrought by invading armies), and Angkorian literature in most forms is lost to us.

Oral tradition is another type of source, useful for the history of recent times, but there is little it can reliably tell us about the period of Angkor. This means that the sources available to us consist mainly of those that were inscribed on stone. The stone inscriptions were normally composed as records of endowments to temples, and they are overwhelmingly skewed to the affairs of religious institutions. This in turn means that our information tells of the official and ritual affairs of the court and great families, and the texture of everyday life is very largely missing.

Nevertheless, there are hints here and there in the inscriptions, and there is much more about the ordinary life of the Khmers in the observations of visiting Chinese, which were neither chiselled nor chalked, but painted with a brush; what preserves these for us is, of course, the archival tradition of the Chinese courts which meant that manuscripts were perpetuated by constant recopying and recompiling in new collections down the centuries. The Chinese references to the life of the Khmers –

especially the detailed record left by Chou Ta-kuan (Zhou daguan) at the end of the thirteenth century – can be supplemented by occasional passing references in the inscriptions, and by a few other sources such as the evidence of sculpture, to yield a quantity of information about daily life in ancient Cambodia.

The most striking portrayals of contemporary life in the period of Angkor are the bas-reliefs of the Bayon, the state shrine established as the ritual centre of the kingdom by Jayavarman VII at about the beginning of the thirteenth century.

The sculptor's chisel has left many vignettes upon its walls. We see the king sitting on a terrace floor surrounded by courtiers, their heads fanned by a thicket of fly-whisks. Before them are paraded for their entertainment a row of animals, including a hare, a buffalo and a rhinoceros. Two fencers are poised in balletic attitudes, and a tightrope walker edges forward along his precarious path. A chamber orchestra provides the appropriate *Tafelmusik*, allowing us to examine the design of the Cambodian violin, harp and cymbals; a juggler lies on his back spinning a wheel that is so much like the emblem of Buddhist teaching in more pious contexts, and an acrobat supports a tower of children.

Plate 19 A cockfight; bas-relief, Bayon

Elsewhere, we see a land battle (with the Cham enemies wearing their characteristic head-dress with floral crests), and a naval battle, in which fierce-prowed longboats are crowded with standing warriors who wield spears above their heads, while shoals of fish below them suggest the otherwise invisible water.

In other scenes, wrestling palace guards amuse themselves by tying one another into knots; and, in the marketplace, pedlars grapple with the baskets, hung from a shoulder-yoke, that are still a familiar sight in monsoon Asia. In such scenes, as nowhere else, we sense a little of the flavour of real life.

The most striking thing about the information we can glean of the ordinary people of Angkor is its continuity with what may be observed about the daily life of ordinary people in the present. This makes a vivid contrast with such matters as political organization, court affairs and priestly religion. In these respects, ancient Cambodia in her heyday was conspicuously different from the state that has survived into modern times. In the life of the people, on the other hand, the

Plate 20 Market scene with food stalls, from gallery walls at the Bayon

fragments of information vouchsafed to us by the historical record convincingly match the rural Cambodia of the the recent past.

Some of the customs recorded by the Chinese are like those of India:

They regard the right hand as pure and the left as impure. They wash every morning, clean their teeth with little pieces of poplar wood, and do not fail to read or recite their prayers. They wash again before taking their meal, and get to work with their poplar-wood toothpicks immediately afterwards, and recite prayers again.[1]

This comes from Ma Tuan-lin (Ma Duanlin), whose thirteenth-century *Ethnography of the Peoples Outside China* included ingredients from various past observations by Chinese about the people of 'Chen-la'. The sentence immediately following also suggests an Indian cultural borrowing, but it is surprising in view of the fact that the Indian taste for milk was not transferred to South-East Asia: 'Their food includes a lot of butter, milk-curds, powdered sugar, rice and also millet, from which they make cakes that are soaked in meat juices and eaten at the beginning of the meal.'

Chou Ta-kuan, the thirteenth-century visitor, observes that the Khmers would bathe several times a day in the hot season, all repairing to the bathing-place in groups; during bathing, men and women were not segregated, but old and young were.[2] Chou Ta-kuan was struck by the amount of washing that was done by the Cambodians, and darkly attributes to it the prevalence of leprosy. According to him people freely mingled with lepers, without catching the disease. However, a former king was said to have contracted it, and it is possible that there was a genuine historical basis to the story.[3]

Chou Ta-kuan was in Cambodia less than a century after the

---

[1] Ma Tuan-lin, *Ethnographie des peuples étrangers à la Chine, ouvrage composé... par Ma Touan-lin*, tr. Le Marquis d'Hervey de Saint-Denys. Paris: Georg, 1876, vol. II, pp. 579f.
[2] Chou Ta-kuan, *Mémoires sur les coutumes du Cambodge de Tcheou Takouan*, tr. P. Pelliot. Paris: Ecole française d'Extrême-Orient, 1951, p. 33.
[3] See D. P. Chandler, 'Folk memories of the decline of Angkor in nineteenth-century Cambodia: the legend of the Leper King', *Journal of the Siam Society*, 67 (1979), pp. 54–62.

reign of Jayavarman VII, who founded 102 medical institutions in all parts of the kingdom. Inscriptions list in detail the provisions that had to be made for the upkeep of these institutions, which required a huge investment in food, furnishings and medicinal herbs. They are usually called 'hospitals', though it is not clear whether they had any in-patients. It is more likely that they were warehouses and dispensaries for medicines.

Related to health is the problem of sewage disposal, a topic which unsurprisingly is not discussed in any inscriptions. Chou noticed the differences of custom from the Chinese, remarking that the Cambodians appeared to make no use of nightsoil as fertiliser. He describes Khmer latrines:

By two or three families they dig a ditch which they cover again with grass. When it is filled, they cover it over and dig another ditch. After having gone to this place, they go to the pond and wash themselves with the left hand, for the right hand is reserved for food. [This is another clear parallel with India.] When they see the Chinese use paper, they mock them and close their doors. There are also women who urinate standing. It is ridiculous.[4]

Chou also comments freely on sexual practices. He refers with intense distaste to the homosexuals who would accost intended partners, making targets of the Chinese: 'In this country, there are many homosexuals, who every day wander by in groups of more than ten in the market place. They constantly try to attract the Chinese, for rich presents. It is hideous. It is vile.'[5]

Inscriptions cannot of course be expected to tell us much about sexual behaviour, but on the matter of dress the bas-reliefs and statuary associated with the temples have a great deal to show; gods and goddesses are depicted wearing clothing and ornaments that reflect the changing fashions favoured by the men and women at court.

There is some evidence that, in very early times, the Khmers were accustomed to go naked. Ma Tuan-lin refers to a seventh-century embassy from a country in the neighbourhood whose envoys 'laughed at the sight of a man dressed'.[6] According

---

4   Chou Ta-kuan, *Mémoires*, p. 25.
5   Ibid., p. 16.
6   Ma Tuan-lin, *Ethnographie*, pp. 484f.

to the legends of 'Fu-nan', indeed, it was the Indian founder Kauṇḍinya who induced the women to put a cloth over their heads, and K'ang-t'ai who persuaded a third-century ruler to order the men to wear waistcloths. Ma Tuan-lin refers to the Funanese as naked, with untended hair and tattooed bodies.

However, such stories are likely to represent Chinese stereotypes of barbarism. From as early as we see Khmers represented in sculpture, they are wearing skirts. All would knot their hair and go bare-shouldered. The Cambodian skirt or kilt, the *sampot*, is a rectangle of cloth which is wrapped around the waist and tied, with a number of folds at the front; these folds may be passed back between the legs and tucked in at the small of the back. Sculpture of the period of the Bakheng makes us familiar with pleated skirts with the upper border turned out over the belt. (The folding over of the cloth at the belt provides, for the modern Cambodian, a convenient pocket in which anything can be carried, most notably his quids of betel.) The sculptures sometimes show the men moustached and with small beards like that of the British monarch Charles I.

Different phases of art show female fashions of the respective times; the variations are most notable in their coiffure: conical in the Bakheng period, or domed, with the hair falling freely around, in the eleventh century. Angkor Wat's sculpture shows a profusion of different hairstyles in the earlier twelfth century; at the time of Jayavarman VII it was common for hair to be drawn up to a point, with many long braids falling to the ground. They wore rows of pearls and heavy pendants and necklaces, and a double chain falling between the breasts.

The Cambodians apparently did not weave their own silk. At the time of Chou's visit, silk clothes were made with the help of the Siamese, who grew the mulberries and were called in as tailors. The thread was spun with hand spindles, and the weaving of the cloth was conducted with backstrap looms – women would fasten the warp to their belts and use hand shuttles. Degrees of gorgeousness went with rank:

Only the prince is allowed materials with dense floral designs. He wears a gold diadem, similar to those that are on the head of the Vajradharas [images of thunderbolt-wielding deities]. When he does not wear the diadem, he simply winds a garland of fragrant flowers into his chignon. The flowers remind one of jasmine. Around his neck he has nearly three pounds of large pearls. On his wrists, ankles, and fingers, he wears bracelets and gold rings set with cat's-eyes. He goes barefoot, and the soles of his feet and the palms of his hands are tinted red with a red dye.[7]

The last detail is interesting: red dye was used also on the soles of commoner women's feet, as well as their palms. According to a sixteenth-century source, the nobles would wear silk or very fine cotton, while the common folk wore coarse cotton.

As Chou Ta-kuan corroborates, the simplicity of basic dress – a mere skirt for both sexes, supplemented by an additional waistcloth for outside wear, and no shoes or coats – was compensated for by an abundance of ornament by those who could afford it. Chou tells us that men and women used perfumes of musk, sandalwood or other fragrances. Bracelets were ubiquitous. (Earlier in the twentieth century, Cambodian dress was less flamboyant. In the countryside, the traditional uniform was plain black. Delvert described Cambodia as *'humanité vêtue de noir'*.[8]

Dress and ornament are ways of bringing a little colour and style into a life that was necessarily always drab for most, toiling in house or field in the enervating heat. Colour and style were to be injected also, with enthusiasm and panache, by the round of festivals which punctuated the cycle of the seasons and the changing conditions of life.

In modern times, the round of festivals begins with the October rituals of Kathen, the giving of gifts of clothing to Buddhist monks at the end of the rainy season; it is something to be found throughout the Buddhist world. In November comes the festival of the retreat of the waters, marking the end of the rainy season. The following dry season is marked by a remission of agricultural activity and a corresponding intensification of recreation and festivals; the month of April as a whole is marked by New Year celebrations. In May, with the recommencement of cultivation, comes the festival of the sacred furrow.

Things were not so different in the time of Angkor. In the hot weather, particularly, Cambodians gave themselves up to

---

[7] Chou Ta-kuan, *Mémoires*, p. 13.
[8] J. Delvert, *Le Paysan Cambodgien*. Paris: Mouton, 1961, p. 143.

festivals and ceremonies. Chou Ta-kuan refers to new year festivities using rockets and firecrackers, a clear case of Chinese cultural borrowing. He also mentions a ball-throwing festivity during the New Year celebrations, a feast of lights, the ceremony of washing Buddha images, celebrations at the royal palace during the eighth month with actors, musicians and fights of boars against elephants; and there was a ritual burning of rice at the end of the harvest, when piles of rice were brought to the south gate of the city and offered to the Buddha.[9]

The festival of floats took place in the sixth month. A description of such a festival on the water, cited by J. Jacob, reveals what a charming ceremony it could be. The festival took place when certain yellow flowers (*Sesbania javanica*) came into bloom just as the floodwaters began to recede. People would set off across the waters in fleets of boats, and 'ahead of them goes a boat in which there is a bowl of batter and a pan of hot fat. The flowers, dipped in the batter and cooked in the fat, are left on the trees so that the pancakes on trees may be collected by those following behind'.[10]

Other forms of celebration attend the rites of passage from birth to death. The most obviously festive are weddings. Until modern times, these have been an occasion for rituals in which the legendary union of Preah Thong the culture hero and the *nāga* princess are remembered. In the thirteenth century, Ma Tuan-lin incorporated a Chinese description of Khmer weddings in his account of the country:

Whoever wishes to marry first of all sends presents to the girl he seeks; then the girl's family chooses a propitious day to have the bride led, under the protection of a go-between, to the house of the bridegroom. The families of the husband and wife do not go out for eight days. Day and night the lamps remain lit. When the wedding ceremony is over, the husband receives part of the goods of his parents and goes to establish himself in his own house.[11]

---

[9]   Chou Ta-kuan, *Mémoires*, pp. 21f.
[10] J. Jacob, The ecology of Angkor: evidence from the inscriptions. In *Nature and Man in South East Asia*, ed. P. A. Stott, London: School of Oriental and African Studies, 1978, p. 113.
[11] Ma Tuan-lin, *Ethnographie*, p. 480.

Funerary customs varied. Burial was certainly known and widespread in prehistoric times. Ancient sources for South-East Asia indicate the prevalence of a custom of putting corpses in lonely places for exposure to birds and animals; when the body was entirely disposed of by scavengers, this was taken as evidence of a fortunate destiny in the afterlife. This custom is, indeed, reported in some Chinese accounts, as well as being evidenced in some parts of the region (for example, in Bali) in modern times. However, in historical times, Indian-style cremation was also practised. The burned remains were treated in different ways. As Ma Tuan-lin reported:

Funerals are conducted in this way: the children of the deceased go seven days without eating, shave their heads as a sign of mourning, and utter loud cries. The relatives assemble with the monks and nuns of Fo [Buddhists] or the priests of the Tao [a term by which the Chinese observer presumably intended sorcerers or shamans], who attend the deceased by chanting and playing various musical instruments. The corpse is burned on a pyre made of every kind of aromatic wood; the ashes are collected in a gold or silver urn which is thrown into deep water. The poor use an earthenware urn, painted in different colours.[12]

The author goes on to refer to the indigenous custom, mentioned above, of exposing the corpse: 'There are also those who are content to abandon the body in the mountains, leaving the job of devouring it to the wild beasts.'

The continuity of prehistoric funerary customs – exposing the corpse to be consumed in the open – is just one of a number of striking continuities which run through Khmer culture over a very long period. So much of what is described in this chapter can indifferently be said about the days of Angkor or 'Chen-la', on the strength of Chinese accounts, or about modern times, on the strength of common observation. Another conspicuous continuity is in the design of the Khmer dwelling. A striking feature of Khmer housing has always been the construction of dwellings upon tall posts which support the roofs and have

[12] Ibid. On Cambodian funerary and other rituals, and the historical and prehistoric origins, see E. Porée-Maspero, *Etude sur les rites agraires des cambodgiens*, 3 vols. Paris: Mouton, 1962–9.

the floors bracketed to them well above ground height. This is a cultural trait; it is in stark contrast to the Chinese style of construction flat upon the ground, even in similar climatic zones. One might think that the purpose of this is simply to raise one's home above the spectacular floods which inundate so much of the country, but in fact, apart from a few fishing villages, Cambodian dwellings avoid floodplains scrupulously. The value of a raised dwelling is, rather, to assist air circulation and freshness in the scorching hot season, to avoid rising damp, and to escape insects, reptiles, rats, boars, tigers and panthers – a reminder of the forest environment from which Khmer culture evolved.

In early times as now, no doubt, the building of a house entailed a scrupulous attention to local spirits. Krun Bali, the *nāga* spirit, owns all the land, and before construction begins an officiant, *acar*, must be employed to divine the disposition of the *nāga*'s body, invisible beneath the earth, so that a house may be properly sited and an auspicious date found for the beginning of building. The floor is hung from columns, which are of a hard timber resistant to termites; usually there are twelve posts. The floor is most often about six feet above ground level, or lower in poorer houses. In front is a verandah, reached by a ladder with an odd number of treads (typically five, seven or nine; an even number is unlucky). In the space beneath the floor may be found ox-pens, mangers, chicken perches, pigsties, ploughs and other agricultural implements, carts, boats, millstones for paddy, big bamboo baskets to store grain, weaving looms and sometimes potting wheels.[13] Furniture is scant and is mostly made of bamboo or rattan. Chou Ta-kuan refers to rattan mats and skins; since his time low tables (about a foot high) have come into popular use, and so have Chinese-made beds as an alternative to rugs on the floor. A type of utensil likely to have been made since very ancient times is the multipurpose food container (modern *kandon*) made of banana or other leaves and sewn by the womenfolk.

Bas-relief carvings on temple walls show pile dwellings very similar to those known today. The most conspicuous differences in dwelling construction, perhaps, would have been in the

---

13　Delvert, *Le Paysan Cambodgien*, p. 181.

houses of the great, and most notably the royal palace. Though these palaces were not built of stone and little or nothing beyond some foundations remains today, the Chinese accounts confirm that they were equipped with every luxury.[14] Walls were sometimes made of ivory; fine decorations in gold adorned every surface, gracefully fashioned with delicate floral designs. Censers wafted exotic fragrances; precious stones gleamed in every corner.

As in other South-East Asian countries, we see among the ancient Khmers the operation of sumptuary laws which placed restrictions on the possessions allowable to different orders of people. Chou noticed, for example, that only the higher orders were allowed to roof their houses with tiles; ordinary people used thatch (as many still do).

It is possible that the Theravāda Buddhist *wats* (monasteries) preserve architectural memories of the palaces of imperial times, but the latter are no more than a memory now, their riches looted by conquering armies, their fabric crumbled or rotted into the parent earth. On the other hand, the way of life of the ordinary villagers in their thatched pile houses continues. The differences between past and present are chiefly in the lives of the great; the similarities are chiefly in the ways of the humble.

In the matter of recreations, for example, village families have no doubt enjoyed the same sorts of pastimes for many centuries. In the evenings, when the light waned, people liked to tell stories about heroes and spirits, just as now; and the asking of riddles has always been a popular literary form.

In the daylight hours the flying of paper kites is a favourite game; a kite could be made to produce musical notes with reeds tied to it. Cockfights, gory battles with spurs attached to the combatants' feet, attracted the gamblers and the vicariously aggressive down the ages. The affluent, meanwhile, could disport themselves on the polo field, while the less vigorous among them could sit back and enjoy listening to the music of the *capi* (a lute with plucked strings), the *tra* (a sort of violin, made of coconut, with a bow of horsehair), the *pi* (an oboe with a reed

---

[14] See for example Ma Tuan-lin, *Ethnographie*, vol. II, p. 461.

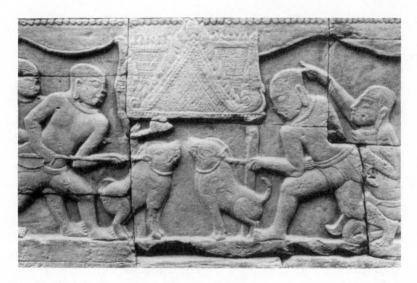

Plate 21 Pig-fighting scene

Plate 22 Scenes of daily life from bas-relief at the Bayon

Plate 23   Musicians at a celebration, Pre Umbel

made from the *papos* leaf), and the *sgar araks* (a pottery drum with a snakeskin membrane).[15]

Children's games, using only the most cheap and rudimentary of equipment, may well have been much the same down the centuries. One game, called *lu*, requires contestants to compete in throwing a coin into a specially made hole that is only just big enough for it; in another, *gap van*, they seek to dislodge a coin or other small object from an outline traced round it on the ground by throwing a piece of brick or tile at it from a distance. Such activities involve no expensive visits to toy shops, but they can engross the energies of teams of youngsters for hours.

Some of these things have changed. The traditions of court music have been disrupted; cockfights are not encouraged. In the villages, however, the general pattern of life today would be reasonably familiar to a visitor transported by a time machine from the days of Angkor. The modern reader of Chou Ta-kuan's chatty description of the Cambodia he saw cannot but recognize

[15]   Khing Hoc Dy, *Contribution à l'histoire de la littérature khmère*, vol. I. Paris: Harmattan, 1990, p. 114.

the Khmers of today in so many details of daily life. In the countryside, some things do not change very fast.

There are two opposite errors. On the one hand, it would be wrong to dismiss the whole record of Cambodia's past as a monotonous unchanging treadmill of battles fought by the same warrior kings and crops harvested by the same toiling peasants – a history without depth or variety, all too easy to understand. On the other, we should not be betrayed by the exotic and mysterious drama of the Khmer past into thinking that these people belonged to an alien species, somehow detached from the humanity we know and motivated by strange half-understood goals. We should never forget that the Khmers of the past lived in much the same sort of environment as their modern descendants, and had the same needs and aspirations. The texture of rural life has qualities that pervade much of human history, reaching across continents and millennia.

11

Farmers

'To study the Cambodians and to study the Cambodian peasant', Jean Delvert has written, 'are one and the same thing.'[1] Cambodians have always been close to the land.

Their agriculture has not always commanded admiration, however. A nineteenth-century Vietnamese emperor, for example, remarked of the Khmers that

The people do not know the proper way to grow food. They use mattocks and hoes, but no oxen. They grow enough rice to have two meals a day, but they do not know how to store rice for an emergency.[2]

The passage shows that, whatever feats of agricultural production may have sustained the might of Angkor, nothing lingered of them that could impress Cambodia's neighbours four centuries later.

But how sophisticated *were* the techniques deployed at Angkor, and how complex the organization? The answers are neither clear nor simple. The agricultural methods actually needed to sustain the panoply of empire were not necessarily elaborate: they might have been elementary and small in scale – like those of Cambodia today, in fact, without some of the modern improvements. Such an economic base could have sustained an elite class which, though small in comparison to

[1] J. Delvert, *Le Paysan cambodgien*. Paris: Mouton, 1961, Introduction.
[2] *Dai Nam Thuc Luc Chinh Bien*, vol. 15, p. 171, cited by D. P. Chandler, *A History of Cambodia*, Boulder, Col.: Westview Press, 1992, p. 101.

the urban populations of modern states, was big enough to run an empire.

As we shall see later, the character of Angkor's agricultural base is subject to debate. The debate concerns the organization of manpower and the likelihood that there were irrigated dry-season crops. Nevertheless, in other respects modern Cambodian farming may offer evidence of a pattern that has persisted since ancient times. In this chapter, we shall first review the Khmer adaptation to local conditions, looking at the whole way of life of the Cambodian farmer as it is known today. After that, we shall consider how different the agricultural life of the Khmers at the time of Angkor might have been.

In mainland South-East Asia, nature has usually been benign and survival has not required as much effort as in many other parts of the world. In the early centuries of 'Chen-la', as in the village environment today, multiple crops in elaborately irrigated ricefields were not a basic feature of the Cambodian farm holding. A single crop raised in rain-watered fields during the wet season would have been as adequate for a family's subsistence then as it is now. Modern Cambodian agriculture is pre-eminently a household activity, each family owning or leasing plots of land which it farms as it wishes.

In modern times, home-made ploughs with wooden shares protected only by scraps of metal, if at all, are still used by some Khmers. These simple ploughs may well be descended directly from those used at the time of Angkor. They often merely scratch a groove in the soil a few inches deep, but in the clay soils where such ploughs are often used the topsoil may be no more than six or eight inches deep anyway; the infertile subsoil is best not brought up to the surface. The case is different in the areas of choice 'red' soil, where a hoe can be used instead.

This agriculture may be simple in its technology, but it yields a rich diversity and normally in the past has been more than adequate to the needs of subsistence. It is based on rice, but there are other crops (many of those cultivated nowadays being post-Columbian introductions from the Americas) to spread risk, vary diet, and make efficient use of the land and the seasons. These include maize, cucumbers, potatoes, pumpkins, beans, onions, mustard, leeks, eggplants, squash, okra or gumbo, marrow and taro. There is a wide range of fruit:

watermelon, *longan* (the pale fleshy fruit known by its Chinese name, 'dragon's-eye'), mangoes, mangosteens, lichees, jujubes, rambutans and guavas. Other important plants are soya and betel. The betel is a shrubby plant, *Piper betel*, whose leaf is wrapped around grated areca nut and lime to make a quid used as a masticatory; the characteristic red stain of the chewed betel is familiar in India too. The sapodilla (*Achras sapota*) is a large evergreen which yields a durable timber and a particularly sweet berry.

Bamboo is vigorously exploited; from it are made household utensils, receptacles, baskets and construction materials. The sugar palm (*Borassus flabellifer*; Khmer *thnot*) is a particularly important sideline for the farmer; it yields not only sugar but vinegar and alcohol; its flowers can be macerated and used as a medicine; its pollen preserves tobacco leaves; its fruit is eaten green or ripe; its fronds are used to make everything from hats and fans to sunshades and roofing. Orchards of various trees are maintained near the homestead, particularly along river banks: areca, citrus, coconut and jack-fruit (the less pungent relative of the durian; its wood, incidentally, is still used for the dye that colours some Buddhist monks' robes). Kapok, mulberry and banana are widely grown. The variety of produce within the Khmer farmer's repertoire, then, is considerable. But the most important crop is, of course, rice.

We know that rice was the staple crop in early centuries. Chinese observers commented upon it. Chau Ju-kua reported that rice was cheap – one could obtain two bushels of rice for an ounce (*tael*) of lead. Rice has long been a fundamental feature of Khmer life; the expression for 'eat', *si bay*, means literally 'eat rice'. The language is as sensitive to varieties of rice as Icelandic is to varieties of snow. There are more than a hundred words for types of rice.

The chief form of rice cultivation is the wet-season (*vossa*) paddy grown in rain-watered fields, but it is worth noticing that the gathering of wild rice (Khmer *srangne*) is still an option to be exploited in the west of Cambodia, though it is not a reliable source of abundant grain.

Another option is the cultivation of rice in dry fields (*chamkar*), where the forest is cleared by burning undergrowth. In the fertile bed thus created a crop can be grown for a few

years without the great input of labour that is required by
wet rice techniques. When the soil is exhausted, the farming community can move on, leaving nature to renew itself
gradually.

This form of agriculture is still carried on in South-East Asia
on higher hill slopes. In Cambodia, it is practised by non-Khmer
communities in some hill districts, principally to the north or
east. It has some advantages: it does not suffer much from
seasonal variation; it requires little labour once the ground is
cleared; and yields of good-quality rice can overlap the lower
parts of the range of yields deliverable by wet field cultivation.

'Floating rice' (Khmer *srauv vea*) has the peculiarity that it
can grow to a height of 5 metres, and can thus be planted in an
area of seasonal flooding so long as the floodwaters do not rise
faster than about 0.1 metres (4 inches) a day, a rate with which
the rice can keep pace. The flooded lands nearest to Angkor
have a relatively steep gradient and are not suitable for floating
rice, which is however quite widely grown elsewhere, in areas of
about two metres flooding.

Floating rice has a growing season of about nine months. Its
yields are not great, and it was probably never the basis of
intensive surplus-producing agriculture in Cambodia.[3] On the
other hand, a variety of 'floating rice' had a successful career
further east: the Chams are known to have had it, and by the
beginning of the eleventh century 'Cham rice' had been imported to southern China, where it was highly regarded as a
source of high yields.

Chou Ta-kuan observed 'a type of natural field where rice
grows all the time without being sown; when the water rises one
fathom, the rice grows with it'. It is not clear exactly what he
meant; Delvert suggests that the Chinese visitor was observing
the exploitation of wild rice, *srangne*.[4]

Before we turn to the rain-fed cultivation that is by far the
most widely practised system, it is desirable to give some attention to irrigated agriculture as it is known today in Cambodia,

[3]   R. C. Ng, The geographical habitat of historical settlement. In *Early South
East Asia: Essays in archaeology history, and historical geography*, ed. R. B.
Smith and W. Watson, New York: Oxford University Press, 1979, p. 266.
[4]   Delvert, *Le Paysan cambodgien*, p. 330.

for this is the system which is often seen as the foundation of Angkor's greatness.

Fields irrigated from ponds or streams in the dry season (*prang*) are known nowadays, though Khmer farmers prefer not to engage in the often very arduous labour that is required for their cultivation; employers of labour sometimes choose to maintain them, however. It is notable that, given freedom to choose how they shall work, few Khmers voluntarily undertake hard work in the hot season to produce large quantities of irrigated crops. In Angkor, of course, it is possible to argue that the apparatus of a successful state was in a position to intervene in the direction of labour and require, on a large scale, the dry-season irrigated field labour that nowadays is carried on only in a small way. Whether this actually happened is a moot point.

Irrigated rice can be grown in a three-month cycle, which makes just possible the claim that Angkor had up to four crops a year. The paddy is grown around ponds in flooded areas, or, in areas of deep or rapid flooding, the receding waters may be

Plate 24   *Irrigating dry-season crop, near Lake Koki*

trapped by minor earthworks thrown up around three sides of a temporary reservoir against the gradient of the flood (*tanub*), or across the course of a stream.

Constant hard work is necessary to keep the field watered by a variety of devices.[5] One consists of a bucket swung in and out of the water by cords that are held by two men standing on either side of a stream. This requires long hours of toil in the heat, and lifts water only a few inches above its original level. An apparatus used to raise water from a pond in the corner of a field is a tripod from which a hollow log is suspended by cords in such a way that it can act as a scoop; or one end of the log can rest on the lip of a bank while the other is lowered into the water and then lifted by a pulley to the required height.

Nowadays, *norias* driven by pedals – an endless chain of scoops or buckets drawing water up a bank, emptying it and returning to river level – are used in some places, primarily on the Siemreap River. These are thought to have been introduced from Vietnam or China. Less labour-intensive, and attractively energy-saving, is the waterwheel *noria*, a waterwheel with buckets or tubes attached to it that scoop up water at the bottom of their rotation and pour it out into a chute at the top. They are driven by the unaided power of the water's current, which is enhanced to a sufficient velocity by building a barrage across the stream, leaving only a narrow gap through which the water surges upon the waterwheel and propels it. They are not the easy answer to all the problems of irrigation, for they will be economical only where there is water throughout the dry season, the banks are not too high, and the irrigated culture is profitable enough to justify the labour.

All in all, irrigated agriculture plays a modest role in the modern agricultural economy, though some reformers seek to enlarge it. If it was at the basis of Angkor's prosperity, we must recognize that it required a pattern of manpower control substantially different from what came before and after Angkor.

The basic system of cultivation uses rain-fed rice fields, *sre vossa* ('wet-season fields'), which is the staple today and may or

---

[5] On the variety of devices used to control water supply – some indigenous, some of Indian or other outside origin – see J. Spencer, La maîtrise de l'eau en Asie du Sud-est, *Etudes rurales*, 53–6 (1974), pp. 73–94.

may not have been so at the time of Angkor. Seeds are sown in nursery beds at the beginning of the rainy season and nurtured until the time is ripe for planting out to ploughed fields, usually in August or September, late enough to be sure of receiving sufficient rain. In the past, much ritual used to surround the planting. Care must be taken that conditions are right; as a proverb has it, 'One must cultivate rice when the earth is warm; one must court a girl when love is quickened.' There is, however, little work to be done in the fields until the harvest. Ducks can be set loose to do the weeding. When the first golden ears appear, the water can be drained. Harvesting is a period of frantic activity, conducted usually in neighbourhood groups with a great deal of sociable good humour.

The allocation to different fields of different strains with different growing periods calls for nice judgement. With some fields sown or harvested later or earlier than others, the risk of loss through shortage or excess of rainfall can be hedged, and the labour of harvesting can be spread over a period. The farmer knows every strain of rice like the back of his hand. Their names are evocative: they include white cat, red cat, parrot's eyebrow, teal's eyebrow, rattan spike, serpent's neck, elephant's tail, iguana eye, little bee, troop of soldiers, and young white girl.

The round of farm activities associated with this sort of cultivation probably resembles that of earlier centuries. Productivity is not very high, but in the absence of abnormal disruptive conditions it is capable of keeping farm families reasonably fed and yielding a surplus that could, in principle, support a small but self-assertive non-productive class. As observed in the middle of the twentieth century, the statistical (albeit imaginary) average farm family contained five and a half people and cultivated two to three hectares, consuming two-thirds to three-quarters of the crop. A single hectare can produce over a ton of rice, enough for the average family's basic needs. In favoured places, such as on river banks and in southern Battambang, farmers in the 1960s were able to produce yields as high as two and even three tonnes of paddy per hectare. Under the Democratic Kampuchean regime in the 1970s, Pol Pot borrowed a slogan from communist China, namely 'three tonnes [of paddy] per hectare', which he proposed as a national *average* yield. The goal was reached in very few

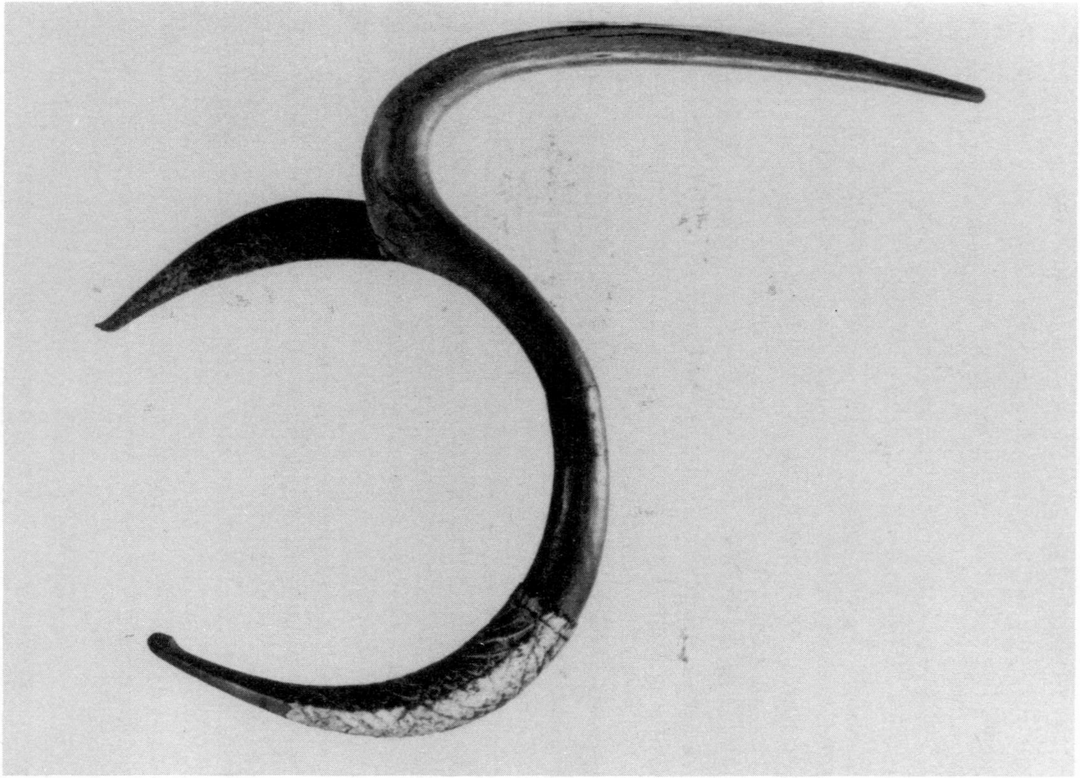

Plate 25 Cambodian rice knife

places, the experiment itself was a disaster, and following the collapse of Democratic Kampuchea, average national yields of paddy dropped back to a little over one tonne per hectare – one of the lowest in South-East Asia.

How different would things have had to be in Angkor in order to support the empire? Was the prosperity of this empire built upon a state-supervised system that raised two or more crops a year, as has sometimes been thought?

In some respects, we might suppose that an Angkor dependent on the *sre vossa* techniques familiar today would have been worse off than modern Cambodia. There would have been a much narrower range of secondary food products to enlarge the diet; and we must allow for the likelihood that farming methods and grain types were somewhat less productive.

On the other hand, the rain regime may have been more reliable, and perhaps the soil better; possibly, also, easily harvested wild rice accounted for a larger proportion of the national diet. The urban population of Angkor, we might conclude, could after all have been supported by a simple rain-field agricultural system.

The traditional agricultural system as it is observed today has not lasted from the dawn of history. In earlier periods of rice cultivation (leaving aside the question whether it began by the coasts or further inland), farming was concentrated in the floodplains of the Mekong delta and the Mun and Chi river drainage system, broadcasting seed and relying on natural flooding; by the tenth century, however, the floodplains were largely abandoned and Khmer farmers increasingly took to reclaiming land for bunded fields in the lowland forest areas of the Mun-Chi system and around the Great Lake, a process that was under way in the eighth century and clearly has much to do with the rise of the Khmer states in the 'Chen-la' and Angkorian periods. Ponds were dug to supply water to groups of families, and earthworks were constructed to retard the dissipation of floodwater in order to enhance the supply for neighbouring fields.

Geographical reasons for this shift are not obvious. It has been suggested that there could possibly have been a change in the flood patterns.[6] Coinciding with the shift was the intro-

---

[6] W. van Liere, Traditional water management in the lower Mekong Basin. *World Archaeology*, 11, no. 3 (1980), pp. 265–80.

duction of new strains of rice: previously, mainland South-East
Asian farmers had used round-grain types of paddy like the
japonica known at present, whereas long-grain rice of the *indica*
varieties gained ground after the tenth century. Its husks have
been found in ruins of structures dating from earlier centuries
in the Mon-Khmer area. Thus there was perhaps a link between
Indian influence (from the Pāllava empire of South India) and
the introduction of *indica* rice.[7]

We now confront the question whether there was a further
and dramatic shift in the character of rice agriculture during
the Angkor period that was brought about by the exercise of

*Plate 26 After the ploughing of the sacred furrow, a rite inaugurating
the rice-growing cycle, the royal cattle 'choose' grain from different
receptacles: their choice is believed to predict the success or failure of
crops*

[7] Tadayo Watabe, *Ine no Michi* (Tokyo, 1977), pp. 129–31, cited by
Yumio Sakurai, Tank agriculture in South India: an essay on agricultural
Indianization in Southeast Asia. In *Transformation of the Agricultural Land-
scape in Sri Lanka and South India*, ed. S. D. G. Jayawardena, Kyoto: Kyoto
University Center for Southeast Asian Studies, n. d., pp. 117–58, at p. 117.

the new imperial power. In the tenth and eleventh centuries, bigger and bigger reservoirs were built, holding huge amounts of water. Were these used to irrigate fields? Were they the foundation of a prosperous state-managed agricultural system?

In the past, most scholars have supposed that the reservoirs supplied the needs of an extensive and elaborate irrigation system which was assumed to sustain the prosperity of the empire by nourishing several crops each year. After all, it would be so much easier to account for the (literally) monumental extravagance of the Angkorian rulers with the manpower they needed to build reservoirs, temples and an empire if we had evidence that the agricultural surplus was greatly enlarged by the growing of two or more crops a year through irrigation in the dry season.

This assumption has recently been challenged. The matter is open to debate. Let us look first at the argument in favour of large-scale irrigation. With assured supplies of water all the year round, it is theoretically just possible to raise up to four crops of rice. If this possibility were realized, Angkor could have supported the hordes of soldiers, labourers, craftsmen and officials on whom the empire depended. We have further the testimony of Chou Ta-kuan, who said that there were generally three or four crops a year.[8]

The irrigation theory appeals to the stark and conspicuous fact that the kings of Angkor built huge reservoirs which required an enormous investment in labour and organization. The process began in the ninth century, when Indravarman I was responsible for the construction of the Indrataṭāka ('Indra's Lake'). As an inscription of Indravarman from the Preah Koh claims, 'From the time when he received the royal power, he made this promise: "In five days from today, I shall begin to dig, etc."'[9] His lake (3,800 × 800 metres) was the largest artificial reservoir yet constructed in the region.

Successive rulers moved step by step upstream to divert the waters of the Siemreap River into progressively more ambitious

---

[8] Chou Ta-kuan, *Mémoires sur les coutumes du Cambodge de Tcheou Ta-kouan*, tr. P. Pelliot, Paris: Ecole française d'Extrême-Orient, 1951, p. 25.
[9] G. Coedès, *Inscriptions du Cambodge*, 8 vols. Paris and Hanoi: Ecole française d'Extrême-Orient, 1937–66, vol. 2, pp. 17–31, verse VII.

hydraulic systems. The process advanced in a great leap with Yaśovarman's construction of the Eastern Baray to grace his new capital of Yaśodharapura. This was 7 × 2 kilometres, raised up above the level of the plain by huge embankments 10 metres high and with a maximum capacity that has been estimated as up to 60 million cubic metres. An inscription refers to 'this divine lake, made as if to drown the pride of all kings, water of *amrta*'[10] – the food of the gods, nectar of immortality.

Yet even this was surpassed in the eleventh century, probably by Sūryavarman, with the Western Baray, which was built to the west of the main capital site and measured 8 × 2 kilometres. Its capacity has been estimated as ranging from 42 million to 70 million cubic metres. Though it eventually lost its capacity, like all the other reservoirs, it was partly restored in 1937, with further work in 1955, and made possible the irrigation of 11,000 hectares with two crops.

This was the greatest reservoir of all, but some later kings made significant additions to the hydraulic system. In the twelfth century, the moats and canals constructed around Angkor Wat by Sūryavarman II were themselves capable of carrying 5 million cubic metres, and around AD 1200 Jayavarman VII constructed another, smaller reservoir, the Jayatatāka, north of the Eastern Baray, which measured 900 × 3,700 metres.

Historians have long supposed that such reservoirs were politically important in a practical way. Philippe Stern detected a rhythm running through the building activities of numerous rulers that demonstrated a threefold pattern: as a first priority, the construction of reservoirs for irrigation; as a second, the consecration of shrines to previous rulers and family members; as a third, a culminating statement of legitimate power, the building of temple-mountains situated at the ritual centre of the kingdom.[11] These were seen as the three steps that an ambitious king must take to secure his power.

---

[10]   B. Groslier, La cité hydraulique angkorienne. Exploitation ou sur-exploitation du sol? *Bulletin de l'Ecole française d'Etrême-Orient*, 66 (1979), pp. 161–202.

[11]   P. Stern, Diversité et rythme des fondations royales khmères. *Bulletin de l'Ecole française d'Extrême-Orient*, 44 (1954), pp. 649–87.

Bernard Groslier argued that these reservoirs, and the elaborate system of canals (revealed by aerial photography) with which they were linked, fed an irrigation system that yielded multiple crops on fields downhill from the storage. On Groslier's reconstruction, water first seeped through the embankments of the reservoirs into the collector channels that surrounded them. Then it was distributed across the fields by an elaborate system of canals. There was no need for sophisticated contrivances to lift water from one level to another (which would be an objection to the irrigation theory if it required an elaborate technology which the Khmers did not possess); gravity could direct the water from bunded field to bunded field, and it could be regulated simply by digging or filling up gaps in the bunds.

Groslier later modified his earlier hypothesis that the reservoirs were used as the main source of water for the irrigation

*Plate 27   Transplanting rice shoots in September. In the background
is a floodgate for irrigation*

of several crops a year.[12] In fact, despite their size, the water thus used would not have watered a very large area. But the importance of the system, he argued in a later article, could have been in providing an assured reserve to supplement when necessary the supplies of rainwater in single-crop fields. Successful harvests brought in year after year with the insurance of this supply, he said, would have been capable of laying a basis of prosperity altogether lacking when farmers had to depend upon irregular monsoon rainfall that came in the wrong quantities or at the wrong time in as many years as not.[13] According to Groslier, the single-crop fields directly benefiting from the system, on this interpretation, would have occupied up to 86,000 hectares. This area could perhaps have supported between a third and a half of a million people.

However, even this modified form of the irrigation hypothesis is untenable according to recent critics. W. van Liere, for example, has argued that the assumption that water would seep into the collector channels from the reservoirs is technically incorrect: no water at all could find its way into the canals alleged to have supplied the irrigation needs of the fields below.[14]

Groslier recognized the problems that must have followed any attempt to sustain intensive agriculture unremittingly on the rather poor soils of the area. Silt blocked the channels through which the water had to flow, causing a progressive breakdown impossible to remedy without massive reconstruction; deprived of the water they needed, the irrigated fields were exposed to the sun, dried out and suffered erosion; solar heat caused the sub-surface water to transpire to the top, bringing up ferrous oxides, and the soil was sterilized. Several factors converged in this process, with the earth suffering erosion, leaching and sterilization. The demands of a dense population for agricultural land, fuel and construction materials inevitably brought about deforestation, and this not only exposed the good topsoil

---

[12]   See B. P. Groslier, *Angkor et le Cambodge au XVIe siècle d'après les sources portuguaises et espagnoles.* Paris: Presses Universitaires de France, 1958, pp. 114, 118.
[13]   Groslier, *La cité hydraulique.*
[14]   Van Liere, *Traditional water management.*

to erosion but probably also had an effect on rainfall, depriving the land at least of convection rains. For Groslier, these problems are part of the explanation of the eventual collapse of the intensive irrigation system. For critics of the irrigation hypothesis, they are reasons why Angkor could not have supported the intensive irrigation system in the first place. In modern times, hydro-agricultural projects have often brought about degradation of the soil in a matter of years; leaching and deprivation of the required nutrients, allied with the inevitable silting up of reservoirs and the deforestation of slopes, would have quickly made high-yielding wet rice cultivation impossible.[15]

What, then, was the purpose of the hydraulic system? For the critics, the reservoirs must have been part of the ritual apparatus of kingship, with its cosmological symbolism that assimilated the ruler to the gods watching over the earth and the surrounding waters. The reservoirs did not help, but hindered, the drainage of water towards the fields. So far as the requirements of agriculture went, the simple small-scale and usually temporary water diversions or dams to trap receding floodwater met all the hydraulic needs of the farmers.

Further arguments have been levied against the multiple-crop version of the irrigation hypothesis. The involvement of the farming population in a centrally managed scheme to grow multiple crops in the dry season did not contribute to efficient agriculture. Farmers seeking to grow more would move out and clear more fields; land was not scarce. Further, compression of the agricultural timetable into successive blocks of time devoted to multiple rice crops would have deprived them of the opportunity to diversify, with different sorts of rice planted in staggered cycles to spread the risk of bad months, and especially to tend orchards, go fishing, and grow other sorts of crops in the slack months left available by single-crop culture. Incidentally, this diversification, with various activities being carried forward by different farmers at the same time, and the cycles of rice

[15] F. Grunewald, A propos de l'agriculture dans le Cambodge mediéval. *Asie du Sud-est et Monde Insulindien*, 13, nos 1–4 (1982), pp. 23–38. Grunewald makes the suggestion that supplies of rice levied as tax to support the capital could have been produced in the productive areas much further south, in the old heartland of 'Fu-nan'.

growing widely staggered, could account for Chou Ta-kuan's impression that there were several succession crops.

The newer criticisms have not convinced all historians. For those who distrust them, the location and scale of the hydraulic works powerfully suggest that these works were directed at least in part to the needs of agriculture. Even if the number of people who could be supported by ricefields watered from the system is much smaller than used to be imagined, the concentration of population which the system made possible in one restricted area might have constituted Angkor as a 'Key Economic Area' on a small scale – that is, a prosperous zone that gave its ruler an edge over would-be rivals in other surrounding zones, enabling him to dominate them.

Critical to the irrigation theory is the question whether Angkor achieved the critical mass for a shift to a new pattern of social and political organization, a pattern that worked according to rules different from those that applied before and after. The emphasis of much modern research is upon the centrifugal forces in ancient Khmer politics – the continuing autonomy of the provincial communities with their leading families and local protective spirits. We need this emphasis to prevent us imagining a monolithic 'oriental despotism' served by a centralized administration. Nevertheless, within the limits imposed by an agrarian and rather segmented society, it is possible to argue that Angkor achieved a concentration of power that made it in some ways qualitatively different from the earlier states of the region – a concentration which, in fact, made it an 'imperial state'.[16] As such, it may have been able to organize manpower in new ways. It may have been able to sustain a much more intensive agricultural system. Some such view must be accepted if the traditional irrigation theory is to be maintained.

It is not clear what conclusion we should draw. Certainly, in recent times the trend has been to deny that Angkor's hydraulic works were for irrigation. Geographers and hydraulic engineers who have observed the terrain often judge it unlikely that the

[16] See Kulke, The early and the imperial kingdom. In D. G. Marr and A. C. Milner (eds), *Southeast Asia in the 9th to 14th Centuries*, Singapore: Institute of Southeast Asian Studies, and Canberra: Research School of Pacific Studies, Australian National University, 1986, pp. 1–22.

Barays served the needs of agriculture. However, such a prodigious expenditure of labour must have served some important
purpose, and the alternative explanation – the needs of ritual –
deserves to be detailed more thoroughly.

The 'ritual' interpretation can be supported by an examin-
ation of the bases of royal legitimacy, which depended upon
massive labour-intensive activities as a manifestation of the
spiritual power concentrated in the person of a ruler. However,
this possibility does not decide the issue. There may well have
been practical benefits from the availability of such a volume
of water as the Barays collected, whether for domestic supply or
for irrigation, and there are still problems to be solved before we
discount the older interpretation altogether.

12

Ruler and State

Only a few generations of people living in modern western countries have ever been able to regard peace as a natural condition with its own equilibrium. Throughout Cambodia's recorded history, the Khmers have had to regard war as a normal state of society and as a factor that conditioned it.

Mainland South-East Asia was an arena where rulers competed for hegemony, reaching out from home territories in fertile river valleys to secure the submission of neighbours or control of manpower. Inscriptional eulogies as a matter of routine describe kings as carrying swords red with the blood of their enemies, felling foes with vibrant blades, and cleaving the bodies of their enemies.

Armies did not consist of permanent standing forces, but were raised *ad hoc* for particular campaigns by the great men in the provinces, who were responsible for supplying troops for royal service. Often enough, huge armies could be raised in this way; Chau Ju-kua claims that the Khmers in his time had 200,000 elephants and many horses (albeit small ones). It is difficult to trust such figures. No doubt there could be enormous hordes of cheaply maintained footsoldiers – Chou Ta-kuan says that there had been universal conscription for a recent exhausting war against the Siamese – though the levies might be ill-trained and poorly equipped. Chou tells us that the Khmer soldiers were unclothed and barefoot; they lacked discipline and were poorly led.[1]

[1] Chou Ta-kuan, *Mémoires sur les coutumes de Cambodge de Tcheou Takouan*, tr. P. Pelliot. Paris: Ecole française d'Extrême-Orient, 1951, p. 34.

The permanent guard maintained at the capital was probably better. Relief sculpture portrays palace guards wearing helmets wrought with elaborate motifs; door guardians carry ceremonial weapons, their points protected by covers; sentinels carry lances, swords and shields. Ordinary soldiers carried lances in their right hands and shields in their left. The arsenal included sabres, swords, shields, broadswords, daggers, catapults and other contrivances.

One type of contrivance, probably a ballista, is illustrated in the relief sculpture. Carried on elephant back or mounted on wheels, it is portrayed in the art of the Bayon and Banteay Chmar; it appears to be a double bow, operated by pulling back the rear bow.[2]

Ma Tuan-lin recounts an episode in twelfth-century military history. A mandarin from Fukien, he tells us, was shipwrecked on the coast of Champa in 1171, while there was war against Angkor. He told his hosts that the Cham forces should rely less on elephants and more on cavalry with bows and arbalests. He taught the Chams how to fire arrows while riding, and arranged for the purchase of some superior horses. These advantages, it was claimed, turned the tide of war in favour of the Chams.[3]

The Khmer sources for this Cham victory refer to a surprise naval attack, sending a fleet up the Tonle Sap to the Great Lake. This illustrates the importance of shipping, for naval warfare as well as commerce; the Khmers, long accustomed to navigation on the Lake and the great waterways that seamed their territory, were not backward when it came to war at sea, and in one twelfth-century war against the Vietnamese it was claimed that they sent a fleet of 700 vessels round the coast.

An ancient Indian manual of statecraft, the *Arthaśāstra*, operates upon the explicit principle that neighbours are automatically potential enemies. In South-East Asia, war was a fact of political life, and the character of kingship was moulded

---

[2] P. Mus, Les balistes du Bayon. *Bulletin de l'Ecole française d'Extrême-Orient*, 29 (1929), pp. 331–41.

[3] Ma Tuan-lin, *Ethnographie des peuples étrangers à la Chine, ouvrage composé ... par Ma Touan-lin*, tr. Le Marquis d'Hervey de Saint-Denys. Geneva: Georg, 1876, vol. II, pp. 555f.

Plate 28 (a) and (b)   Warriors with ballistae going into battle

Plate 29   Mounted warriors, Angkor Wat bas-relief

Plate 30   War chariot, Angkor Wat bas-relief

by preparations for armed conflict. An attempt to understand kingship needs to begin from this point.

Enemies were not only to be found beyond a country's borders. They lurked within each kingdom, within the capital, even within the court where rival members of the royal family and all their supporters occupied the hot days with games of intrigue. How did kingship work in these circumstances? How did people come to be kings? Having succeeded, how did they try to secure their authority?

There is a legend about a man in ancient times who began his career at court as the custodian of the royal cucumber garden. The king was especially fond of the cucumbers grown in it, and gave strict instructions that nobody should be allowed into the garden on pain of death. The gardener was ordered to kill intruders on sight. One day, the gardener saw an unidentified intruder skulking among the cucumbers; being nothing if not loyal, he killed the stranger on the spot. Unfortunately the victim was the king himself. Hauled before the authorities, the gardener explained that he had been doing his duty. This defence, in the Gilbertian world of legend, could elicit but one sequel: there was nothing for it but to make the gardener king, complete with the widowed queen as his consort.

The story, told in Burma as well as Cambodia, is a piece of local legend. What is worth noticing about it is its pitiless logic. He who kills the king becomes king. This principle is grounded in the politics of succession disputes in so many kingdoms, where intriguers struggle for power and feel little compunction in murdering anyone in the way in order to take the throne for themselves. They, in their turn, are murdered by the next successful contestant.

As for succession in the Khmer kingdoms, no one knows exactly what rules of succession, if any, were recognized. Neither patrilineal nor matrilineal descent was a dominating principle of legitimacy. Some kings of Angkor (but not all) claimed links to Jayavarman II, founder of the kingdom. Marriages forged bonds of alliance between kings and the great families at court, many of them having royal ancestors (whether Angkorian or pre-Angkorian royalty).

It has been argued that there was a way of reckoning descent that was essentially bilateral;[4] it has also been argued that there could have been a form of reckoning based on a 'conical clan', whereby succession passed through all male members of one generation before descending to the next.[5]

It is possible to demand too much precision: as C. Jacques has reminded us, only eight out of twenty-six rulers of Angkor were sons or brothers of their predecessors, and one of these, Yaśovarman I, had to fight his way to a throne which his father sought to deny him.[6] Genealogies frequently appear in royal inscriptions, but we may suspect that they are partly fiction: occasionally mythical beings are listed as ancestors.

The death of a ruler – transpired or imminent – was often enough to turn the rivalry between his brothers and his sons (who were usually half-brothers by a number of queens) into armed conflict. A seventh-century Chinese account tells of the custom of kings of 'Chen-la' to mutilate or confine their brothers in order to keep rival claimants at bay. Ma Tuan-lin tells us: 'A finger is cut off one, a nose off another.' This observation lacks independent corroboration, though.

Authority and loyalty worked between persons rather than between offices. Dignitaries gave their support to a ruler (or less openly to a rival) because of personal ties that were cemented by family connections and hopes for advancement. The inscriptions do not record the details of court faction and intrigue, but

[4] Thomas A. Kirsch, Kinship, genealogical claims and societal integration in ancient Khmer society: an interpretation. In *Southeast Asian History and Historiography: essays presented to D. G. E. Hall*, ed. C. D. Cowan and O. W. Wolters, Ithaca, N. Y.: Cornell University Press 1976, pp. 190–202.

[5] M. Vickery, The reign of Sūryavarman I and royal factionalism at Angkor. *Journal of Southeast Asian Studies*, 16, no. 2 (1985), pp. 226–44. Vickery observes that, in this situation, genealogies 'will more often be fictional than historically true' (p. 243).

[6] C. Jacques, *Angkor*. Paris: Bordas, 1990, pp. 22f. For some relatively recent views on succession in Angkor, see Vickery, The reign of Sūryavarman I; idem, Some remarks on early state formation in Cambodia, in *Southeast Asia in the 9th to 14th Centuries*, ed. D. Marr and A. Milner, Canberra: Research school of Pacific Studies, Australian National University, and Singapore. Institute of Southeast Asian Studies, 1986, pp. 95–115; O. W. Wolters, Khmer Hinduism in the seventh century, in *Early South East Asia: Essays in archaeology, history and historical geography*, ed. R. B. Smith and W. Watson, New York: Oxford University Press, 1979, pp. 427–42, at p. 429.

the evidence of internecine strife is often indirect. The partial effacement of an inscription of Indravarman I may suggest that his successor, Yaśovarman I, did not succeed peacefully. Harṣavarman II came to the throne 'thanks to a friend and his two arms'. The inconsistent references in inscriptions to the transition from Rājendravarman (*d.*966 or 967) and Jayavarman V (who acceded sometime in the period 968–70) may well mask a period of strife. Yaśovarman II was described as gaining the throne by his own efforts, a hint that he had to fight his way up. Jayavarman VII had to spend years fighting a multitude of foes even after driving out the Chams who had conquered Angkor. Claude Jacques has directed attention to such episodes as these, reading between the lines of the bland record of all-conquering rulers to detect a much more fluid political situation.[7]

Such research has an important bearing upon our interpretation of Angkor's political history. There was rarely if ever a stable, assured succession by a single legitimate heir to dominion over an integrated, well-defined territorial state. Regional centres such as the old city of Bhavapura, the base from which Rājendravarman climbed to the throne, competed with each other, and the lords of the realm were jealous of the regional balance of power. Rājendravarman probably did more than any ruler to create a genuinely centralized administration; but as late as the twelfth century, Jacques has suggested, one can see evidence of groups of landed great families with independent bases of power.[8]

There was a symbiosis between the interests of the king and those of the great lords. They supported him so long as his policies favoured them; he bestowed patronage upon those he felt he could trust. High position was a matter of nearness to power, and those given the most exalted positions were, or became, part of the king's party, the group of kin and clients on whom the ruler thought he could rely. Chou Ta-kuan tells us that the great officials were mostly princes; when they were not,

---

[7] C. Jacques, Nouvelles orientations pour l'étude de l'histoire du pays khmer. *Asie du Sud-est et Monde Insulindien, Cambodge I,* 13, nos 1–4 (1982), pp. 39–58.
[8] Ibid., pp. 55f.

they had their interests tied to those of the palace by offering daughters to the king. The king needed to keep the great families of the land on his side by giving them honours and bestowing the revenues of territories upon them. In principle, it appears, the bestowal of such revenues could be recalled at any time; but so far as inscriptions show, kings only rarely and cautiously attempted to withdraw such grants. As time passed, we might suppose, successive generations of endowed families came to regard their grants as private property.[9] Rulers had to buy loyalty afresh in every generation.

High rank was marked by court ceremonial rather than by status in any impersonal state machine. Great officials were preoccupied with the ceremonial indices of their positions, and sumptuary laws governed the insignia of rank, particularly the design of their parasols (of red Chinese taffeta, with fringes falling almost to the ground) and their palanquins that declared their dignity on public occasions.[10]

As for the mass of the subjects, who lived for the most part in tiny agricultural settlements dotted over the landscape, what did they think about their kings?

Take the case of the claim made for Jayavarman V. According to one inscriptional eulogy he had compassion for those he ruled: 'Like a father cherished by his children, he dried the tears of his afflicted subjects.' Solange Thierry remarks sardonically: 'Inscriptional figure of speech: the kings dried the tears of their subjects by making them build cities and temples, reservoirs and embankments. Either they enjoyed it, or they died of it.'[11] The comment is apt as well as pithy, but whatever we might claim about the attitudes of ordinary people to their kings is based upon ignorance. There are two opposite sorts of naïveté: to suppose that, because the kings appear in the historical record as great beings with semi-divine status, their subjects must have

---

[9] S. Sahai, *Les Institutions politiques et l'organisation administrative du Cambodge ancien.* Paris: Ecole française d'Extrême-Orient, 1970, pp. 144f; I. W. Mabbett, Kingship in Angkor, *Journal of the Siam Society*, 66, no. 2 (1978), pp. 1–58, at p. 24.

[10] 'All parasols are made of red taffeta from China, and their flounces fall to the ground. Oiled parasols are all made of green taffeta, with a short flounce' (Chou Ta-kuan, *Mémoires*, p. 14).

[11] S. Thierry, *Les Khmers.* Paris: Seuil, 1964, pp. 85f.

loved them and given all their toil willingly; and to suppose on the contrary that, because they had to toil, they must have hated their rulers and wished for a less hierarchical order of society. Both these views are the products of culture-bound imagination.

We can only suppose that, for all sorts of particular reasons (generally no doubt connected with the ramification of patron-client relations in the countryside) which are obscure to us, some kings were well-loved, others were detested, and yet others were regarded with indifference. Our own preferences among the Cambodian rulers are not likely to be a guide to those of the ordinary subjects.

On what did the authority of the ruler actually depend? Two different answers have been given; both have been made problematic by recent research. The first is religious symbolism. It apeals to the notion that rulers surrounded themselves with impressive rituals that assimilated them to gods, and were thereby able to present themselves as more than human. We have already noticed here that the *devarāja* cult, instituted by Jayavarman II, was once seen as the cult of the king himself turned into a god. However, it can scarcely be so regarded any more, for the 'god' of the cult is unlikely to be the ruler, and the cult must be inserted within the network of regional spirits which could be given concrete reality as protectors of individuals or families.[12] The second is the control of a centralized irrigation system. However, as was pointed out above, the reality of such a system is now in doubt.[13]

There is no agreed way of analysing the authority of the kings of Angkor. Structures and institutions of government might be described as totalitarian (lacking formal checks upon a king's power), but the Khmers did not have despotic god-kings exercising totalitarian power in practice. Society was too fragmented for that, and there was too much rivalry, always

---

[12] On this see also A. Forest, Cambodge: pouvoir du roi et puissance de génie. In Forest (ed.), *Cultes populaires et sociétés asiatiques: appareils cultuels et appareils du pouvoir*, Paris: Harmattan, 1991, pp. 169–83.

[13] On the relationship between religious symbolism and control of manpower in securing royal authority, see P. J. Wilson, *The Domestication of the Human Species*. New Haven, Conn.: Yale University Press, 1989, esp. pp. 90–1.

latent and ready to break out into conflict even under the strongest of rulers.

Nevertheless, it would probably be wrong to regard the ancient South-East Asian states as weak and decentralized polities of one type, with a single pattern of power and authority. Indeed, the period from the reign of Rājendravarman to that of Sūryavarman may mark a genuine breakthrough to a new sort of polity. This interpretation has been urged by H. Kulke, who distinguishes between three types of state. The first is the local chiefdom, confined to a limited home territory around a chieftain's fortified settlement. The second is the regional kingdom, which consolidates a number of contiguous localities by conquest into a kingdom ruled by a *rāja*, who exercises authority over outer territories only indirectly, through local vassals. The third is the imperial state, which draws the aristocracies of outlying vassals into an imperial court and integrates their territories into the imperial administration.[14] This third sort of state represents a new type of political power, in which rulers command a much more centralized apparatus of administrative control than existed in the clusters of principalities which they replaced.

It can be argued that the strongest of them, certainly including Angkor at its height, made a qualitative shift, acquiring a more integrated political structure with a large and self-sustaining bureaucracy capable of acting upon society in new ways. Economically, the region of Angkor possibly supported a sufficiently dense and well-supplied population (until the forest was denuded, the soil degraded, and the possibilities of intensive wet rice cultivation largely exhausted) to give it the needed edge over neighbouring regions. Culturally, a vocabulary of religious grandeur was needed in order to give expression to an identity that could transcend the loyalties of the city states upon which Angkor was built.

Whether or in what ways Angkor was qualitatively different from earlier states is open to debate. The old picture of a centralized and more or less totalitarian state under an 'oriental despot', as we have already noticed, needs to be discarded:

---

[14] H. Kulke, The early and the imperial kingdom in Southeast Asian history. In Marr and Milner, *Southeast Asia in the 9th to 14th Centuries*, pp. 1–22.

Khmer society was a patchwork of communities with powerful traditions of autonomy under the protection of local patron spirits. But this does not exclude the possibility that, by virtue of its superior resources and strategic position, Angkor was able to create new institutions of hegemony structurally different from what had gone before.

One major feature of the 'imperial state' was its maintenance of a large court and a corps of officials. Angkor had a sizeable bureaucracy staffed by officials of many sorts. Like so much about the Khmer kingdom in ancient times, the structure of government and the categories of the civil service are known to us through the temple inscriptions, which frequently name various types of official or local dignitary in listing those present to witness the formal demarcation of land bestowed upon religious foundations; they mention a variety of grades and titles, some of them obscure. The *khloñ rājakārya* was responsible for the administration of 'royal work', probably corvée among other things. The *tāmṛvāc* was an inspector; the officials who swore allegiance to Suryavarman I had this title, for example. The *guṇadoṣadarśin* (assessor of virtues and defects) was concerned with temple property. A variety of functionaries were called *khloñ* (inspector) and had responsibilities in various areas such as grain, temple dues, management of religious foundations, and several aspects of court proceedings.[15] Revenue was usually in kind, being paid in grain, but some special districts paid in other commodities such as honey and wax.

There is evidence that some of the categories in which officials were placed were not types of professional specialization but divisions of the government service placed under the patronage of particular chiefs belonging to the royal family, a system that was indeed known in later centuries.[16] Some of the groups of dignitaries named in the inscriptions, again, appear to have been the bearers of hereditary privileges in the royal household;

---

[15] On these *khloñ*, see H. de Mestier du Bourg, La première moitié du XIe siècle au Cambodge: Sūryavarman Ier, sa vie et quelques aspects des institutions à son époque. *Journal Asiatique*, 258 (1970), pp. 281–314, at p. 302.
[16] On the four appanages in the nineteenth century, see A. Leclère, *Recherches sur le droit des cambodgiens*. Paris: Challamel, 1894; cf. Mabbett, Kingship in Angkor, p. 32.

the term *varna*, for example, designates any of a number of
orders of dignity, which have such official functions as religious
teachers, performers of rites, door guardians, garden keepers,
palace servants, bearers of flywhisks, and artists.[17]

It was probably Rājendravarman who, more than anybody
else, inaugurated the institutions of centralized administration
and entrenched the power of Angkor in the provinces through
the agency of teams of officials. The empire was divided into
areas and districts, but the terms used in the inscriptions are
inconsistent, and there is doubt about their precise meaning.
Ancient principalities, with the scions of their royal lineages still
eager for local autonomy, began to be absorbed within the
apparatus of a national monarchy – though it can be disputed
whether the absorption of the lordly families was ever complete.
Up to the end, kings had to compete with rivals who had
regional power bases.

At any rate, administrative divisions were standardized. On
one widely shared interpretation the designation of many territories as *viṣaya* where previously there had been *pramān* indicated that formerly autonomous princely fiefs were integrated
as provinces. It appears likely that the former was primarily a
geographical term, while the latter came to refer to a specific
administrative division, possibly equivalent to a province.[18]

In the thirteenth century, Chou Ta-kuan writes that there
were over ninety provinces, each with a fortified citadel. At the
level of the locality, there were officials whom he called *mai-
chieh* in the villages, possibly equivalent to *me srok*, custodians
of settlements. Village elders, *grāmavṛddha*, are mentioned in
the epigraphy, and appear to have had official responsibilities
such as delivering criminals, suitably caged, into the custody of
royal officials.

Justice was administered according to principles about which
we have little detailed information, though certainly such Indian

---

[17] These *varṇas* have been discussed by I. W. Mabbett, in Varnas in Angkor
and the Indian caste system, *Journal of Asian Studies*, 36, no. 3 (1977), pp.
429–42.
[18] S. Sahai, Territorial administration in ancient Cambodia. *South East
Asian Review*, 2 (1977), pp. 35–50; C. Jacques, Sur l'emplacement du
royaume d'Aninditapura. *Bulletin de l'Ecole française d'Extrême-Orient*, 59
(1972), pp. 193–205.

texts as the *Manusmṛti* lawbook were known. The king was recognized as the final court of appeal and final authority in law. Before a case reached the king, it might go through various lower courts; inscriptions frequently mention officials who appear to have functions connected with courts of law.

There is no way of measuring the extent of discrimination and corruption in the administration of justice. The ideal of fairness to all was certainly recognized; one judge, or example, is declared to have been appointed on the strength of his impartiality.

Judicial procedure sometimes involved ordeals, a feature of Indian law. References to the practice in the earlier 'Chen-la' period were noticed above. As for Angkor, Chou Ta-kuan refers to a proceeding known as 'celestial judgment', whereby in some difficult civil cases the litigants would be confined for a few days in the belief that the guilty one would become subject to diseases.[19] Penalties were harsh by modern standards, but not random. Chou mentioned burial, amputation, fines and judicial torture. Chau Ju-kua, not much later, observed that theft was punished by cutting off a hand and foot and branding on the chest. In the sixteenth century, San Antonio referred to impalement, flaying and exposure to mosquitoes as varieties of sentence.[20]

These are reports by foreigners. Inscriptions show that a wide range of penalties could be imposed, especially fines in silver ingots, known as *palas*. In such cases, the normal (but not invariable) principle in the Indian lawbooks was to vary fines according to the rank of the offender, to the benefit of the higher ranks; this principle may have operated in Cambodia, but an inscription of Yaśovarman decreed a scale of fines that increased with social rank (and presumably with deemed ability to pay): royal princes paid twenty *pala*, ministers and members of the royal family paid ten, and so on down to ordinary people who paid just five-eighths of a *pala*, or received a hundred blows of the bamboo cane instead.

Flogging was well known, with about a hundred blows

---

[19] Chou Ta-kuan, *Mémoires*, pp. 22f.
[20] Gabriel Quiroga de San Antonio, *Brève et véridique relation des événements du Cambodge*, tr. A. Cabaton. Paris: Leroux, 1914, p. 99.

specified in a number of cases; or an offender might receive blows on the face, or amputation of fingers, hands, feet or nose. One escaped slave was condemned to have his nose and ears cut off. An inscription of 1006 refers to a commoner who was deprived of both hands and both feet. There are references to local lock-ups (but there were no regular prisons, just as in mediaeval Europe). Adultery could be punished by having the aggrieved husband squeeze the offender's feet in a wooden vice until, unable to bear the pain, the miscreant made a gift of his property to the plaintiff.[21]

All the institutions of government reviewed above give the impression that they belong to an apparatus of (at least potentially) oppressive, even totalitarian, power. Indeed, it is altogether likely that after the time of Rājendravarman the kings of Angkor presided over a much more centralized regime than the Khmers had known before. Institutions of government embodied no principles of constitutional checks upon royal power beyond the notion of religious morality. An impulse to totalitarian government was present, and found expression whenever rulers found themselves temporarily without dangerous rivals still at large. We must remember, though, that this state lacked all the advantages of modern communications and technology to assert its control in detail, and that all sorts of regional, personal and factional loyalties were liable to obstruct the impulse to totalitarianism before too long.

[21] Sahai, *Les Institutions politiques*, pp. 94–8.

13

Society and Economy

The land of the Khmers, as we have seen, was not one great farm beneath the control of the ruler; nor on the other hand did its inhabitants live in totally autonomous communities untouched by the demands of any central authority. There was a constant tension between impulses towards unity and disunity. What sort of society lived under the uncertain protection of such an unstable polity?

Farming communities could often move away and open up new land if they were disgruntled. Numerous land transactions were made quite independently of state initiative; a large proportion of all the inscriptions recorded have to do with the disposition of privately owned land. On the other hand, as in India, the ruler had recognized rights over all cultivated land. He did not 'own' it in the modern legal sense, which did not accord with the Khmer world view, but he was, in a moral sense, master over it and could make claims upon its produce and the labour of the people who worked upon its surface.[1] Often enough, kings could create new settlements by shifting communities bodily from elsewhere; there is a probable example as early as the reign of Jayavarman II, who summoned

---

[1] Sanskrit lawbooks acknowledged the role of the ruler as master, *svāmi*, over the land, with certain rights but not ownership. See S. Sahai, *Les Institutions politiques et l'organisation administrative du Cambodge ancien*, Paris: Ecole française d'Extrême-Orient, 1970, pp. 146f; M. Ricklefs, Land and the law in the epigraphy of tenth-century Cambodia, *Journal of Asian Studies*, 26, no. 3 (1967), pp. 411–20.

migrants from his old home territory to new lands in the north-west.

But the demographic history of the Khmers was not essentially the work of kings; it was a story of growth and territorial expansion in response to people's interaction with their environment. We can recognize that shifts took place with population growth, migration and sometimes state colonization of new lands. From the eleventh century, there is clear evidence of a movement to the west and north-west; it has been suggested that in the eleventh century the Khmer heartland extended from Sambor and Kampong Cham in the east to as far as Preah Vihear in the north and Battambang and Sisophon in the west, with an extension into Mon territory, in the area of Lavo, during the reign of Sūryavarman I.[2]

Our view of the articulation of Khmer society needs to be nuanced. Rulers could use their power of patronage to alter, even drastically, the distribution of power and wealth among the lords of the land – but only so long as they played the game cannily and did not antagonize the wrong people.

The same was true of India, which supplied so much of the vocabulary of Khmer culture, but Cambodian social organization was not Indian. In the caste system of India there was a network of endogamous communities rigorously stratified in ritually defined classes. Some of the Indian terminology of caste was borrowed – *varṇa*, *brāhmaṇa* (priest), *kṣatriya* (warrior-noble) – but there was no equivalent of the separate and hereditary Indian classes of warrior-nobles and priests. Elite families provided members in both categories, frequently endowing religious foundations in which their own kin officiated as priests.

Thus priests were not an order of society separate from the nobility. Inscriptions suggest that the history of the temples was bound up with the history of landed families and their political fortunes. The bestowal of land upon religious foundations, an activity to which the historical sources are overwhelmingly skewed, played an important part in articulating Khmer society. It supported a class of literate men who were indispensable for the ritual and administrative underpinning

---

[2] H. de Mestrier du Bourg, La première moitié du XIᵉ siècle au Cambodge. *Journal asiatique*, 258 (1970), pp. 281–314.

of the state. It provided careers for the sons of aristocratic families in the provinces; it was an instrument for colonization and migration, in so far as the establishment of temples was a mechanism for creating communities in new areas; it maintained and protected the interests of a lordly class which kings were reluctant to plunder. In many cases, religious settlement could promote economic settlement, with well-endowed new temples becoming the hubs of whole communities; it has been suggested that religion came before economics in this way in the development of Preah Vihear under Sūryavarman I, and eleventh-century inscriptions such as that of the Sdok Kak Thom stele record successive royal endowments of temples in northern and western territories that were being opened up to Khmer settlement.[3]

It is no wonder that the temples received such largesse, from rulers and wealthy families alike. Donors seldom relinquished all rights over donated lands unconditionally; they had a continuing interest in them. Many endowments by private individuals were designated, by royal permission, as 'royal foundations', which has been seen as a device to secure the king's guarantee of the legitimacy and permanence of the terms of these transactions.[4] From the point of view of the king, a royally endowed foundation was a permanent instrument of patronage. From the point of view of noble or official donors, there were tax advantages (kings often approved the exemption of land made over to temples from official demands for tax and corvée); there was the prestige attaching to acts of conspicuous piety; there was a benefice for kin and clients following religious careers; and there was a continuing economic interest in the form of a share of produce or of the labour that went with the endowed land.

The inscriptions recording the details of endowments were politically and socially important documents. They often ended with curses upon any who in future should violate the terms of the endowment, commonly employing the formula that a

[3] G. Coedès and P. Dupont, Les stèles de Sdok Kak Thom, Phnom Sandak et Prah Vihar. *Bulletin de l'Ecole française d'Extrême-Orient*, 43 (1943–6), pp. 56–134.
[4] Sahai, *Les Institutions politiques*, p. 147.

violator should be accursed 'as long as the moon and sun shall last'.

Between royalty and villagers, then, there was a stratum of lordly families with ancestral territories living in symbiosis with the network of prospering religious foundations. Beneath them, there was a population of free farmers about whose affairs we know very little. It is entirely possible that they were recruited into more or less formal groups of clients attached to patrons at court, especially members of the royal family, for there are traces of such a system in later centuries; in these client–patron relationships, the clients owed periodic services to their patrons, who protected them in return.[5] The presence and character of such a system during the period of Angkor is, however, a matter of speculation.

The free population was not the base of the social pyramid. What of the slaves, bondsmen or serfs? To what extent was Angkor founded upon slavery? Records of endowments commonly include lists of the names of people whose labour the donors made over, at least in part, to the beneficiaries. In the Khmer inscriptions they are simply called men and women; in the Sanskrit inscriptions they are called *dāsas*, 'slaves', and it has been normal among scholars to identify such people as temple slaves. Some, though, have argued that this is the wrong word to describe their status, since being a temple 'slave' could be an honour: the names of the people entering temple service were inscribed in stone as part of the record of endowment, within sight of the gods; although the field labourers merely performed agricultural tasks there were others whose functions were ritually important, such as preparing food for the gods; there were cases of women, presumably of landed families, soliciting the honour of entering temple service; sometimes such 'slaves' bought their own land and even had their own slaves.[6]

[5] See A. Leclère, *Recherches sur le droit des Cambodgiens*. Paris: Challamel, 1894; cf. May Ebihara, Societal organization in sixteenth- and seventeenth-century Cambodia, *Journal of Southeast Asian Studies*, 15, no. 2 (1984), pp. 280–95.

[6] C. Jacques, A propos de l'esclavage dans l'ancien Cambodge. In *XXIXe Congrès International des Orientalistes. Asie du sud-est continental*, vol. 1, ed. Pierre-Bernard Lafont, Paris: L'Asiathèque, 1976, pp. 71–6.

What this shows is that, whether or not we apply the term 'slave', the Khmer institution of temple service was complex, involving various types of status, sometimes ritual and honourable. For such reasons, some scholars prefer to call these temple workers 'servants'.

Quite apart from temple service, though, there were certainly domestic servants, often recruited from among captured hill tribesmen and thereafter bound to hereditary service, who can perhaps quite appropriately be called slaves. Chou Ta-kuan, once more, is our chief source of information:

As slaves, one buys savages who perform this service. Those who have many slaves possess more than a hundred; those who have few possess ten to twenty: only the very poor have none at all. The savages are the people of the maintainous wastelands . . . When they are young and strong, they are worth a hundred strips of cloth each; when they are old and weak one can buy them for thirty to forty strips. They can sit or lie down only beneath the raised floor. To perform their duties they can go upstairs, but then they must kneel, put their hands together, and prostrate themselves; only after that may they go on . . . If by chance a Chinese arrives and, after his long enforced celibacy, should inadvertently have intercourse just once with one of these women, and the master finds out, then the next day the latter will refuse to sit down in the newcomer's company, because he has had intercourse with a savage . . . If slaves run away and are caught, their faces are marked with blue, or alternatively they are branded on the neck in order to keep them; others have branding on the arms or legs.[7]

This testimony comes from a late stage in the history of Angkor, and does not necessarily apply to all stages. We cannot know for certain what proportion of the population at any stage was constituted by domestic slaves, or by temple servants, or by the combination. It does appear altogether probable, though, that at least a part of the greatness of Angkor was built upon the availability of easily captured labour from the hill communities in the neighbourhood. If so, is an apt reminder that the underlying factors of history are not necessarily those which were most clearly stated in the historical record.

[7] Chou Ta-kuan, *Mémoires sur les coutumes de Cambodge de Tcheou Takouan*, tr. P. Pelliot. Paris: Ecole française d'Extrême-Orient, 1951, p. 19.

Whether or not the wealth of Angkor was built by the exploitation of toiling slaves or bonded labourers, wealth there certainly was: 'They eat from bowls and vases of gold. From that comes the proverb of the rich Chenla. The people are in fact rich. The weather is always hot. Neither ice nor snow is found there. . . .'[8]

By the thirteenth century, Angkor was known to the Chinese as Cambodia the Rich. The wealth of Angkor at its height was bravely displayed in public magnificence: in the luxurious appointments of the palace, for example, with its ivory screens, its silk hangings, its hordes of ceremonial attendants standing sentinel with ornate weapons, or stirring the hot still air with fans, or waiting upon the great men and women of the realm with trays of betel. Ceremonial processions, such as those described by Chou Ta-kuan, demonstrated the wealth of the nation to its citizens. Temples, too, were storehouses of treasures. A single foundation possessed assets including thirty-five diamonds, 40,620 fine pearls, 4,540 precious stones, 967 *voiles de chine*, and 512 silk beds.[9] It has been argued that the tremendous expenditure on religious foundations in Angkor had short-term beneficial effects in stimulating economic activity, but in the long run inhibited the development of the economy because it did not promote new sorts of production or create new wealth.[10]

Angkor was an agrarian state *par excellence*, but trade played an important part in the economy, and perhaps influenced the course of history more than is generally recognized. Trade routes carried goods in all directions, linking Angkor with the coast via the Tonle Sap and the Mekong; overland routes led westwards to the area of Phimai (which was eventually dominated by Khmer settlement) and the Mon states beyond, and eastwards across the Annamite Cordillera to Champa and the Vietnamese territories.

The line between imports and exports can be difficult to draw, because many traded commodities (notably slaves, deerskins and forest products) came from the hilly and unsettled regions that were not definitively Khmer, but many of which

[8] Ibid., p. 11.
[9] S. Thierry, *Les Khmers*. Paris: Seuil, 1964, p. 117.
[10] De Mestier du Bourg, La première moitié.

were progressively assimilated as the empire grew. Cardamom and aloes wood, for example, were sought from the Cardamom Hills by the Khmers of the 'Chen-la' period in the course of foraging expeditions, accompanied by rituals and prayers directed to profitable trade. Villages developed craft specializations that gained them reputations for particular products, and sometimes their wares were traded far afield. Some villages, for example, specialized in particular sorts of metal goods, such as cartwheel rims.

Barter was the normal market exchange mechanism. After the Angkor period, gold coins marked with symbols made their appearance, but until then gold or silver ingots with measured weights functioned as currency (the earliest evidence of the use of bullion in exchange dates from the period of 'Fu-nan'). Small-scale transactions were conducted with rice, pieces of cloth, glass, pearls or beads. Temple inscriptions often refer to exchanges involved in the acquisition of land to bestow upon religious foundations, and, from 'Chen-la' times onwards, we see land being obtained in exchange for miscellaneous valuables including carts, blocks of laterite, husked rice, quantities of alcohol, and the rights to let goats or pigs scavenge.

The Khmers had a complex variety of weights and measures, many of the details of which are obscure to us; they mixed together various Khmer and Sanskrit terms.[11]

In the markets of Angkor one could obtain precious stones, pearls, cotton cloth, the finest silks, spices, ceramics, aromatic wood (an important export item), rice, silver, gold (pieces of which were often a sort of currency) and slaves. Livestock included cows, buffalo, elephants, horses and pigs. San Antonio's account, from the sixteenth century, mentions silk, incense, benzoin, rice, lacquer-ware, gold and silver.[12] In the workshops

---

[11] J. Jacob, The ecology of Angkor: evidence from the inscriptions. In *Nature and Man in South East Asia*, ed. P. A. Stott, London: School of Oriental and African Studies, 1978, p. 116. Field areas were measured in *sare* or *samre*; weights included the Sanskrit *bhara* and *tula* and the Khmer *jyan*, 'balance'; a dry capacity unit, the *je*, was also used from 'Chen-la' times. Measurement of surviving buildings has made it possible to define precisely the *hat* or cubit used by architects: it was 0.43545 metres.

[12] Gabriel Quiroga de San Antonio, *Brève et véridique relation des événements du Cambodge*, tr. A. Cabaton. Paris: Leroux, 1914, p. 94.

of the city, craftwares were turned out by painters, lacquerers, joiners and carpenters, smiths working in bronze, silver and gold, masons, sculptors, weavers and jewellers.

Angkor was well known for the aromatic timbers (*gharu*, aloes wood, lakawood, sapan-wood and so forth) that were traded across the Indian Ocean and across the South China Sea. Elephant tusks and rhinoceros horns were also exported, as were cardamoms, pepper, ginger peel, beeswax, kingfisher feathers, dammar resin, vegetable oils (including chaulmoogra and lucrabau seed oil), raw silk, cotton fabrics, gamboge and lacquer.

Imports came from many of the lands around the Indian Ocean and South-East Asia, but China figured particularly as an exporter of craft or manufactured goods. Gold and silver were not mined in the immediate vicinity but possibly were imported from an area to the west, in Vietnam. It is possible that an Indian type of design for bellows attached to smelting furnaces, known in nineteenth-century Cambodia, was imported during the Angkorian period.[13] Commodities and wares imported included porcelain (including fine celadons), kittysols (Chinese-style umbrellas made of bamboo and oiled paper), drums, samshu (rice spirit), sugar, preserves, ginger, tinware and lacquered trays. Most of these are mentioned by the Chinese Chau Ju-kua and Chou Ta-kuan; the latter provides a long list of goods, some of which (such as ginger) figure elsewhere as exports.[14]

From the untamed forest of South-East Asia came some of the products (animal, vegetable and mineral) that were most valued throughout the old world, from China to the Mediterranean. The rhinoceros, for example, was quite important in the luxury trade because of the properties attributed to its parts, including its horn, skin, blood, tusks, teeth and the nail of its left foot, all of which were valued antidotes for maladies of any sort. A seventeenth-century European comment on the reputation of

[13] B. Bronson, Patterns in the early Southeast Asian metals trade. In I. Glover, Pornchai Suchitta and J. Villiers (eds), *Early Metallurgy, Trade and Urban Centres in Thailand and Southeast Asia*, Bangkok: White Lotus, 1992, pp. 63–114, at pp. 106f.
[14] Chou Ta-kuan, *Mémoires*, p. 26; Chau Ju-kua, p. 53.

the rhinoceros is interesting for more than its quaintness – it illustrates the importance of forest products in the international trade:

They say that the skin of this animal infused at length, boiled in water and let sit for three continuous days, and then drunk, is an utterly reliable medicine for those who suffer from haemorrhoids and those who, because of a delicate stomach, or for some other reason, have no taste at all for food, and are tormented by constant lack of appetite . . . [I have not] seen the slightest indication that the horn of this great beast can combat epilepsy, in spite of what Olao Vormio writes . . . The prescription, however, that one must use the horn of a beast killed around the beginning of September is not generally accepted; rather, there are certain people who hold that only those which die naturally are suitable. And others, more superstitious still, confine themselves to saying that the power to cure epilepsy derives only from the right horn, the left being quite useless.[15]

There is an anthropological theory that trading activities, by their nature, engender distrust and conflict, so a culture has to embed them in elaborate ritual regulatory mechanisms; quite often they are left to aliens so that the social contamination should be contained.[16] On this view, foreign trading communities such as the Chinese may have been playing a functional role in Khmer society. Certainly, Chou Ta-kuan attests the lurking dangers of conflict arising from trade when he tells us that Khmer traders were not to be trusted – because they always cheated the Chinese! Epigraphy offers passing references to a Cham, to a Vietnamese, and to a 'Vāp China' who dealt in slaves, gold and silver.[17] Generally, though, it was the Khmer women who predominated among the market stalls, handling the commerce while their husbands toiled in the fields or loafed

[15] This comes from the the account of Atanasio Chircher, published in Florence in 1671; cited by San Antonio, *Brève et véridique relation*, p. 94n. Translation kindly supplied by Carolyn James.
[16] B. L. Foster, Trade, social conflict and social integration: rethinking some old ideas on exchange. In *Economic Exchange and Social Interaction in Southeast Asia: Perspectives from prehistory, history and ethnography*, ed. K. Hutterer, Ann Arbor, Mich.: University of Michigan Press, 1977, pp. 3–22.
[17] K. Hall, Khmer commercial development and foreign contacts under Sūryavarman. *Journal of the Economic and Social History of the Orient*, 18, no. 3 (1975), pp. 318–36, at p. 321.

Plate 31   Rice vendors in Phnom Penh market, 1981

at home. This is another feature of daily life which has not changed much since Chou's time, for, as in so many societies, it is still normal in Cambodia for the womenfolk to take goods to market.

So far, the commerce of the Angkor period has been considered here as a single topic, though most of the evidence comes from relatively late in Angkor's history. Future research may well demonstrate the importance of shifts in trade patterns.

Indeed, increased trade had a major impact upon all the seaboard South-East Asian states. It is likely to have had ramifying effects upon their history, as a major shift took place in distribution of wealth and power. It is therefore important to take account of the economic developments taking place throughout the region. These developments were powered by events in China.

It was during the Northern Sung dynasty (AD 960–1127) that the demographic balance in China tipped towards the south, with the lush green paddies of the monsoon lands gradually realizing their potential for intensive cultivation and dense population. The tempo of long-distance trade throughout South-East Asia was necessarily affected. The indigenous evidence of increased activity is patchy and uncertain, but the epigraphy of the period from 922 to 1071 in Cambodia shows a much greater concentration of references to merchants than in previous centuries, and many of them fall within the reign of Sūryavarman I (early eleventh century).[18] Further, de Mestrier du Bourg has pointed out that inscriptions refer to forty-seven cities (settlements whose names end in '-pura') in the time of Sūryavarman, as against only twenty or so in any of the previous three reigns.[19] Urbanization is not identical with increasing trade, but we may well suppose that the two went together. Kenneth Hall has suggested that in the eleventh century the Khmers were active in the trade of the Malayan Peninsula, drawing the northern part of this area into its own commercial orbit and away from the Sumatra-based Śrīvijaya.[20]

It was in 1127 that invaders put an end to the Northern Sung, and the Chinese dynasty was reinstalled in the south; the very next year, it bestowed ceremonial dignities upon the Khmer ruler, designating him 'Great Vassal'. Between 1131 and 1147 problems of trade between China and Angkor were resolved by negotiation. Communities of Chinese merchants (or, in the archipelago, quite often pirates) henceforth became more familiar as a part of the economic fabric of South-East Asia.

The development of commerce through the area is conspicuously illustrated by the very great increase in the sophistication of merchant shipping that took place in the thirteenth to fifteenth centuries. Pierre-Yves Manguin has described the longstanding indigenous tradition of shipbuilding that prevailed before the fourteenth century (and still persisted, alongside new techniques, into the twentieth century).[21] In the next couple of

---

[18] Ibid., p. 320.

[19] De Mestrier du Bourg, La première moitié, at p. 308. The numbers of references to *pura* are: in the reign of Jayavarman IV, about a dozen; Rājendravarman: 24; Jayavarman V: 20.

[20] Hall, 'Khmer commercial development', at pp. 329f.

[21] The structure evolved from the dug-out by raising planks on either side of the keel piece, made from a tree-trunk; there were no iron nails, and no outriggers; there were multiple masts and sails, and typical lengths were fifteen

centuries, large junks (such as are described later by Portuguese sources) became familiar in South-East Asian waters. These vessels, according to surviving descriptions, weighed from 400 or 500 tons and up to 1,000, and were capable of carrying a thousand people.[22]

The Mongols when they conquered China (Yüan dynasty, 1279–1368) showed a strong interest in maritime contacts to the south, and the following Ming dynasty, established in 1368, was marked in its early years by an unprecedented fit of naval activity which saw relations between China and the states of South-East Asia and the Indian Ocean made stronger than ever before. Famous are the seven voyages of great fleets sent out as far as the coasts of the Indian Ocean (even reaching Africa) by two successive emperors under the command of the Grand Eunuch Admiral Cheng Ho (Zheng He) between 1405 and 1433. These and other voyages promoted closer and closer commercial contacts. Chinese activity in South-East Asia is evidenced by a whole series of reports and gazetteers written by Chinese travellers and officials, most of them connected with Cheng Ho's expeditions: Wang Ta-yüan described ninety-nine localities and reported on his own travels; Ma Huan, attached as an interpreter to Cheng Ho's voyage of 1413, wrote the famous *Ying-yai-sheng-lan*, a detailed account of the countries in the area; a number of other travellers described journeys far afield.

Angkor played a part in this commercial intensification. By the thirteenth century there was a well-established Chinese community in Angkor, as Chou Ta-kuan tells us: 'Chinese who follow the sea like this country, where little clothing is necess-

---

to twenty-five metres: Paul-Yves Manguin, The trading ships of insular southeast Asia: new evidence from Indonesian archaeological sites. In *Proceedings, Pertemuan Ilmiah Arkeologi V*, Yogyakarta: Ikatan Ahli Arkeologi Indonesia, 1989, pp. 200–19. As early as 'Fu-nan' times, the report of K'ang-T'ai refers to boats made from long trees, ninety-six feet long and six wide, decorated with iron ornaments and carrying a hundred men each with a long oar, a short oar and a gaffe: P. Pelliot, Le Fou-nan, *Bulletin de l'Ecole française d'Extrême-Orient*, 2 (1902), pp. 248–303, at p. 253.

[22] Manguin, The trading ships. On the Chinese developments in marine technology, see J. Needham, *Science and Civilization in China*, vol. 4, part 3. Cambridge: Cambridge University Press, 1971, pp. 379–699.

ary. Rice is easy to obtain, commerce easy to direct. So, they
constantly go to this country.'[23]

Cambodia offered the Chinese visitors something very different from their own cultural environment. On the whole, they
liked it; and we need to take account of the influence of Chinese
involvement in the economic life of the country, an obvious
enough fact in modern times when the bulk of the population of
the main urban centres is of at least partly Chinese descent, but
likely to have been significant even in Angkorian times, when it
is less conspicuous from the historical sources and easily overlooked. One theory, as we shall later observe, is that the commercial intensification of the thirteenth to fifteenth centuries
created a new social magnetism, attracting urban populations to
the coasts, and thus playing a part in the decline of the old
inland agrarian society of Angkor and the rise of Phnom Penh.

[23] Chou Ta-kuan, *Mémoires*, p. 34.

14

Artists and Craftsmen

A *Who's Who* of the ancient Khmer kingdoms, listing all the people known by name, would not fill a thick volume, but it would certainly identify many individuals. There would be entries for many kings, with rich, fulsome (and generally fictitious) biographies. There would be large numbers of ministers, councillors, courtiers, lords-in-waiting and senior officials of all types. (The inscriptions recording Sūryavarman I's oath of allegiance would alone furnish us with about 400 names.[1]) There would be huge numbers of temple servants, although their biographical entries would be short, for they are known of only by the lists attached to endowments. But there would be virtually no poets, artists or architects.

This must seem odd at first sight, because among all these people it is the artists and architects whose creations alone survive for us to admire. We know the names of some court priests who planned and organized the construction of monuments, and it may be that these priests supplied the master schemes for the symbolism of their constructions; but they were served by hosts of lesser beings who were responsible for the creation of these works in detail. Perhaps these lesser beings are the people whose work we admire.

In part, this anonymity must be seen as a result of the royal monopoly on glory. All the great things done in the kingdom had to be seen as achievements of the ruler; artists, craftsmen

[1] G. Coedès, *Inscriptions du Cambodge*. Paris and Hanoi: Ecole française d'Extrême-Orient, 1937–66, vol. 3, pp. 205–216.

and poets were instruments of ideology. But there is an important religious dimension too. The anonymity of the artist reflects a particular, entirely rational, attitude that belongs to a pre-scientific, traditional world view. It is not very different, after all, from the world view embodied in the religious architecture of mediaeval Europe, where craftsmen toiled just as anonymously to raise soaring cathedrals in praise of God.

What went for Christianity went for the religion of the Khmers. The principle at work was that a teaching ideally gains all its conviction, its moral force, from its conformity to a known canon that tells eternal truths; it gains none from the original thought of its merely human author. This is true for builders as well as writers. So things made with the hands evoke the divine only to the extent that (by a sort of sympathetic magic) they capture the divine energy that lives in a known pattern or symbol.

A shape or image that has not been seen before is not likely to tune in to the divine, for the forms of the divine are already known. Hence the need for iconography. So an artist's success lies in his ability to distil the essence of a familiar formula. His individuality is irrelevant. *Ego feci* is misleading. In a deep sense, *dei fecērunt*.

In prehistoric times, Khmer artists and architects, necessarily anonymous, made and decorated jewellery, beads, clay models, tools and utensils; they hewed wood into shapes that were prescribed by unquestioned standards and joined them to make houses that were not expected to last very long.

When the Indian traditions came, the craftsmen remained anonymous, while they learned new techniques. We have reviewed here the problem of assessing the mechanisms by which the Indian contributions were made, but, however the Khmers and other peoples of South-East Asia came to acquire their knowledge of Indian art and architecture, local genius aserted itself.

The gods alone were housed in imperishable stone; mortals, even kings, lived in wooden structures, and nothing of them survives for us to admire except where (like the 'flying palaces' mentioned above) they are modelled in relief on stone.

The fact that only religious buildings were of stone possibly has something to do with the limits of architectural technique.

A royal audience hall or banqueting chamber required, ideally, a great deal of uncluttered space. Timber columns, beams and rafters would do this job; stone ones were too heavy and could bridge only narrow spaces. Workers in the Indian architectural tradition of the early centuries, during the formative stages of South-East Asian styles, did not make use of the arch or vault that can be used to roof the space above the heads of a multitude. Unlike European cathedrals, Indian temples, on the other hand, required no large spaces for congregations; the gods were tucked into dark spaces in a womb of stone, and a temple sanctuary, gallery or access corridor could well be spanned by masonry lintels and corbelling.

Buddhism had its own traditions. In India, early forms of Buddhist stone architecture, within the first few centuries after the Buddha's death, included the rock-cut cave shrine and the stone-clad dome-shaped mound called the *stūpa*. The latter were originally modelled on burial mounds, but came to be erected as marks of devotion without necessarily containing relics. Cave shrines did not persist as a major architectural form to be exported elsewhere (though the Burmese temples called *ku*, whose shrine chambers are secreted within great masses of stone, echo this motif; a prime example is the Ānanda temple at Pagan, built about the end of the eleventh century). The *stūpa* travelled wherever Buddhism spread, though in the process it evolved into many forms, some far removed from the original masonry-covered dome with a terrace and spire on the summit. But the Khmer kingdoms did not much favour the endowment of *stūpas*. It was common for a foundation of any sort to contain images of deities freely drawn from Hindu and Buddhist lore alike. Buddhist foundations commonly resembled Hindu temples in general plan. However, there are some *stūpa* remains from the twelfth century.[2]

Hindu temples were a more influential paradigm among the Khmers. Stone Hindu temples in India evolved in the north during the Gupta dynasty (fourth to sixth centuries AD), at a time when South-East Asia was particularly receptive to Indian culture and the early kingdoms were taking shape. The

---

[2] They usually have many mouldings and treat the motifs of design rather freely. See J. Boisselier, *Le Cambodge*. Paris: Picard, 1966, pp. 97f.

Gupta temple was basically an enclosed rectangular hall with multiple stepped stone roofs. In time, it became more elaborate, especially by reduplicating its own features within itself: the corners were multiplied by a proliferation of re-entrants in the plan; the roofs were multiplied by the addition of more and more false storeys, diminishing upwards in a pyramid shape; the platform on which it stood was multiplied by additional terraces. Wall spaces were covered by intricate relief carving, often smothering all available surfaces in busy detail. Statues were placed in niches, on pedestals, beside doorways.

This was the legacy upon which the Khmer imagination set to work. The materials were to hand: bricks from the clay soil; laterite, a red ferruginous rock or subsoil, characteristic of some tropical zones, that is easy to mine and hardens in the air; sandstone quarried not far north of Angkor, in the Kulen hills. The laterite was coarse-textured and very rarely used by the sculptor; it came to serve chiefly in foundations and terraces. The sandstone, a soft grey lit to golden by the sun, was used for door piers, lintels, tympana, roofs, decorated surfaces, and eventually indeed for superstructures generally. Big blocks of it could be brought at least part of the way to each building site by water, using the network of canals.

The techniques of masonry architecture for a long time imitated those of timber, often quite inappropriately, with stone beams, mortises and tenons. Some Angkorian temples had stone beams reinforced with wood; when these rotted away, the structure above them collapsed.

As in India, the favoured technique to cover a space between two walls, providing roofs for corridors and cloisters, was corbelling: successive courses of brick or stone on either side jutted out each above the one below it, so that the courses rising from the two walls eventually met in the middle.

Construction in stone was constrained by the limits of its architecture. Khmer temples were single-storey towers, whose tiered roofs, often decorated with a profusion of ornament and projection, rose high above.

Khmer architects found various ways to ring the changes on this basic design. For one thing, the platform on which a tower stood could be itself raised up in successive tiers, to any extent, so that the sanctuary tower might become simply the crowning feature of a stepped pyramid. In Angkor, the great central shrines imitating Mount Meru were constructed on this principle, beginning with the Bakong at Hariharālaya and the Bakheng at Yaśodharapura.

Towers could be grouped on a single platform. This was favoured for some groups of shrines dedicated to past royalty, such as Indravarman's Preah Koh, described below.

Again, smaller towers could serve as subordinate shrines in a symmetrical arrangement around a sanctuary platform, or in tiers upon the terraces of a pyramid. (The Bakheng had numerous towers around it, both at ground level and on its terraces.) Such multiple towers could be linked by corridors or cloisters, forming galleries enclosing the central shrine. Towers could be placed at the corners of these enclosures, and in the middle of each side, their door openings making them gateways that gave access to the courtyards within. Angkor Wat is the most famous temple using these features.

Lengths of corridor might turn into free-standing narrow buildings within such a courtyard. Such structures may well have been libraries, and are generally so called.

These are the ingredients of Khmer temple architecture; they offered little scope for the deployment of inner space, and in fact many Khmer monuments have gallery interiors that are inaccessible unless, in some cases, one chose to climb through a window; an example is the Ta Keo, built by Jayavarman IV, whose second level has galleries lacking any door. This was not a problem, however, because there was no reason for anyone to be inside the galleries. The style encouraged the elevation of elaborate masses designed to impress the viewer at a distance. The genius of the Khmer architect was to exploit the possibilities of these ingredients with brilliance and finesse, taking heed of the principle (known to the ancient Greeks) that the majestic aspect of a monument is best appreciated from a distance of twice its greatest dimension.[3]

The history of Khmer temple architecture perhaps found its beginnings in 'Fu-nan'. Several brick monuments associated with 'Fu-nan' and 'Chen-la' survive in the lower Mekong valley and up the Tonle Sap towards the Great Lake. They are square

[3] S. Thierry, *Les Khmers*. Paris: Seuil, 1964, p. 110.

brick towers with undecorated wall panels and stacked multiple roofs rising in a steep pyramid.

In the 'Chen-la' period, some of the distinctive features of Khmer religious architecture began to develop. Towers became more slender. Temples used laterite and sandstone, but bricks were in this period the basic materials for walls; they could be carved by the sculptor after construction and could be covered with a stucco finish that lent itself to painting. Bricks were bonded with a remarkably powerful adhesive, probably a vegetable cement; the joints are barely visible, and chunks of brickwork cemented with it can remain unshattered after a fifty-foot fall.[4]

The most celebrated achievements of Khmer architecture belonged of course to Angkor. Here, there were two basic patterns. One was that of a group of tower sanctuaries standing together, dedicated to a group of deities (sometimes with each god matched by a companion shrine for his consort) and at the same time to human ancestors or predecessors on the throne. The other pattern was that of the central sanctuary, raised on a pyramid and in later developments surrounded by increasingly elaborate complexes of walls, galleries and subordinate tower shrines; it was dedicated to a patron god, usually Śiva in the form of a *liṅga* (two important exceptions are Viṣṇu at Angkor Wat and Lokeśvara at the Bayon) set in the *sanctum sanctorum* at the top. Those kings who had the time and resources constructed such monuments as symbolic centres of the kingdom, with the capital city rearranged about them, and after their deaths their relics were installed in stone receptacles beneath the icons of their patron deities.

An example of the former type is furnished by the Preah Koh, built by Indravarman I and dedicated in 879. It was surrounded by four courtyards, the outermost enclosure measuring 450 × 800 metres and surrounded by a moat. The sanctuaries comprise six towers on a platform, the three larger, dedicated to forms of Śiva, in a row running north to south and open towards the east, and behind them were placed three smaller towers dedicated to forms of the consort of Śiva, Gaurī. At

---

[4] L. P. Briggs, *The Ancient Khmer Empire.* Philadelphia, Pa: American Philosophical Society, 1951, p. 70.

the same time, the central Śiva shrine was dedicated to the king Jayavarman II, the northern to Indravarman's maternal grandfather Rudravarman, and the southern to his father Pṛthivīndravarman; the rear towers standing behind these were dedicated similarly to their wives. The shrines were built of brick, covered in plaster. The Preah Koh has given its name to one of the styles into which Khmer art history is divided by historians.

One other example of a group of towers demands a mention; it has a special charm that has made it a favourite with many students of Angkor. It is the Banteay Srei, initiated by the king's preceptor Yajñavarāha in the reign of Rājendravarman II and completed in the reign of Jayavarman V. It lies at a distance of about 20 kilometres (12 miles) to the north of the Angkor complex, in woodland solitude; its moat holds water still and offers bright reflections of the little towers.

What is remarkable about it is that, though it occupies a precinct about 200 metres in length, it is all in miniature. The doorway of the central sanctuary is only just over 1 metre in height. The gateway tower giving access to the first enclosure has an interior space that can barely be squeezed into, being about 30 centimetres wide. Apart from this, the most striking feature of this cluster of low towers and library buildings within an enclosed courtyard is the richness of their bas-relief decoration. Tympana over the doorways are graced by delicately carved scenes from myth, showing episodes from the legends of Viṣṇu and Śiva and from the epics. The demon Rāvaṇa attempts in vain to shake the divine mountain Kailāśa. Kṛṣṇa prepares to kill the evil demon Kaṃsa who was incarnated as the wicked king of Mathurā. Indra, guardian of the east, gazes out majestically from the shoulders of his three-headed elephant Airāvata.

The other type of monumental complex is the pyramid sanctuary marking the ritual centre of the kingdom. Its history is long and complex, marked by many stages of elaboration as towers, galleries, enclosing courtyards and other buildings were incorporated in new ways into the design. Here we can notice only a very few examples.

The first stage is marked by the Bakong, built by Indravarman I, dedicated in 881. The pyramid consists of five laterite terraces, bearing the remains of statuary and small subordinate towers. The single great tower on top is a later construction, as we noticed above.

With the move to Yaśodharapura at the end of the ninth century, the capital was centred upon a natural hill topped by a great pyramid shrine, the Bakheng. This monument can be read as an elaborate ritual statement assimilating the royal shrine to the divine order of the cosmos.

A contrast is presented by another, smaller, pyramid, the Baksei Chamkrong, built by Harṣavarman I (son of Yaśovarman) and incomplete. It consists of a single tower upon a pyramid of four laterite terraces uncluttered by super-structures. It has a special charm of its own, for the plainness of the terrace sides brings out to best advantage the warm reddish glow of the laterite, especially when it is lit by late afternoon sunlight.

In the following reigns there was a series of pyramid shrines upon increasingly elaborate foundations. They were political statements, and some of them have already been referred to here as royal achievements. Here it is appropriate to give special attention to the best-known of them all, Angkor Wat, which was built as the temple-mausoleum of Sūryavarman II in honour of his patron god Viṣṇu.

The complex was surrounded by a moat 180 metres wide. Within lay, possibly, a whole city, contained by a laterite and sandstone wall bounding an outer enclosure measuring 815 × 1,000 metres. The moat has helped to keep the jungle out and allow the buildings of the temple complex to remain so well preserved. Part of the moat still holds water. This is why so many of the photographs are taken from the north-west; they exploit the afternoon light and the water which fills the fore-ground. Soft blue sky is duplicated in a shimmering looking-glass world where golden cloisters and towers hang upside down. Above, arranged by perspective into an artful com-position, the great central sanctuary and its four subordinate shrines that are the foothills of Mount Meru reach up above the surrounding maze of stone; their many-tiered towers curve gently inward as they rise, converging upon a point, so that they are like so many rockets aimed at heaven.

Plate 32   Royal temple mountain: the Bayon

How to describe Agkor Vat without the risk of being false to its beauty? From the west of the temple, we cross the moat, two hundred metres wide, by a causeway; we pass through the *gopura* with its five passages; and then at last, in a magnificent perspective, we have the entire temple in front of our eyes. More than four hundred metres distant, it is brought before us by a sandstone-paved carriageway a metre and a half above the ground. Early in the morning, the temple vanishes into the dawn mist; at midday, it is hammered by fierce sunlight; but, in the evening, gilded by the setting sun, it is a scene from fairyland that fades little by little until there is only a silhouette remaining in the black night.[5]

The causeway by which one enters the complex leads from the west straight towards the central mountain with its five towers, crossing concentric courtyards. The second enclosure is 270 × 340 metres and the whole of it is raised 2 metres above the ground outside. The pyramid at the centre rises in three terraces each surrounded by cloisters and galleries, the first 187 × 215 metres, the second 100 × 115 metres, the third 75 × 73 metres. The topmost tower is 42 metres high and 65 metres above the ground level.

Figures like these exorcise the fairyland magic and reduce Angkor Wat to a drab blueprint. It is worth remembering, though, that it is just such figures that created the magic, in a probably quite literal understanding of the expression, for the builders of the monument. A shrine was a cosmogram, an embodiment of a transcendental order, and every calculation that entered its design had a part to play in creating in stone the proportions of a myth. Recall the modern explanatory legend: Indra's horses rode out from the heavenly prototype of this place; Angkor Wat was intended to shake the earth with the reverberation of their hoofs.

One essay in the interpretation of Angkor Wat's numerical symbolism has been offered by a group of scholars who examined closely the geometry of the monument's design; their conclusions are intriguing and ingenious, though debatable. According to this interpretation, Angkor Wat was, among other things, an observatory: at the equinox and at the solstice the rising sun was aligned with important dimensions converging

---

[5]   C. Jacques, *Angkor*. Paris: Bordas, 1990, p. 112.

upon the western entrance, and the movements of the moon could be measured from various points within the temple. On the new reading, the monument was an elaborate cosmogram, designed to superimpose the world of the king, Sūryavarman II, upon the world of the gods under the creator and supreme lord Viṣṇu, and the present age of mankind upon the golden age of virtue, the Kṛta Yuga. However, the measurements cited to support this set of interpretations are not precise enough to compel general acceptance.[6]

Earth and heaven are brought together by their juxtaposition in the relief carvings that extend around the cloister walls enclosing the pyramid. They stand more than 2 metres high and extend in long sections totalling 1,600 metres. Lower reaches of these shallow reliefs are blackened and shiny from the touching of devotees down the centuries. They show scenes from Indian epic and contemporary Angkorian court life side by side: Sūryavarman reviewing his troops; the king seated on a mountain, addressing his officials; the myth of creation by the churning of the ocean of milk; the great battle of Laṅkā from the *Rāmāyaṇa*; the battle of Pāṇḍavas and Kauravas from the *Mahābhārata*; scenes from heaven and hell; Viṣṇu riding on his mount Garuḍa – the mythical creature that is half bird, half man, and carries Viṣṇu across the heavens.

The evidence of Portuguese and Spanish visitors in the sixteenth century suggests that at that time the towers of Angkor Wat were still covered in gilt, and crowned with globes, banners and gilt bronze tridents. In the 1870s E. Aymonier saw at Angkor Wat a tower with two metal balls raised above its peak. There are inscriptions suggesting that such ornaments were the gifts of post-Angkorian kings.

Angkor Wat marks a peak of achievement, although Jayavarman VII certainly tried to outdo his predecessors in magnificence. The general consensus on Jayavarman is that, however grandiose, his hastily built central shrine, the Bayon, falls short

---

[6] See R. Stencel et al., Astronomy and cosmology at Angkor Wat. *Science*, 193 (1976), pp. 281–7; E. Morón, Configuration of time and space at Angkor Wat. *Studies in Indo-Asian Art and Culture*, 5 (1977), pp. 217–267. The conclusions of these sources are summarized by D. P. Chandler, *A History of Cambodia*, Boulder, Col.: Westview Press, 1992, pp. 49, 51, 53.

Plate 33   Two figures of garudas (flying deities), Angkor Wat

of Angkor Wat's controlled, uncluttered majesty; it is impressive none the less.

Jayavarman's capital city, Angkor Thom, was again re-centred, with a new ritual focus inserted between the Eastern and Western Barays. The surrounding wall, built of laterite, was a novelty; it rose to a height of 7 or 8 metres, with an embankment 25 metres wide at the top running along it on the inside. The square it defined had a circumference of 13.2 kilometres, and around the outside ran a moat 100 metres wide, crossed at five points by great causeways which were bordered by elaborate carved balustrades representing gods and goggle-eyed demons holding the body of a serpent. These causeways led to massive gateways whose towers were topped by gigantic sculpted heads with four faces gazing serenely out over the four directions of space.

The symbolism of the whole is rich and elaborate, and has attracted a great deal of scholarly attention. The four faces suggest the god Brahmā, but are nowadays thought to represent a form of the Buddhist divinity Avalokiteśvara as well as incorporating the king himself. The serpent balustrades evoke the myth of Indra's rainbow, which leads to Indra's heaven, to which the city of Angkor Thom is thus assimilated. On another level of symbolism, the serpent body, projecting on opposite sides of the city and held like the rope in a tug-of-war by its supernatural bearers, suggests the myth of creation which tells of the churning of the ocean of milk: gods and demons used the serpent lord Vāsuki as a cord to wind round Mount Mandara and churn with it the ocean of milk from which all things came, including the nectar of immortality which the gods drank.

What symbolism did the architects actually intend? It is likely that they were conscious of all the resonances of Indian myth that occur in their work, and more besides. One might well add that the notion of Jayavarman's city as an epitome of cosmic creation, presided over by Indra, is reinforced by the frequent recurrence of the three-headed elephant Airāvata in the sculpture of gateways and terraces. Airāvata was the white elephant with four tusks who came out of the ocean of milk at its churning and became the mount of the god Indra. He is the king of elephants, and stands as archetype for the sixteen elephants which support the whole world on their backs. The significance of this cannot have been far from the mind of Jayavarman as he sat before his palace reviewing parades and sports staged to bring the world before the eyes of its august monarch and sustainer.

This persistent symbolism, assimilating the city to the abode of the gods and the king to the lord of creation, is especially manifest in the Bayon, the great shrine at the heart of the city. It was built hastily, and time has done its worst; walls sag, lintels totter, and it is in much worse condition than many earlier structures such as Angkor Wat. The design of the Bayon embodied a number of patterns simultaneously and resists simple description; but the dominant motif is clear enough: courts and cloisters, punctuated by towers, cluster around a central massif, rising about 45 metres above ground level, that stands for the mountain of the gods and served as shrine for an image of the Buddhist divinity Lokeśvara. A Buddha image was installed in the central shrine; subsequently, probably during the Hindu backlash later in the thirteenth century, it was thrown down into the pit beneath and broken. In the 1920s it was rediscovered and restored. The sanctuary tower at the heart of the construction, surrounded by eight of the Lokeśvara towers to represent the radiation of this *bodhisattva*'s compassion to all directions of space, is based upon a circular design, with an indoor *pradaksiṇa* path encircling the central sanctum. However, the irregular complex of galleries built around this shrine, and the extension of this complex into halls and gate-houses on the approach side, the east, makes it all a bewildering confusion.

On top of this shrine, and crowning about forty-nine smaller towers around the pyramid, appear multiples of the same four-faced giant head that the gateways of the city display; in all there are nearly 200 faces. Here, gazing serenely over the whole of space, the Buddha-to-be extends his infinite compassion to all beings in the universe.

The art of the reign of Jayavarman VII is characterized by a profusion of construction. It is tempting to speculate upon the possibility of a connection between this extravagance of creation and the sudden dearth of building in the reigns that followed. The rest of the thirteenth century is a mystery. At

Plate 34   Detail of a lintel, Banteay Srei

any rate, Angkor's long chapter of architectural and sculptural achievement came to an end.

What has not yet been adequately evoked by this outline is the minuteness of artistic detail with which the sculptor's craft was bent to the service of religious symbolism on walls, in niches, on lintels and tympana, on capitals and entablatures; indeed, wherever a chisel could be inserted, so that the walls, terraces and shrines of each complex became an encyclopaedia of sacred lore twined in rich foliate decoration.

Bas-relief carving in Angkor, as in India, was busy and florid, covering the wall space with floral, animal, mythical and divine motifs. Lintels in particular exhibit powerful images in arrangements that vary according to periods and styles. Lintels frequently portray *makaras*, marine monsters that originated in India in part from crocodile images and acquired large birdlike tails as they evolved; they represent the watery chaos which is the matrix of all being. They also portray *kālas* (the word means 'time'), bodiless monster faces that seem to vomit serpent bodies, symbolizing the circular endlessness of time which swallows up and brings forth all that is.

A function of the *kāla* is to keep all evil spirits away from the sacred space of the temple. The same function is performed by guardian deities standing in niches on either side of doorways, or sometimes as free-standing lion statues in the space before them. Female divinities are ubiquitous, full-bosomed and slender-waisted. Notable are the specimens of the type of celestial nymph called *apsaras* (which is the singular form of the word, often mistaken for a plural) who grace the walls of temples, richly jewelled, naked above the waist and wearing a long skirt. They are the mistresses of the celestial musicians, and they dance in the clouds in Indra's heaven. The walls of Angkor Wat are covered with *apsarases* carved in relief, all different, yet sharing one doubtless painful disability: the sculptors have felt unable to adapt them to the very shallow relief employed without bending their feet to one side at right angles. For all that, they are remarkably graceful.

Statues abound of gods, of men and women, of deities to whom men and women are assimilated, of divine animals and of ambiguous demon-creatures. There are many *Nāgas*. Some temples have *nāga* bodies running alongside causeways and

Plate 35 Detail of a lintel showing makara *(marine monster),
Banteay Srei*

Plate 36   Lintel with kāla *head, Roluos*

Plate 37   Apsarases (celestial nymphs), Angkor Wat

rearing up huge cobra hoods with seven heads at the outer end; those at Angkor Wat rise nearly 4 metres (12 feet) high.

Gods have their mounts (Śiva's bull Nandin; Viṣṇu's bird Garuḍa; Brahmā's goose Haṃsa; Indra's elephant Airāvata) and their goddesses, in different forms (Viṣṇu's consort Lakṣmī; Śiva's Umā or Gaṅgā or Parvatī; Brahmā's Sarasvatī).

Their iconography is meticulous, for it is the attributes of the gods which, created on earth, make their presence real. The rules observed by the sculptor are not really a separate subject of study outside religion; they are religion in practice – the carving of a correctly formed image is a sacramental act. In a sense, therefore, iconography belongs just as much with the study of the gods as in this chapter, but it is convenient to notice here some of the characteristics of the gods embodied in stone, since this is a part of our appreciation of the achievement of Cambodia's ancient artists.

Indra is important in Cambodia as a symbol of majesty; he guards the east and is chief of the guardians of the four quarters (and hence of cosmic space).

Brahmā is the god of creation; he is represented at Angkor

Plate 38   Causeway, Angkor Thom, showing nāga *head*

particularly by his consort Sarasvatī, goddess of wisdom. He has four faces, looking out over his creation, a motif which is re-embodied in Lokeśvara who presides over the Bayon.

Śiva has an abundant mythology and numerous attributes to embody it. He may be shown with a trident, or with a third eye in the middle of his forehead, or with heavy curling hair, or a lotus. With his mount Nandin (Indravarman I's foundation the Preah Koh is named after the Holy Bull), with his consorts, and in many a legendary scene taken from myth, Śiva is one of the most popular divinities represented at Angkor.

So is Viṣṇu, the god who presides over the cycles of creation and destruction of the world; between cycles he sleeps, reclining on the coils of the cosmic serpent Ananta. A standing Viṣṇu statue can commonly be recognized by the mitred head-dress, or by the emblems carried in the statue's hands: conch, disc, lotus and club. He presides over the churning of the ocean of milk. A lotus grows from his navel. His association with waters and with *nāga* spirits made him popular in Cambodia.

Buddhism was an important but lesser stream in the art of Angkor. The Buddha's iconography was standardized in India. Sculptors worked with a list of thirty-two characteristics by which the Buddha could be recognized; the most conspicuous of these are the protuberance on top of the head (the *uṣṇīṣa*) and the *ūrṇā*, originally a circle of hair between the eyes but eventually a sort of third eye, the Buddha Eye.

The form of Buddhism which came to prevail among the Khmers after Angkor – the Theravāda school – does not encourage elaborate art or grand stone temples. It was the Buddhism of the Mahāyāna – the schools which came to prevail chiefly in northern countries, notably China and Japan – which is represented in the art of Angkor, notably at the time of Jayavarman VII.

In Mahāyāna Buddhism, a *bodhisattva* is a heavenly being who out of compassion uses his store of grace to help all beings in the universe work towards their own nirvana. In a sense, Buddhist doctrine can be argued to deny the worship of gods, but in practice the Buddha himself and a host of *bodhisattvas* likewise came to be cult figures, treated in religious art exactly as are the gods of Hinduism. The Buddha is often represented in the *abhaya* posture, with hand raised to drive out fear. Among *bodhisattvas*, the figure of Avalokiteśvara, lord of the Western Paradise and hearer of prayers, had some popularity; he first figured in images from the end of the seventh century, generally marked by a miniature representation of Amitābha (the Buddha of infinite light) above his brow. Avalokiteśvara was popular in the art of Jayavarman VII's reign, in the form of Lokeśvara. The *bodhisattvas* Vajrapāṇi (the thunderbolt-wielder), Maitreya (the next Buddha who will appear in the future) and Mañjuśrī (*bodhisattva* of wisdom) are also found, as is the female divinity Prajñā, embodiment of wisdom. She is popular in tantric schools, and tantra is represented by various figures including bronze images of the deity Hevajra.

All these elements of religious art were familiar to the craftsmen who made the monuments of Angkor. Their use of such symbols shows us what sort of world they lived in. It is important not to treat Khmer religious art as a set of odd and arbitrary symbols belonging to an inscrutable alien culture. The culture was like that of other parts of the world at the same time, notably mediaeval Europe, where the craftsmen who worked on such monuments as the Cathedral of Chartres were

Plate 39   Royal terrace: row of portrait heads

just as much concerned to embody divine powers in stone according to a meticulous iconography. Their symbols were not for them, as symbols are in modern culture, objects that merely pointed to other objects not present. They were objects which, by taking the form of the thing symbolized, made that thing real and present. What was symbolized in the art and architecture of Angkor was an invisible order whose existence patterned and made comprehensible the world in which people lived. A craftsman, then, was not just a man with a chisel: he was priest, thaumaturge, psychopomp, nuclear scientist. Yet, because his work was no more than a vessel for pre-existing ideal forms, he did not care to leave his name for us to read.

15

Jayavarman VII and the Decline of Angkor

Much of what can be said about the career of Jayavarman VII is derived from an inscriptional eulogy by his queen, Indradevī. It claims that Jayavarman, as a prince, was conducting a military campaign in Champa when he learned about the upheavals which led to the death of his father and the accession of Yaśovarman II. 'He returned in haste to aid King Yaśovarman, but Yaśovarman had been stripped of throne and life by the usurper [Tribhuvanādityavarman], and Jayavarman remained in Cambodia waiting for the propitious moment to save the land heavy with crimes.'[1]

These events were in the mid-1160s. It was to be over a decade before Jayavarman found his opportunity to bid for power – the Cham invasion of 1177 mentioned earlier (see pp. 106, 157). Jayavarman VII made it his task to rid Cambodia of these foreigners, and was later able to represent himself as saviour of the nation through his victories over them in a series of battles. One naval engagement is vividly depicted in relief carving on the walls of two of his temples. By 1183 he was able to have consecrated his dominion over the Khmers as a whole. The fact that he had to take several years to fight his way to power even after disposing of the foreigners is a reflection of the persisting danger of political fragmentation, not suppressed even in the twelfth century.

Much is doubtful about Jayavarman's origins and earlier

---

[1] G. Coedès, *The Indianized States of Southeast Asia*, tr. S. Cowing, Canberra: Australian National University Press, 1968, p. 169.

career. It is possible that while in Champa he had gained his close sympathy with the values of Mahāyāna Buddhism. As for his legitimacy as ruler, he could evidently claim kin links through mother and father with Sūryavarman II, with the Mahīdhara line, and with earlier royalty; but the claims of numerous princes were probably just as good.

At all events, the imperial unity that the second Jayavarman had so proudly celebrated, ardently pursued by subsequent kings yet never irrevocably mastered, required a mighty effort if it was to be seized once more. Jayavarman VII was the man for the occasion. His reign was grander than any other. His inscriptions declared a loftier and more inspiring ambition. The sheer massiveness of his monument-building rivalled the total of all that had gone before, so that it took a long time for historians to recognize that the building of so many structures had been initiated or completed in a single reign. Throughout the lands of the Khmers, wherever the instruments of Angkor's power had disappeared, perhaps believed gone for good, his armies came in triumph bearing the banners of empire.

The Chams, of course, had to be punished; between 1203 and 1220 Jayavarman VII was able to subject Champa to Khmer dominance, putting his own nominee upon the throne. An inscription from Say Fong, opposite Vientiane, attests the extension of Jayavarman's administration to present-day Laos. A later Chinese record lists the dependencies of Angkor at the time, enumerating the suppliers of the emperor's daily washing-water (an act of homage by vassals); the list includes what it calls the king of Java (possibly a Malay ruler), the king of the Yavanas (the Vietnamese), and the two kings of Champa. The borders of the Khmer empire were probably never very secure or precisely defined, depending largely upon the political calculations of local chieftains in choosing patrons, but Jayavarman's empire appears to have been as great as Angkor had ever been.

This empire was held together by roads that were built on embankments above flood level, 5 or 6 metres high. They crossed rivers by ornamental bridges. One went north about 225 kilometres towards Phimai; one went west towards Sisophon, one east towards Champa, and another south-east to Kompong Thom, 150 kilometres.

Inscriptions record the erection of 121 'fire-houses' along

major routes, many in the north. It is not clear whether these were resthouses or shrines where rituals were performed. They are not entirely unprecedented – such an institution is known from the reign of Sūryavarman I – but so far as the evidence shows, no network of 'fire-houses' on this scale had been constructed before.

Also recorded is the construction of 102 'halls of diseaselessness' (*ārogyaśāla*). These are usually referred to as hospitals in modern literature, whether or not they actually had resident patients; but the maintenance of them was clearly a major public enterprise. There were four categories. The first, a group of four institutions near the capital (with a staff of 200 each), were directly endowed by the king; the others were smaller. Three times a year, the king would donate a set of medicines for the benefit of these 'halls of diseaselessness'; the list of products donated includes only thirty-six items, a small part no doubt of the range of Khmer pharmacology, but doubtless enough to symbolize the compassion felt by the august ruler for all who suffered.[2]

As was mentioned above, Jayavarman built his own reservoir, the Jayataṭāka. Though much smaller than the Eastern and Western Barays, it was graced by an attractive complex of grottoes and statuary on an island at its centre – the Neak Pean, which incorporated icons of Hindu gods, although the central shrine (which used to be enveloped in the roots of a rubber tree until the tree was destroyed by a storm in 1935) was Buddhist, containing an image of Lokeśvara. It has been argued that the design of the Neak Pean symbolizes the celestial Lake Anavatapta, source of India's four sacred rivers, above which rises Mount Meru. The lake is associated in myth with the sun, with light, and in Buddhism with enlightenment. But the symbolism is ambiguous. Some scholars have tended to regard Jayavarman as exclusively Buddhist, and his early sojourn in Champa may well have helped to familiarize him with the resources of Mahāyāna Buddhism, but the evidence of his monuments is that he patronized as wide a variety of sects as any of his predecessors. He certainly gave special favour to the Buddha. According to the Preah Khan stele inscription, he

2   C. Jacques, *Angkor*. Paris: Bordas, 1990, p. 157.

learned his Buddhism from his father, who 'found his satis-
faction in this nectar that is the religion of Śākyamuni [the
Buddha]'.[3]

The maintenance of religious institutions required a considerable logistic commitment. The headquarters of the 'hospital'
system was at the Ta Prohm, a temple foundation dedicated to
Jayavarman's mother. It was a regular town, with a staff of
12,640, and the services of 79,365 people in villages attached
for its support. Today, much of it has succumbed to the forest,
crumbling stone walls now penetrated and embraced by great
mallows.

A companion foundation, the Preah Khan, dedicated by the
king to his father, housed images of 20,400 deities. Many of
these icons doubtless embodied territorial spirits indigenous to
the Khmer land, who were honoured along with the Indian
gods. Viṣṇu and Śiva were worshipped here, as well as other
Hindu deities, while (as in so many of Jayavarman's foundations) the Buddha had pride of place: at the centre was an
image of Lokeśvara, surrounded by 182 subordinate divinities.
To support this establishment 13,500 villages and 97,840
people were committed to supply six tons of rice a day. It clearly
was no ordinary temple-monastery: staffed by a thousand
religious teachers, it has been described as a university.

Prodigious effort was lavished upon the construction of
Jayavarman's capital city, Angkor Thom, which lay in a square
walled enclosure measuring over 3 kilometres on each side;
this great wall represents the first real city fortification at
Angkor (after the tenth-century embankment that enclosed
Yaśodharapura).

The Bayon, Jayavarman's central shrine, also has an important political dimension. The temple has been called a 'forest of
heads', for the central shrine with its surrounding jumble of
courtyards is studded with towers, each sculpted with four faces
of Lokeśvara gazing out serenely in all directions. Some believe
that all these faces represent the king himself – full-lipped, with
heavy-lidded eyes. Just as, in Orwell's dark fantasy *1984*, Big
Brother has his eyes and ears trained upon the lives of all the
toiling citizens, so in the Angkor of Jayavarman VII the pre-

[3] Coedès, *The Indianized States*, p. 173.

Plate 40   Head of Lokeśvara, Ta Prohm

siding *bodhisattva*, fused symbolically with the ruler himself, extends his vigil in all the directions of space. The idea is taken from the mythology of Mahāyāna, according to which the *Bodhisattva*'s eyes send rays of all-seeing compassion into the whole of space, filling it with the light of his boundless merit. In the same way, Jayavarman saw himself as a presiding angel, taking a share of his subjects' suffering and bestowing upon them a share of his inexhaustible treasury of merit. It is a conspicuous feature of the symbolism of his court ritual and architecture that he regarded the *bodhisattva* Avalokiteśvara, particularly in the embodiment known as Lokeśvara, as his special patron.

However, as we have noticed, Jayavarman was not exclusively Buddhist. Angkor was home to innumerable celestial or supernatural powers of many sorts, Hindu, Buddhist and local (particularly the ancestral spirits, *nak ta*). As king, Jayavarman was a focus for them all; the ritual of his dominion was a bridge between the great gods and the spirits of communities. No doubt he wished to be known by posterity as a being whose transcendent compassion had a supernatural effect upon the destiny of his kingdom and his subjects: 'The bodily suffering of men became the suffering of his spirit, and afflicted him all the more: for it is the grief of their subjects that causes the grief of kings, and not their own grief'.[4]

Perhaps it seemed to those who read this inscription while the marks of its chiselling were still fresh and clean that such a great king must be the founder of a glorious epoch. Angkor was at the peak of its glory. The institutional reforms of Rājendravarman were secure, giving a measure of centralization to the administration of the empire. A large hydraulic system had been created; it was unlike anything else in the region and it bestowed a powerful increment of prestige upon its masters. Gilded temples everywhere testified to an impressive nexus between the wealth and the piety of benefactors past and present. Luxuries and curiosities from the whole of the known world converged upon the capital by barge and cart. There was no rival power close enough to be a serious threat except for the Chams, and for the time being the Khmers had the upper hand. It must have seemed to many that the empire would never know a twilight.

Yet some at least of the underlying factors of Angkor's decline were emerging even now. In some ways the reign of Jayavarman VII stood at an end, not a beginning. After him, indeed, the decline seen with hindsight by the historian was probably not manifest to the inhabitants of Angkor, and the realm did indeed remain prosperous and proud for a century or more; but the foundations of its pre-eminence were being eroded, warfare was to become increasingly defensive and damaging, and no sub-sequent ruler was able to scale the heights of magnificence reached by Jayavarman VII.

There is a way of taking Jayavarman's professions of responsibility for the lives of all his subjects that accuses him of presuming too much. In his victory, it might be said, he was

---

[4] Inscription of Say Fong, stanza XIII: L. Finot, L'inscription sanskrit de Say-Fong (Notes d'epigraphie, 2). *Bulletin de l'Ecole française d'Extrême-Orient*, 3 (1903), pp. 18–33. Jacques, *Angkor*, p. 157 (whose reading and translation are followed here) points out that this sentiment is not necessarily and specifically Buddhist. In the Indian tradition, a king of any religious leaning might profess such an identification with the *karma* of his subjects.

deluded into thinking himself invulnerable; in his royal wealth and pomp, he came to believe himself divine; and to sustain an illusion he wore his kingdom down into poverty. For all his monuments and all his victories had to be paid for in the sweat of those who were made instruments of his leaping ambition. In the end, some have argued, it was the exhaustion of the kingdom brought about by Jayavarman's extravagance that set it upon its downward course.[5]

There may be some truth in this interpretation, but it is not obvious *prima facie* that an over-exploitation of human resources about AD 1200 should bring about Angkor's abandonment two centuries later. Jayavarman's immediate successors may have found it unwise to attempt to imitate his achievements, but that is another matter. There must be other parts of the explanation which bear more directly upon the events of the fourteenth and fifteenth centuries.

After Jayavarman, although the age of mighty deeds and massive endowments recorded in Sanskrit inscriptions came to an end, Angkor continued to be known as a prosperous kingdom. Even if the outer territories of the empire were asserting their autonomy, Angkor itself continued to be a bustling, prosperous city; quite apart from the fragments of evidence in isolated inscriptions and various Chinese sources, the clear testimony of Chou Ta-kuan confirms as much. Yet the production of inscriptions and monuments virtually came to an end; nothing of consequence was produced in the reign of any later king. Indravarman II (*r. c.*1220–43) may or may not have been a son of Jayavarman VII; he made no attempt to imitate his predecessor's style. There was a Hindu backlash, evidenced by deliberate defacement of the Buddhist art of Jayavarman's reign, and it is possible that this occurred in the time of Indravarman. There is an intriguing local folk memory of a leper king which was reported to Chou Ta-kuan at the end of

---

[5] For example, L. P. Briggs wrote: 'All the great monuments of antiquity were built by forced labor and the almost necessary consequence of a prolonged period of architectural greatness was an exhausted, spiritless people. The people became dissatisfied with the greedy gods for whom they must continuously toil and fight and give ...' (*The Ancient Khmer Empire*, Philadelphia, Pa: American Philosophical Society, 1951, pp. 258f).

the century. Some think that, just possibly, there really was such a king, and the dramatic change in the style of Cambodian kingship may reflect the psychology of a ruler whose career was cruelly blighted by the undeserved humiliation of a disease he could not understand. If so, this king may well have been Indravarman II.[6]

Indravarman III (*r.*1295–1308) was on the throne when the Chinese visitor Chou Ta-kuan came in 1296–7. The description he gives does not suggest that court life was less grand. Everything that could be gold was gold; and state ceremony was staged with a fine sense of occasion:

When the prince goes out, troops head the escort; then come the standards, the pennants, and the music.

Young girls of the palace, three to five hundred in number, who wear floral materials and flowers in their hair and hold candles in their hands, form one troop; even in broad daylight their candles are lit. Then come girls of the palace carrying gold and silver royal utensils and a whole series of ornaments, all of a very peculiar shape and the uses of which are unknown to me. Then there are the girls of the palace carrying lances and shields, who comprise the private guard of the prince; they also form a troop. Following are goat-carts and horse-carts, all decorated with gold. The ministers and princes are mounted on elephants; in front of them one can see from afar their red parasols, which are innumerable. After them come the wives and concubines of the king, in palanquins, in carts, on horses and elephants. They have, certainly, more than a hundred parasols flecked with gold. After them is the sovereign, standing on an elephant and holding the precious sword in his hand. The tusks of the elephant are also sheathed in gold. There are more than twenty white parasols flecked with gold, with handles of gold. Numerous elephants crowd around him, and there are more troops to protect him. If the king goes to a nearby place, he uses only gold palanquins carried by ten girls of the palace. Most frequently the king, on his outings, goes to see a small gold tower in front of which is a gold Buddha. Those who see the king must prostrate themselves and touch the ground in front of them. This is what is called *san-pa* (*sampeah*). If they do not, they are seized by those in charge of the ceremonies, who do not let them go until they have paid for their transgression.

[6] D. P. Chandler, Folk memories of the decline of Angkor in nineteenth-century Cambodia: the legend of the Leper King. *Journal of the Siam Society*, 67, no. 1 (1979), pp. 54–62.

Twice each day the king holds audience for the affairs of government. There is no fixed agenda. Those officials or commoners who wish to see the sovereign sit on the ground to wait for him ... Two girls of the palace raise the curtain with their tiny fingers, and the king, holding the sword in his hand, appears at the golden window. Ministers and common people clasp their hands and strike the ground in front of them; when the sound of the conches stops, they can raise their heads again. Immediately thereafter the king sits down. In the place where he sits there is a lion skin, which is a hereditary treasure.

When business is concluded, the prince returns; the two girls let the curtain fall, and everyone rises.

We see from this that, even though this is a barbarous kingdom, these people know what a prince is.[7]

Nor were the kings of Angkor yet unable to maintain their dignity in their dealings with the outside world. Between 1371 and 1403, even well after Chou Ta-kuan's visit, there were ten embassies to China, often taking rich presents. Not for nothing did China know Cambodia as 'Chen-la the wealthy'.

Yet the signs of decline were perhaps there to be read. Chou Ta-kuan says that when he was in Cambodia there had recently been a particularly debilitating war against the Siamese; according to report, 'the whole population was required to fight'.[8] This was the time when independent Thai kingdoms were appearing in the Chao Phraya valley – Sukothai in the middle of the thirteenth century, and a hundred years later the much more powerful state of Ayudhya, which directly challenged Angkor. In 1369 the capital of Angkor was temporarily abandoned. In the fifteenth century, the decisive move was made by the court to the south, and Angkor ceased to be the centre of an empire.

The circumstances of the end of Angkor are equivocal. For one thing, the date of the retreat from Angkor is not at all certain; conventionally it is considered to have taken place in 1430–1, following a Thai siege and conquest by a king Paramadhiraj, but the sources – Cambodian and Thai chronicles composed much later – are unreliable, and calculations founded upon their authority are precarious.

---

[7] Chou Ta-kuan, *Mémoires sur les coutumes du Cambodge de Tcheou Takouan*, tr. P. Pelliot. Paris: Ecole française d'Extrême-Orient, 1951, pp. 34f.
[8] Ibid., p. 34.

Further, it was not a matter of straightforward military conquest; Thai invasions clearly played a part, but they did not lead to permanent occupation and were not necessarily decisive. Angkor was not definitively abandoned; it remained a provincial outpost that was refurbished and occupied temporarily by some later kings.

What probably happened is that, early in the fifteenth century, Khmer rulers shifted to the south-east, establishing themselves in the area of Phnom Penh, and with this shift the character of the kingdom changed. There were no more big stone Hindu temples. Theravāda Buddhism had taken over, and the saffron-robed monks observed by Chou Ta-kuan were from then on the custodians of the country's established religion. Pāli, the language of Theravāda scriptures, replaced Sanskrit as the vehicle of religious culture. Whether or not stone was obtainable for the building of new great temples, Theravāda Buddhism simply did not call for them. Magnificent victories and imperial aggrandisement were no longer recorded. Cambodia ceased to be one of the great powers in the region. By anybody's standards, a new period of history began.

One of the main problems in Cambodian history is the assignment of causes for this shift. The Siamese threat in the north-west is one obvious reason for it. However, some historians deny that it should be seen as a sufficient cause. It is true that, according to Chou Ta-kuan, the Siamese war that had taken place not long before his visit had required all-out involvement, but, in the long run, it is not clear that the Thais were overwhelmingly more successful than the Khmers in the wars between them, and their campaigns did not lead to annexation of territory. Like so many of the conflicts between neighbouring South-East Asian powers, they were essentially looting raids followed by retreat. Parts of the former Khmer empire in the Chao Phraya basin (chiefly around Lopburi) demonstrated their independence by sending their own tribute missions to China from the thirteenth century onwards, but the rivalry between the Khmer kingdom and the Thai state founded at Ayudhya continued without a decisive victor until the eighteenth century.

Michael Vickery has suggested that it is necessary to look elsewhere for an explanation of the shift from Angkor to the middle Mekong,[9] and he has argued that Ayudhya and Angkor were not two monolithic competing entities with clearly distinct territories. There came to be a mixed Mon–Khmer–Thai aristocracy, which provided some of the rulers on both sides; such a one was Bāña Yāt, who led Khmer forces against the power of Ayudhya in the fifteenth century. 'The conquest of Angkor was not so much an international war as a conflict of rival dynasties for control of mutual borderland.'[10]

Another line of thought, propounded by Bernard Groslier, attributes the abandonment of Angkor to the eventual failure of its elaborate hydraulic system, which on his view was an essential part of the irrigation network that served the densely populated capital territory. This argument proposes that the hydraulic system, by its nature, required more and more work to keep it free of silt and able to function. Like the Red Queen in *Alice*, the Khmers had to run faster and faster in order to remain in the same place. Eventually, the argument runs, the task became too great and the whole system broke down. A number of ecological factors combined to make Angkor's agriculture unsustainable. These problems were described above, in chapter 12. As Groslier put it, 'Angkor's hydraulic system and its agriculture literally *killed* the soil.'[11] This interpretation was advanced by Groslier as part of his view of Angkor's agricultural history. According to him, the reservoirs were part of an elaborate irrigation system, which served the state well until the problems became overwhelming. The critics of the irrigation theory would agree in seeing these problems attendant upon any attempt to sustain a dense population upon Angkor's much-abused natural resources for very long; they would differ in denying that an effective irrigation system actually supported Angkor's agriculture in the first place.

The gradient of the land around Angkor, averaging about

[9]   See M. Vickery, *Cambodia after Angkor: the chronicular evidence for the fourteenth to sixteenth centuries.* Ann Arbor, Mich.: University Microfilms, 1977.
[10]   M. Vickery, The 2/k125 fragment: a lost chronicle of Ayuthaya. *Journal of the Siam Society*, 65, no. 1 (1977), pp. 1–80, at p. 61.
[11]   B.-P. Groslier, Agriculture et religion dans l'empire angkorien. *Etudes rurales*, 53–6 (1974), pp. 95–117, at p. 105.

9:10,000, hastened the silting up which the Khmers must have found so difficult to control, and, as the water became more stagnant, the soil lost more of its nutrients.[12] This allows one to hypothesize that malaria could have played its part in the state's downfall, for these stagnant waters would have been an excellent breeding-ground for the malaria-carrying mosquitoes known to have penetrated Asian waterways in this period. Rhoads Murphey has pointed out that malaria could have contributed to the decline of Rome, and that it reached Sri Lanka by the thirteenth or fourteenth century; sometime thereafter it would have reached Burma, Thailand and Cambodia, where the mosquitoes would thrive in disused irrigation works.[13] However, there is no clear evidence to support the theory, and it remains a speculation.

Another way of looking at the problem of Angkor's decline appeals to the broader international context. No national history is completely self-contained, and the agents of change often hatch out elsewhere, well beyond the borders. In the case of Angkor, we need to take account of the inevitable influence of developments in China, a regional super-power at least as important to the rest of Asia as the USA is in the world at large today.

It was during the Sung dynasty that a decisive demographic shift took place in China, with the bulk of the population henceforth concentrated in the south, where well-watered monsoon paddies helped to underwrite the prosperity that Marco Polo was to admire later, during the ascendancy of the Mongol conqerors. The Sung 'commercial revolution' and the temporary residence of the court in the south gave added energy to the trade of the south seas.

These developments gave advantages to *coastal* power, and it is possible to see them as at least a partial explanation of the rise of South-East Asian cities downriver from the older centres and in easy reach of the coasts. In the middle of the fourteenth

[12] B.-P. Groslier, La cité hydraulique angkorienne. Exploitation ou surexploitation du sol? *Bulletin de l'Ecole française d'Extrême-Orient*, 66 (1979), pp. 161–202.
[13] See Rhoads Murphey, The ruin of ancient Ceylon. *Journal of Asian Studies*, 16 (1957), p. 199.

century, Sukothai and the other northern Thai principalities were superseded by Ayudhya, and not long afterwards the rulers of the Khmers retreated to the Mekong. The area of Phnom Penh became the new centre of strategic importance, and attracted attacks from Ayudhya that were evidently directed to suppressing its economic rise.

This retreat could thus be seen as a response to changing economic circumstances rather than, or as well as, a strategic move in the face of the Thai military threat. In an important study, Michael Vickery has argued for this view.[14] According to it, what is significant is the shift in orientation from agriculture to trade. Between 1378 and 1415 there were more exchanges of missions with China than in the previous 500 years; there was a new interest on the part of the rulers and nobility of Angkor in the resources of the outside world. For Vickery, the problem for future research is to gain some understanding of the changes in economic and social structure that can explain the new economic orientation.

It is unlikely that historians will agree confidently on a single main cause for the decline of Angkor. The evidence they must use is fragmentary and ambiguous, and they are thrown upon speculations that vary according to individuals' assumptions about the way history works. It may well be that Angkor's glory came to an end for a combination of reasons, none sufficient.

Perhaps we should consult the views of the Cambodians themselves. Chou Ta-kuan reported the Khmers' own version: the fate of their kingdom depended upon the ruler's constant renewal of a covenant with the spirits of the territory, the *nāga* rulers.

There is a gold tower [the Phimeanakas] at the top of which the King sleeps. All the natives claim that there is a spirit in the tower, a serpent with nine heads, which is the master of the soil of the whole kingdom. It appears every night in the form of a woman. It is with this spirit that the King first sleeps and unites himself. Not even the wives of the King may enter here. At the second watch the King comes forth and is then free to sleep with his wives and his concubines. Should the spirit fail to appear for a single night, it is a sign that the King's death is at hand.

---

[14]   Vickery, *Cambodia after Angkor*.

If, on the other hand, the King should fail to keep his tryst, disaster is sure to follow.[15]

We should not overlook the significance of such testimony. As with the legend of Kauṇḍinya and Somā, so with the thirteenth- and fourteenth-century rulers – their power depended upon their ability to unite themselves with a spirit that transcended the particularisms of locality. The Khmer empire began and ended with the relationship between the ruler and the sacred soil of his kingdom. So long as the imperial state could compel the loyalties of most of the Khmers in the once-independent communities dotted about the countryside, it could command an apparatus of government more unified and powerful than those of neighbouring kingdoms. When that magic was lost, Cambodia reverted to the status of a regional kingdom engaged in a struggle for survival with its neighbours.

15   Chou Ta-kuan, *Mémoires*, p. 12.

16

From the Fall of Angkor to 1945

Cambodia's history between the abandonment of Angkor and the end of the Second World War suffers from a shortage of usable sources and a lack of scholarly attention. Studying even more recent events, on the other hand, is affected by an overwhelming quantity of relevant material and by the dark shadows cast across our vision by the 1970s, when Cambodia almost disappeared. Although '1945' offers perhaps the sharpest turning point in Cambodia's political history prior to the 1970s, there are several earlier phases and turning points that need to be identified and examined.

The first period, which is poorly documented, lasted roughly from the abandonment of Angkor in the mid-fifteenth century until the end of the sixteenth century, when the Cambodian court fell under Thai domination. Between the early seventeenth century and the 1860s, Cambodian history can be seen as a tug-of-war between the Thai and the Vietnamese. In the early nineteenth century, the country was the scene of fighting between these two powers, whose rivalry ended only with the establishment of a French protectorate in 1863. Cambodia was awarded its independence temporarily in 1945 by the Japanese forces that occupied the country. The French returned to power a few months later. Over the next thirty years, Cambodia toyed briefly with a parliamentary system, gained its independence, lost its monarchy, became a republic and succumbed to a communist revolution. This in turn was halted by a Vietnamese invasion. Cambodia's history since 1979 is by definition open-ended and requires an open-ended approach.

Alongside this periodization and these turning points, there are many continuities between Cambodia in Angkorian times and Cambodia today. Some of these in the realm of work and social behaviour are depicted in the bas-reliefs at the Bayon, and have already been discussed. Other themes include the role played by Theravāda Buddhism, which became influential in Cambodia in the thirteenth century; the country's continuous demographic weakness *vis-à-vis* its neighbours Thailand and Vietnam; its hierarchical, personalized form of government and, more recently, the way Cambodians perceive their distant past. These continuities – social inertia, Buddhism, a shortage of people, deference, and a tendency to look back rather than ahead – converge when we examine Cambodian society and politics today.

Whether we approach the 500 years since the 'fall' of Angkor as a series of phases or as a whole, it is crucial to see the period in its own terms, rather than weighed in the balance against Angkor, or against Cambodia's neighbours, and found wanting. It is unhelpful to perceive this half millennium in terms of Cambodia's 'decline'. After all, we seldom speak of 'post-Hellenic Greek history', 'post-seventeenth century Holland', or 'post-nineteenth century Britain'. Moreover, it seems likely that the 'post-Angkorian' quality of Cambodian life was already noticeable before Angkor was abandoned. Because of that abandonment, perhaps, and because the French were convinced that they had 'discovered' the ruins in the 1850s, when they were well known to local people, historians in the colonial era often spoke of Cambodia's 'decline', suggesting that Angkorian grandeur was the country's natural or preferred condition, and also justifying the embrace of French colonialism.

The shift of the Cambodian elite from the Angkorian region to the vicinity of Phnom Penh in the fourteenth and fifteenth centuries, as we have seen, has been chronicled by Michael Vickery, mastering a range of scrappy, bewildering and unreliable sources.[1] The inscriptions, chronicles and myths he has examined tell a confusing story, but concur that Angkor

---

[1] Michael Vickery, *Cambodia after Angkor: The chronicular evidence for the fourteenth to sixteenth centuries*. Ann Arbor, Mich.: University Microfilms, 1977, pp. 500ff.

stopped being the home of Cambodia's kings and its elite at some point in the 1400s. Some writers have suggested that a plague (malaria? smallpox?) may have killed off tens of thousands of its people. It is more likely that thousands were taken off as prisoners to Siam by Thai invading armies. But these population losses in themselves do not explain the shift of Cambodia's centre of gravity southward, or its transformation at the top from a Hindu–Buddhist theocracy to a small-scale, more constrained Theravāda Buddhist kingdom. Indeed, it seems likely that the 'miniaturization' of the Cambodian court had begun well before the abandonment of Angkor, as part of the kingdom's ideological shift away from Hinduism and from its emphasis on priestly castes. The shift to supposedly 'peaceable' Theravāda Buddhism is an insufficient explanation for Cambodia's diminishing power. After all, Angkor was repeatedly invaded, and beaten, by armies from Theravāda Buddhist Siam.

As we have noted, Angkorian power-brokers, who were probably large land-holders and traders at Angkor, almost certainly Chinese, found trading opportunities along the Mekong more lucrative than they had been at Angkor. By shifting to the south-east they could link into trading networks being developed elsewhere in the region by Malay, Indian and Chinese merchants. Strategic considerations probably also played a part: in the vicinity of present-day Phnom Penh, the Khmer were much less vulnerable than they had been at Angkor to Thai military excursions.

In any event, Cambodian legends date the foundation of Phnom Penh to the mid-fifteenth century. Its suitability as a capital sprang from its location at the confluence of the Mekong and the Tonle Sap. A fortified city built at this point – known as the 'four faces' in Cambodian, and as 'four arms' in French – could control the riverine trade from the Lao states to the north, as well as trade in pottery and dried fish from the Great Lake, while serving as an entrepôt for such traditional exports as cardamom, stick-laq and other forest products. The port could also receive incoming goods, primarily Chinese in origin, approaching from the mouth of the Mekong, still inhabited in the fifteenth and sixteenth centuries largely by Khmer. Once the choice had been made for Cambodia to become a trading kingdom – and it is impossible to say when or by whom the choice was made – locating a capital at Angkor was no longer realistic. By the mid-sixteenth century, however, the royal and ceremonial capital of Cambodia had shifted some fifty miles north of Phnom Penh, near present-day Longvaek, and the kingdom had earned a reputation among foreigners for its great wealth.

For the first time since the era of 'Fu-nan', Cambodia was primarily a maritime kingdom, with the prosperity of its elite dependent on seaborne overseas trade. The rest of the population, untouched by foreign trade, remained subsistence farmers, monks and officials.

Because so much South-East Asian trade in the sixteenth and seventeenth centuries was in foreign hands, foreigners played an important part in the life of Phnom Penh. Speakers of Malay from the Indonesian islands have left such words behind in the Cambodian languages as *kompong* or 'town' and *psaa* or 'market', as well as several administrative terms. The Malay legacy may well have been deeper than this, for European descriptions of Cambodia strongly resemble descriptions from this era and later of riverine Malaya.[2] Indeed, much of what we know about this period comes to us from Spanish and Portuguese accounts. By the 1650s, foreigners at Phnom Penh included traders from Europe, South-East Asia, the Persian Gulf and Japan, and missionaries from Portugal and Spain.

In the mid-sixteenth century, a Cambodian king from Longvaek, in the course of a hunting expedition in the northwest, stumbled across the abandoned temples of Angkor. In the words of a Portuguese visitor, Diogo do Couto, writing in the 1590s, the King

went to the place . . . and ordered people then and there to cut back the undergrowth. And he remained there, beside a pretty river while the work was carried out, by five or six thousand men, working for a few days . . . And when everything had been carefully cleaned up, the

[2]   See M. Gullick, *Indigenous Political Systems of Western Malaya*. London: Athlone Press, 1958, esp. pp. 125–43.

King went inside [the city] and was struck with admiration for the extent of these constructions.[3]

Do Couto adds that the King decided to transfer his court to Angkor, and inscriptions there suggest that he may have done so briefly in the 1570s, when some additional bas-reliefs of mediocre quality were also carved at Angkor Wat.

Interestingly, this brief period of Cambodian autonomy (and royal adventurousness) coincided with a time of uncertainty and trauma at the Thai court of Ayudhya, devastated by a Burmese attack in 1569. Perhaps the Cambodian King found himself in the Angkor region after (or before) leading a military incursion into Siam. In any case, his stay among the temples was brief. Ayudhya soon regained its strength, and a Thai army besieged Longvaek unsuccessfully in 1587. Foreshadowing the conduct of nineteenth- and twentieth-century Cambodian leaders, the Cambodian king sought help from a distant country – the Spanish Philippines – even promising to become a Catholic if sufficient military help arrived. It never did; instead, the Thai returned in 1594 and sacked the capital.

Two Cambodian myths associated with this event have retained their currency in Cambodia until today. One relates that Longvaek sheltered two spiritually powerful statues, one known as *preah ko* (sacred cow) and the other as *preah kaev* (sacred jewel). Inside the bellies of the statues, the legend relates, 'there were sacred books, in gold, where one could learn sacred formulas, and books where one could learn anything about the world'.[4]

The Thai king wanted the two statues. According to the second myth, when the Thai were besieging the city, their cannons (a weapon which had arrived in South-East Asia earlier in the century from Europe) fired silver coins, rather than shells, into the bamboo hedges that served as ramparts for the city. The Thai armies then pulled back, and the Khmers from the city cut down the hedges to reach the coins. They were defenceless when

[3] See B.-P. Groslier, *Angkor et le Cambodge au XVIe siècle*. Paris: Presses Universitaires de France, 1958, pp. 142–4.
[4] The legend is contained, in Khmer and a French translation, in G. Janneau, *Manuel pratique pour le cambodgien*. Saigon: Imprimerie Coloniale, 1876, pp. 87–8.

the Thai returned, several months later, to take the city. At that point, according to the other legend, they carried off the *preah ko* and *preah kaev* to Ayudhya. After cutting them open

they were able to take the books . . . and study their contents. *For this reason* [emphasis added] they have become superior in knowledge to the Cambodians, and for this reason the Cambodians are ignorant, and lack the personnel to do what is necessary, unlike other countries.[5]

The legends provide a persuasive rationale to many Khmer for their post-Angkorian loss of power. The statue of *preah ko*, it seems, is a metaphor for Cambodia's Indian heritage, while *preah kaev* was probably a metaphor for Buddhism, embodied in a jewel-like Buddha-image. The seepage of Cambodian literary skills – including the Khmer alphabet – to Siam is condensed in the myth into the theft of a pair of statues that had allegedly given the Angkorian Khmer their extraordinary power.

The capture of Longvaek opened up a period of Thai suzerainty over the Cambodian court that lasted, with some short interruptions, until the arrival of the French in the 1860s.

What did Thai suzerainty amount to? Throughout the seventeenth century, the Thai citadel of Ayudhya, centred a short distance north of present-day Bangkok, was a flourishing port and could mobilize considerable military power. As an expression of its monarch's overwhelming fund of merit, conceived in spiritual and material terms, the Thai court sought and received tributary gifts on a regular basis from rulers of weaker states such as Cambodia and Laos, as well as from several riverine sultanates in Malaya. When faced with another 'universal monarch' in neighbouring Burma, the Thai kings resorted repeatedly to war.

Tributary gifts transmitted to Ayudhya were often of considerable value – in some cases miniature metal trees decorated with gold and silver leaves. The gifts expressed the patron–client relationship between Ayudhya and the donor-states. The Cambodian kings, whose capital had moved to Udong after the fall of Longvaek, were allowed to rule the kingdom without much interference from Ayudhya, but were expected to honour Thai requests for troop levies, tribute and pledges of support. It

5 Ibid.

was during this period that many Cambodian and Thai words – and, one supposes, Buddhist monks and other members of the elite – passed back and forth between Cambodia and Siam. The high cultures of the two countries as expressed in palace dances, royal language, court ceremonial, temple paintings and Buddhist sculpture became all but undistinguishable, and impossible to call either 'Cambodian' or 'Thai'.

Cambodian social structure, perhaps because of the kingdom's isolation from the outside world, seems to have been more rigid than its counterpart in Siam. A late sixteenth-century visitor to Cambodia, the Spanish missionary San Antonio, described two classes of Khmer:

Among them are nobles and commoners . . . All the nobles have several wives, the number depending on how rich they are. High ranking women are white and beautiful; those of the common people are brown . . . The nobles dress in silk and fine cotton and gauze . . . The people pay the principal officials, and the king, one tenth of the value of all goods taken from the sea and the land.[6]

These hierarchical divisions of society resembled those that governed Cambodian society into the nineteenth century and beyond. Because popular thinking among Theravāda Buddhists tended to equate worldly power and status with spiritual merit, earned in previous existences (although even higher merit was attributed to living Buddhist monks), what held the society together was a shared belief that people's social positions were more or less permanent. Society was divided between a small number of 'haves', perceived from 'below' as meritorious, and an undifferentiated mass of 'poor', seen from the top as undeserving of respect. The division was embodied in linguistic terms, whereby different verbs and names of body-parts were used for monks, royalty, common people and animals. The harshness of the system was reduced somewhat by the respect granted to elderly people of any social origin, by the egalitarianism implicit in Buddhist worship, by the power of women in everyday village life and marketing, and by the fact that Cambodia's poor had rich cultural traditions of their own.

[6]   See A. Cabaton (ed. and tr.), *Brève et véridique relation des événements du Cambodge*. Paris: Leroux, 1914, p. 100.

These included ceremonies honouring village and local spirits, as well as a fund of oral folk-lore where a favourite hero was the clever slave, Tmenh Chey, who outwitted the rich and powerful. Moreover, occasionally individuals from 'below' could enter the elite by coming to someone's notice – as an attractive girl of marriageable age, for example, or as a literate former monk. The society was hardly characterized by anything like the kinds of mobility (or chaos) with which we are familiar today, but there was a certain amount of movement up and down the social ladder – enhanced by a bilateral kinship system, which worked against primogeniture, and by the uncertainty of royal patronage from one reign to another. As we have seen, each new reign inaugurated a new patronage network, raising or demoting members of the elite, favouring or displacing those from certain regions, 'playing favourites', which in a sense changed society, at least near the top, from one reign to the next.

Many of the norms and values of seventeenth-century Cambodia are displayed in the *chef d'oeuvre* of Cambodian literature, the Khmer-language version of the *Rāmāyana* known as the *Reamker* ('The Glory of Rama') and in collections of didactic poems known as *chhbab*.[7] These poems, taken together, display and suggest a good deal about the lopsided way Cambodians viewed society, and each other, in those days.

One relationship which they stress is the one between teachers (*kru* in Khmer: cf. Sanskrit *guru*). These genteel, authoritarian figures, in a partly literate society, were often, if not always, Buddhist monks. They were the curators and transmitters of normative values. The teacher – pupil relationship was lopsided, determined by differences in age, learning, merit and status. The teacher bestowed, recited and commanded; the student listened, memorized and obeyed. The proper relationship between the two sprang from their relative positions; protection and knowledge were exchanged for obedience and respect. Similarly, Prince Ream (Rama), the hero of the *Reamker*,

---

7 Saveros Pou's magisterial three-volume edition, French translation and critique of the *Reamker* was published by Ecole française d'Extrême-Orient, Paris in 1977–9. For an alternative version, see F. Bizot (ed.), *Histoire de Reamker*, Phnom Penh: n.p., 1973. See also Saveros Pou, *Une guirlande de cpap*, 2 vols. Paris: CEDORECK, 1988.

was thought to have much to teach us by his exemplary conduct, seen in a way to flow from his high position.

The version of the *Reamker* that has survived appears to be incomplete. It contains only a few of the incidents in the Indian original, and the text as a whole has been refocused to accommodate a Theravāda Buddhist perspective. The mythical plot, of a high-born man seeking to reunite with his wife and triumphing over evil forces along the way, draws its richness from what Indians refer to as 'the ocean of stories' that have captivated people everywhere throughout history. Exiled unjustly from the kingdom he is about to inherit, Prince Ream (Rama) travels in the forest with his wife Sita and his brother Leak (Laksmana). Sita is carried off by the wicked Prince Reap (Ravana) who rules the kingdom of Langka. Aided by a monkey prince named Hanuman, Ream attacks Langka to regain his wife, and wins a series of battles. The Cambodian poem ends at this point, with its central crisis unresolved. In other versions that have survived in oral tradition, the couple is reunited.

The role played by the poem in present-day Cambodia resembles that played by the shadow-puppet theatre, or *wayang*, in Java and Bali. As with *wayang*, hearing the poem, or seeing segments of it acted out by dancers, has always been a quasi-religious experience for Khmers. Reciting or dancing out the poem had supernatural value. Doing so was an attempt, like some Angkorian art, to bring spirits out of the sky and the earth not only to entertain an audience but so that they could help the audience to deal with everyday affairs. The poem also portrays the supernatural world where forces of good and evil are perpetually at war, and thus in a kind of permanent balance.

At another level, the *Reamker* was concerned with the activities of meritorious members of a small elite, whose exemplary behaviour embodied hierarchical, 'lopsided' values. The normative poems known as *chhbab* that also date from the sixteenth and seventeenth centuries convey moral values that include unquestioning respect for those with higher social positions, and the muted suggestion that privileged people have a duty to protect less-fortunate Khmers.

The linguistic polish of the *Reamker* and the *chhbab*, the sureness of their moral position, and the elegance of the slow dances performed in Cambodia for centuries to relate the

Rāmāyana story, contrast sharply with what we know from Cambodian texts and from outside observers about politics and everyday life in post-Angkorian Cambodia. These sources depict a country whose royal capital was out of touch with its hinterland, whose rulers were murderous, devious and short-sighted – a kingdom which was at the mercy, much of the time, of factional warfare, natural disasters and invasions. Scattered inscriptions at Angkor, a handful of elegant eighteenth-century Buddhist monasteries and the persistence of overseas trade suggest that Cambodia periodically regained its prosperity, and that its people were occasionally at peace.

Aside from the question of Thai influence, already mentioned, probably the most important event affecting Cambodia before the nineteenth century was the expansion of Vietnamese authority southwards into the Mekong delta. The process was well-advanced by the mid-seventeenth century, after repeated wars had led to the collapse of the intervening kingdom of Champa. By the 1680s, the Cambodian port of Prey Nokor (present-day Saigon) had come under the administration of the Nguyen overlords who dominated southern Vietnam. The change sealed off Cambodia's access to the sea. Smaller Cambodian ports along the Gulf of Siam were soon occupied by Vietnamese troops and Chinese traders. In the process of Vietnam's expansion, thousands of ethnic Khmer came under day-to-day Vietnamese control. The 'Vietnamization' of southern Vietnam left a legacy of resentment among Cambodians there and inside Cambodia that flared up in the nineteenth and twentieth centuries.

By 1700 or so Cambodia, for the first time in its history, was menaced on two sides by more powerful, potentially hostile neighbours. One effect of this development was that factions at the court, and in the provinces, soon tended to split along pro-Thai or pro-Vietnamese lines, depending on which was thought by factional leaders to be the likelier source of patronage. By and large, western Cambodia was subject to Siamese influence, and the parts of the country east of the Mekong succumbed to Vietnamese pressure and protection. The court at Udong was caught in the middle.

It is not surprising, therefore, that the history of Cambodia between the mid-seventeenth century and the arrival of the

French was one of invasions from Vietnam and Siam, preceded and followed by civil wars. In the process the king's authority, and his ability to rally followers, decreased, although regional leaders were occasionally able to raise troops to fend off foreign invaders.

The last thirty years of the eighteenth century were particularly tumultuous for Cambodia. In 1767, a Burmese army sacked Ayudhya. A new Thai dynasty, under a provincial governor named Taksin, soon established itself in the vicinity of Bangkok and Thai armies invaded Cambodia several times, in search of manpower and to take advantage of a burgeoning crisis in Vietnam, where a widespread populist rebellion, known as the Tayson, had broken out. In 1772 a Thai army destroyed Phnom Penh. In the succeeding decade, Vietnamese armies, pursuing Tayson forces, swept across the Mekong. Members of the decimated Cambodian royal family went into exile in Siam. The Cambodian monarch, King Eng, barely twenty years old, returned to Cambodia under Thai protection in 1794. Sensing Cambodia's weakness, and in exchange for this protection, the Thai took over most of north-western Cambodia, including the province of Siem Reap that contained the ruins of Angkor. The provinces were returned to Cambodia only in 1907.

Over the next half century, buffeted by its neighbours and subject to internal pressures, Cambodia almost disappeared. Rivalries between the newly installed Vietnamese and Thai royal houses, exacerbated by factional rivalries inside Cambodia itself, led to repeated invasions by Thai armies and for many years to a kind of Vietnamese protectorate that, in terms of its paternalism and cultural superiority, foreshadowed the French protectorate later as well as the period of Vietnamese-installed Cambodian government in the 1980s.

Most scholars agree that had the French not imposed their protectorate upon a Cambodian king in the 1860s, Cambodia would have broken into two zones of influence, with those parts east of the Mekong being administered by Vietnam and those to the west by Siam.

The early nineteenth century bequeathed several contradictory legacies to Cambodians in the colonial and post-colonial eras. One of these was a resentment of Vietnam and a fear of Vietnamese intentions, contrasted with a failure to blame the

Thai for their misconduct. Another was an awareness on the part of elites and monarchs that to survive they needed outside patrons who could protect them against neighbouring powers. These were hard to find, and their commitment to Cambodia was seldom deep. Hatred of the Vietnamese, the chronic need for patrons, and a sense of Cambodia's uniqueness have permeated the country's politics throughout the twentieth century. At the same time, it is important to stress that for most Cambodians politics itself, as understood in western countries, is often of less concern than politicians, scholars and journalists tend to think. Growing food, raising families and performing rituals still take up much more time and energy. 'Politics' is often left to those with the leisure or inclination to engage in it.

The first fifty years of the nineteenth century also witnessed a decline in the power and prestige of the Cambodian monarchy as an institution. Because the monarchy came under French control soon afterwards, it can be argued that it never regained the lustre or the freedom of manoeuvre that it seems to have enjoyed as late as the early eighteenth century.

One reason for the monarchy's loss of credit was the unfortunate choice made by Eng's successor, King Chan (*r.*1806–34) to resist Siam by seeking the countervailing patronage of Vietnam. Chan's rationale is unclear. Short-term considerations were probably paramount. Chan may have personally offended the Thai monarch, Rama II. He certainly resented the loss of territory in Cambodia's north-west. Conceivably, economic links between his court and Saigon were also important. In any case, by 1811–12, following a brief Thai invasion, Cambodia's capital had moved from Udong to Phnom Penh, three of Chan's brothers had fled to Siam, and a Vietnamese garrison had been installed to protect the king. Chan's fear of being overthrown by his brothers drove him further into the arms of the Vietnamese.

For several years, Vietnamese patronage was not especially far–reaching, and became systematic only after a Thai attack on Cambodia and southern Vietnam in 1833 that coincided with an anti-dynastic rebellion in southern Vietnam. The Thai monarch, Rama III, believed that the time was ripe 'to restore the kingdom of Cambodia and to punish the insolence of Vietnam' – connected in his mind with removing the Cambodian court from the orbit of the Thai. A large Thai army swept

down the southern shores of the Tonle Sap and occupied
Phnom Penh. Chan had been taken off beforehand into Vietnam. A few months later, however, after the rebellion in the
Saigon area had collapsed, the Thai army retreated, after burning down Phnom Penh and driving out its population.

The response of the Vietnamese emperor Minh Mang to
these events was to place Cambodia under more-systematic
Vietnamese control, administered by the military bureaucrat
who had crushed the Saigon rebellion, Truong Minh Giang.
Before Giang could get started, King Chan died suddenly. To
retain a semblance of legitimacy, Giang installed Chan's second
daughter (he had no sons) as queen, while proceeding with what
the French would later call, referring to their own regime, a
'civilizing mission' intended to turn Cambodia into a submissive
and prosperous province of Vietnam.

The civilizing mission included sending Vietnamese settlers
into Cambodia, training a Cambodian militia, and reforming
what Giang and the emperor considered to be their barbarous
customs and behaviour. As Minh Mang wrote to Giang on
one occasion, 'The barbarians [in Cambodia] have become my
children now, and you . . . should teach them our customs.'[8]

The process failed because Cambodian provincial officials
were unwilling to exchange their royal titles and their patronage
networks for Vietnamese-dependent, supposedly meritocratic
positions. Uprisings against Vietnam broke out in the late
1830s, and a larger one, encouraged by the Thai, occurred
in 1840, soon after the Vietnamese had decided to install a
Vietnamese taxation system and to administer Cambodia's
provinces directly, instead of using local officials.

At that point, the Vietnamese imprisoned the Cambodian
queen, whom they thought un-co-operative. The disappearance
of their monarch, however ineffectual she had been, enraged
and terrified many Cambodian provincial officials, who led
their followers into rebellion. In early 1841, a Thai army
invaded Cambodia for the third time since 1811, and for the
next five years Cambodia was a battlefield, with the advantage see-sawing between the Thai and the Vietnamese, with

[8] David P. Chandler, *A History of Cambodia*, 2nd edn. Boulder, Col.:
Westview Press, 1993, p. 128.

the casualties largely Khmer, in an eerie foreshadowing of twentieth-century events. In 1847 the Vietnamese lost momentum and withdrew, allowing the Thai to install Chan's youngest brother, Duang, on the Cambodian throne.

The reassertion of Thai dominance depended on Cambodian acquiescence and Vietnam's loss of interest in the country. For the next thirteen years, King Duang was a talented and popular ruler who presided over Cambodia's coming back to life. This was symbolized by the reconstruction of Buddhist temples ravaged by neglect and war, by a revival in Cambodian literature, and by Duang's assiduous performance of rituals associated by his subjects with the welfare of the Kingdom. Duang also welcomed French Catholic missionaries to Cambodia, and with their encouragement wrote to the French monarch, Napoleon III, asking for his friendship, a euphemism for protection. The presents accompanying Duang's letter were lost en route, and the French did nothing to protect the unknown monarch. In the late 1850s a second attempt to make contact with France was foiled by Duang's Thai mentors.

During Duang's reign two Frenchmen, the missionary Bouillevaux and the naturalist Mouhot, visited the ruins at Angkor; both later claimed to have 'discovered' them. Mouhot's writing fired the imagination of European scholars, already thrilled by recent archaeological work in ancient Egypt and the Maya kingdoms of central America, among others. Scholars were also drawn in by what they assumed were the sociological similarities shared by these ancient empires.

When Duang died in 1860, his eldest son Norodom was unable to take the throne in the face of a rebellion led by Cambodia's Moslem minority, descendants of the Chams who had been driven from Vietnam 200 years before. By then, French forces had landed in southern Vietnam, and France had annexed the provinces adjoining Saigon. French expansion into the rest of what they were to call Indo-China began with an exploratory mission to Cambodia in 1863. Norodom, still uncrowned, agreed to accept French protection, assuming that this would involve military assistance and no interference in his style of rule. He was correct, for the next twenty years at least, and France acquired what they thought would be a valuable possession without paying any money or firing a shot. Because the upper reaches of the Mekong remained unmapped, the French mistakenly considered that Cambodia might constitute a lucrative 'back door' to China. The assumption proved untrue after a costly expedition to map the river – which originated in Tibet – was mounted in 1866. In the meantime, Norodom's willingness to forgo his independence was in sharp contrast to the difficulties the French were encountering with the Vietnamese rulers in Hue. He was crowned in Udong, with French naval officers in attendance, in the middle of 1864.

Over the next twenty years, as France consolidated its holdings in Vietnam, Cambodia remained a backwater. Several scholarly missions to the kingdom copied, catalogued and deciphered hundreds of inscriptions that had been found at Angkor and elsewhere. Little by little, Cambodia's sumptuous, half-forgotten past was brought to light, largely for the edification of Europeans. As we have seen, the French were struck by the contrast they perceived between nineteenth-century Cambodia and the grandeur of Angkor. Obsessed with the dimensions and beauty of the ruins, they invariably saw the contrast in terms of Cambodia's 'decline'.

During these years, French officials sought to limit Norodom's powers and to expand their own. In 1884, when the king refused to allow them to collect customs fees (a lucrative form of revenue), the French sent a gunboat to Phnom Penh (where they had moved the capital in 1866) and forced Norodom to sign a humiliating document that led to systematic French controls. Almost at once, an anti-French rebellion broke out in the provinces, sparked by the French decision to abolish slavery throughout the kingdom. The decision cut into the interests and followings of provincial officials. Norodom probably supported the rebellion in secret, but his younger brother, Sisowath, helped the French to put it down. Sisowath was rewarded by French promises that he would succeed his brother as king. The re-bellion lasted three years, and cost several hundred French lives. Cambodian casualties, of course, were far higher. When it was over Norodom became a powerless hostage of the French, maintained by a generous cash allowance extracted from the population in a variety of taxes. He lived out the remaining twenty-five years of his life in some bitterness, addicted to opium, surrounded by the trappings of absolute power.

Soon after Sisowath came to the throne in 1904, the French negotiated with the Thai to regain the provinces of Battambang and Siem Reap that had been annexed in the 1790s. The provinces were restored to Cambodia in 1907. One effect was to return the Angkorian ruins to Cambodian soil. Another was to add the prosperous rice-producing province of Battambang to the kingdom. Over the next fifty years Battambang provided the bulk of the Cambodian rice exports, that formed the economic basis for the country.

French colonialism was a relatively painless affair. From a Cambodian perspective its advantages probably outweighed its defects. Perhaps the main legacy of the protectorate, mentioned already, is that Cambodia enjoyed continuous peace for the first time in centuries. Even more importantly, the country continued to exist, unworried by its powerful neighbours. Other advantages included the provision of an infrastructure of roads, provincial cities and bureaucrats. Less dramatic advances were made in the fields of health, agriculture and primary education. Cambodia's economy, over the colonial era, was transformed from one based on trade and subsistence agriculture to one based on the export of agricultural commodities, principally rice and, after the 1920s, high quality rubber.[9]

In political terms, the colonial period was remarkably serene. National sentiment or anti-French behaviour in Cambodia were slow to develop, and violence against the French was very rare. At the same time, a disadvantage to Cambodia in the long term sprang from the way the French integrated the kingdom into 'Indo-China', inevitably dominated by Vietnam. By emphasizing this process, the French caused considerable resentment among Cambodia's small elite. Vietnamese bureaucrats staffed the middle ranks of the French administration in Cambodia, as they did in Laos, and continued (or so it often seemed) to consider themselves endowed with not only a different, but a superior, form of civilization.

In the 1920s, King Sisowath, an octogenarian, presided benignly over an economic boom engineered by the French and by rice farmers expanding their holdings to grow crops for

---

[9]   On the colonial period, see especially Alain Forest, *Le Cambodge et la colonisation française*. Paris: l'Harmattan, 1980.

export. When he died in 1927, French rubber plantations in eastern Cambodia, worked by Vietnamese indentured labour, had added greatly to the prosperity of the kingdom. To pay for the expansion, Cambodians paid more taxes on a *per capita* basis than other inhabitants of Indo-China. Under Sisowath's successor, Sisowath Monivong (*r*.1927–41), the process of modernization continued, although the depression in the early 1930s affected rice prices and led the French to reduce taxes for a while on hard-hit farmers. For his part, Monivong was an active patron of Cambodian culture, and during his reign the royal ballet reached a high level of professionalism. Two dancers in Monivong's troupe, ironically, were close relatives of the young boy who was, forty years later, to become the communist dictator of Cambodia, Pol Pot.

The 1930s witnessed a gradual growth in Cambodian nationalism, focused among the Buddhist clergy and a privately sponsored Khmer-language newspaper named *Angkor Wat* that began to appear in 1936. As the urban Khmer elite became more numerous and better educated, some of its members began considering the possibility of independence, but no thought was given to armed rebellion, and the communist movement in Vietnam made very little headway among the Khmer. The defeat of France in 1940, and the arrival of Japanese occupying forces throughout Indo-China in 1941 (the French retained administrative control), encouraged nationalists to make slightly bolder statements; following an ill-advised anti-French demonstration in Phnom Penh in July 1942 several prominent Khmer were imprisoned and the newspaper *Angkor Wat* was shut down.

In 1941 the Thai took advantage of French defeats in Europe and attacked French positions in Laos and Cambodia. Thailand thus regained control over most of Cambodia's north-west, and King Monivong, who died soon afterwards, was replaced by his nineteen-year-old grandson, Norodom Sihanouk, then a high-school student in Saigon and considered pliable by the French. Over the next few years, Sihanouk proved a willing student of the French, and the nationalists remained quiescent, in exile or in jail.

In March 1945 the Japanese suddenly imprisoned French administrators throughout Indo-China and informed local authorities that Vietnam, Laos and Cambodia had become

Plate 41 (a) and (b)   Palace mural, Phnom Penh

independent. Sihanouk's cabinet proceeded cautiously until September, when on the eve of Japan's surrender a more nationalist cabinet under a former editor of *Angkor Wat (Nagara Vatta)*, Son Ngoc Thanh, held office briefly, and sought to open relations with the communist government in southern Vietnam. Time soon ran out. Thanh was imprisoned by the French in October 1945, when they returned to the area in force. Sihanouk and most of the elite, however, had gained a taste for independence. To regain control, and to buy time, the French decided to open up their administration to permit political parties and a constitution.[10]

Although the year 1945 is not as sharp a turning point in Cambodian history as it is, for example, in Vietnam or Indonesia, there are several reasons for closing a narrative of post-Angkorian Cambodian history at this point, and opening another with the post-war period. For one thing, the range of available sources changed dramatically as Cambodia emerged, tentatively and without much enthusiasm, into a wider, more violent and inattentive world. Political experiments of the 1940s and early 1950s, while unsuccessful, had far-reaching effects on subsequent political choices made by Sihanouk in the first instance and later by people who opposed him. The political history of Cambodia after 1945 differs also from pre-colonial history, despite many continuities, because Vietnamese and Thai behaviour towards Cambodia responded to international pressures and foreign ideologies as well as to precedents from the past. After 1945 Cambodian history became a portion of world history, affected by decisions taken in Washington, Moscow and Beijing as well as in the capitals of Thailand and Vietnam. That many Cambodians failed to perceive these changes, and proceeded instead along lines laid down for them by tradition, meant that outside power impinging on Cambodia took many Cambodians by surprise. The results of the encounter, as we shall see, were often extremely painful for the Khmer, even when the rationale of the external powers was not understood.

---

[10] On events in Cambodia in 1945, see David P. Chandler, *The Tragedy of Cambodian History*. New Haven, Conn.: Yale University Press, 1991, pp. 14–28.

17

Cambodia since 1945

In the aftermath of the Second World War, politics in Cambodia were dominated by French attempts to buy time, by the newly established, moderately pro-independence Democrat Party, which won elections in 1946, 1947 and 1951, and by armed resistance to French rule. By 1950, the resistance had come under the control of the Vietnamese communist movement.[1]

In 1945 the French were unwilling to consider granting independence to their possessions in Indo-China. Militarily, however, they were for the moment too weak to enforce their will, so in Laos, Cambodia and especially Vietnam they went through the motions of negotiating with independence-minded groups (and in Vietnam's case with an incumbent communist regime) while concealing their intention to retain power throughout the region for an indefinite length of time.

The Democrat Party was founded in Phnom Penh in 1946 by a group of intellectuals and civil servants. Many of them had been associated in the 1930s with the newspaper *Angkor Wat*, and in 1945 with Son Ngoc Thanh. The leader of the Party was a young prince, Sisowath Yuthevong, who had recently returned from over a decade of advanced study in France. Yuthevong had made friends in French government circles, and especially in the ranks of the Socialist Party there. After his own Party had won a majority in the Constituent Assembly elected toward the end

[1] The political history of this period is covered in detail by David P. Chandler, *The Tragedy of Cambodian History: Politics, war and revolution since 1945*. New Haven, Conn.: Yale University Press, 1991.

of 1946, Prince Yuthevong and his colleagues drafted a constitution for Cambodia, modelled closely on the one recently
promulgated by the Fourth Republic in France. King Sihanouk,
entranced for the moment with the idea of democratic reform,
and perhaps by the thought of independence, agreed to pro-
mulgate the text, which gave greater powers to the National
Assembly than to the King, who figured as a ceremonial chief of
state, like the French President at the time. The French authorities in Cambodia concurred with the text, which failed to
undermine their control. The powers granted to the Assembly
did not include fiscal independence, or jurisdiction over foreign
affairs, and the Constitution placed Cambodia formally in the
recently formed French Union, which had its headquarters in
France. Because of the Democrats' nationalist, law-abiding
credentials and the Party's organizational flair, their candidates
won large majorities to the National Assembly in 1947 (shortly
after Yuthevong's untimely death) and again in 1951. No other
political parties – including those clandestinely financed by the
French – attracted significant support.

Throughout the late 1940s, Democrat 'governments' pursued
negotiations with the French, rather than armed struggle, and in
1949 the French allowed Cambodia some control over minis-
tries not essential to France's Indo-China War. In Cambodia,
fighting was less intense than in Vietnam and more sporadic. In
the north-west it was encouraged by the Thai, anxious to retain
control over Battambang and Siem Reap, which they relinquished with bad grace under international pressure at the end
of 1946. Along the Vietnamese border, Vietnamese communist
influence was widespread. In other sections of the country, more
or less autonomous bands, some more nationalistic than others,
harassed French outposts and pillaged local people. By 1950
many of these bands had rallied to the King, while others had
fallen under the control of the Indo-China Communist Party,
dominated by Vietnam. In 1951 a separate Cambodian Party
was founded by the Vietnamese, to support Vietnam's struggle
and to conduct armed resistance to the French on Cambodian
soil. Most of the men placed in charge of the new Party by the
Vietnamese were Cambodians born in southern Vietnam. As
we shall see, the close but often abrasive relationship between
the movement and its Vietnamese patrons was an important
ingredient of its history.

In 1951–2, as the war dragged on, King Sihanouk became more popular, more active and more self-confident. The Democrats evolved into a more sophisticated, quasi-republican movement. Sihanouk resented them, as his French advisors had always done, and sought to gain control of Cambodia's campaign for independence. As he moved closer to genuine power he overrode the 1947 constitution, claiming to be within his rights because as King he had promulgated the document. His increasingly dictatorial style, encouraged by anti-Democrat French and Khmer advisors, alienated many promising young Cambodians, and drove some, who were studying in France, into the French Communist Party. One young Cambodian to take this route was Saloth Sar (1928–), known since 1976 by his revolutionary pseudonym, Pol Pot.[2] Others, later prominent in the Cambodian Communist movement, included Khieu Samphan, Son Sen and Ieng Sary.

In 1952 the King dissolved the Democrat government and closed down the Assembly, ruling by decree until the kingdom gained its independence. In effect, this move turned the 1947 Constitution into an instrument of Sihanouk's will, and put an end to political pluralism in the country. The King's Royal Crusade for Independence was a clever and intense public relations campaign that surprised and angered the French, who had taken Sihanouk's francophilia for granted. In late 1953 France caved in and granted Cambodia almost complete independence. As a quasi-independent state, Cambodia sent a delegation to the Geneva Conference in 1954, and withstood Vietnamese pressure to have Cambodia's communist guerrillas recognized as a legitimate political force. The Conference stipulated, however, that national elections be held in Cambodia in 1955.

In early 1955, Sihanouk suddenly abdicated the throne, turning it over to his father, Norodom Suramarit. Soon afterwards, he founded a national political movement that aimed to overshadow and obliterate existing political parties. In elections held in 1955 Sihanouk's movement, the Sangkum, gained all

---

[2] For a path-breaking history of Cambodian radicalism, see Ben Kiernan, *How Pol Pot Came to Power*. London: Verso, 1984. See also David P. Chandler, *Brother Number One: a Political Biography of Pol Pot*, Boulder, Col.: Westview Press, 1992; and Serge Thion, *Watching Cambodia*; Bangkok: 1993, a stimulating collection of essays.

the seats. The election was marked by widespread fraud and violence on the part of Sihanouk's supporters. Its short-term effect was to discredit the Democrats and a communist front party, which had unsuccessfully run candidates in the election. Sangkum candidates, hand-picked by Sihanouk, repeated the sweep unopposed in 1958 and 1962. In 1966 the Prince opened up the balloting to allow Sangkum candidates to compete against each other in electorates. The result was a more representative, less radical Assembly that owed little allegiance to Sihanouk.

The fifteen years that followed the 1955 elections are often referred to as the Sihanouk era. They were marked by political stability, except towards the end, and by considerable economic advances. During these years Cambodia prospered from taxes levied on exports of rice and rubber and from substantial infusions of foreign aid. The period was also stamped with Sihanouk's volatile, patriotic, narcissistic personality. For several years, opposition to the Sangkum was never tolerated and seldom voiced. Taxes gained from exports, supplemented by foreign aid, paid Cambodia's bills, improved its infrastructure, and allowed the Prince to direct Sangkum budgets toward educational and public health projects as well as towards often ostentatious public works. In many cases, Sihanouk's fondness for public relations and his impatience with advice undermined the Sangkum's successes. Because the Prince was not interested in genuine social change (although he favoured educational institutions that produced it), he failed to address issues of social equity or human rights. Freedoms of association, expression and assembly, guaranteed by the 1947 Constitution which remained in force, were curtailed. Sihanouk sought and accepted very little advice, except in the realm of foreign affairs. He dominated the media and ran the country like a personal possession. Disagreement with the regime, as so often in Cambodian history, was considered tantamount to treason.[3]

In foreign affairs, the Prince pursued a supposedly neutralist

[3] See Norodom Sihanouk, *Souvenirs doux et amers*. Paris: Fayard, 1981, which should be used with caution; and Charles Meyer, *Derrière le sourire khmer*. Paris: Plon, 1971.

policy aimed at obtaining foreign aid from as many countries as possible and at maintaining Cambodian independence *vis-à-vis* its pro-American neighbours, Thailand and South Vietnam. The policy led the Prince into an alliance with communist China, and friendship with nations in the Soviet bloc, at the height of the Cold War. The bias of his supposed neutrality enraged policy-makers in the United States, but for several years his policies had the advantage for Cambodia of keeping the country out of the Vietnam War.

Domestically, Sihanouk in his speeches and writings stressed Cambodia's past greatness, its high status in the developing world, and his own indispensability. His voice, photographs and writings blanketed the Cambodian media. Emphasizing the importance of education and self-reliance, he probably increased the self-confidence of thousands of his subjects, inured by centuries to defer to their superiors and to 'know their place'. Referring to himself as 'Prince Papa' (*samdech euv*) he seemed reluctant to allow his 'children' to mature, preferring them to act as permanent extras in the musical called 'Cambodia' which he staged and starred in. In student and intellectual circles, his popularity, never strong, began to fade in the mid-1960s, particularly when chances of employment for high school and university graduates declined.

Sihanouk called his mixture of policies 'Buddhist socialism' and claimed that the doctrine, inherited from Angkorian practice, would keep Cambodia from becoming either a capitalist or a socialist nation. Very little socialism or Buddhist thinking was involved. The doctrine, such as it was, allowed Sihanouk considerable freedom of manoeuvre.

When his father, King Suramarit, died in 1960, Sihanouk moved to occupy the newly created position of Chief of State, while retaining his mother, Queen Kossamak, as a ceremonial monarch. In effect, the Prince's decision, which met his own short-term political requirements, put an end to royalty in Cambodia – a form of government that had persisted there for well over a thousand years. Unfortunately, the absolutism that had often characterized the monarchy remained in place. The move freed the Prince from any ceremonial responsibilities, and his behaviour soon became, from the perspective of his opponents, even more authoritarian and erratic.

Plots to overthrow Prince Sihanouk in 1958–9 were hatched in Saigon and Bangkok, with US knowledge, but they failed, and Sihanouk became increasingly convinced of his invincibility and political *savoir-faire*. His self-estimates were echoed by solicitous advisors, journalists and foreign dignitaries who had their own scenarios for Cambodia. To many of these figures, and to Sihanouk himself, the Prince and 'Cambodia' were one and the same thing. Craving approval, he allowed himself to be compared to the Angkorian kings, and claimed that his subjects' attitudes toward him were identical to those their ancestors had held toward their monarchs in Angkorian times.

As the Second Indo-China War (1960–75) intensified in Laos and Vietnam, Sihanouk decided in 1963 to break off US military and economic aid, so as not to offend the Vietnamese communists. Sihanouk hoped to prevent Cambodia from becoming a battlefield. He also presumed that China and France, which shared his anti-Americanism, would step in to make up for the money he had lost. American aid had been used for many years to balance the national budget and pay his armed forces. Not enough money and very little equipment were forthcoming from France and China. The Cambodian army under General Lon Nol, who was chosen to lead it because of his loyalty rather than his competence, became more ineffective than ever, and the North Vietnamese, after coming to secret agreements with the Prince, began to use Cambodia as a conduit for troops and military supplies. Their bases in Cambodia, photographed from the air by the United States, made Americans even more contemptuous of his 'neutrality'.

Cambodia's clandestine communist movement, led from the shadows by Saloth Sar, was hamstrung by Sihanouk's popularity among Cambodia's poor and by its own alliance with the Vietnamese, which made the Cambodian communists unable to oppose the Prince publicly. Sihanouk kept the movement off-balance by his pro-communist foreign policy, and domestically by threats and intimidation. In 1963 Saloth Sar and several other high-ranking party figures, fearing for their lives, sought sanctuary in a Vietnamese communist encampment on the Vietnam–Cambodia border.

From there, Saloth Sar travelled in 1965 to Hanoi and

Beijing, probably at the request of the Vietnamese communist authorities. When he arrived in Hanoi, he was chastised at length by high-ranking Vietnamese communists for the manifesto which he and his colleagues had drawn up for Cambodia, in secret, five years before. The text called for the liberation of Cambodia from feudalism, and made no reference to the Indo-China War. The Vietnamese called the document naïve and theoretically unsound. A Vietnamese document reporting the encounter stated that at the end of the Vietnamese tirade 'Saloth Sar said nothing'. After five more months in Vietnam, when nothing is known of his activities, Saloth Sar went on to China. His visit was secret, for the existence of the Cambodian party was still concealed, and officially the Chinese were allied to Sihanouk. At the same time, the Cultural Revolution was about to sweep through China. Sar found the Chinese approach to revolution more authentic than Vietnam's, more radical and more to his taste. There is some evidence that Chinese officials found him sympathetic. In any case, Sar soon abandoned his dependence on Vietnam, without revealing his change of heart to his patrons in Hanoi. In June 1966, when Sar returned to Cambodia, he moved his headquarters away from Vietnamese troop concentrations into the heavily forested Cambodian province of Ratanakiri.[4]

By that time Sihanouk's balancing act had begun to fail. In early 1968 the Cambodian communists opened up armed struggle against his regime – a move that probably had Vietnamese approval. Communist attacks tied down Cambodian military units in costly operations in the north-east. Rice sales to Vietnamese communist forces depleted the surpluses Cambodia had counted on to earn export taxes. Following the Tet Offensive in Vietnam in 1968, Vietnamese pressure on Cambodia's resources intensified, and Cambodia's export economy also began to falter, alienating Cambodia's small entrepreneurial class. Students and intellectuals were already disillusioned with Sihanouk's regime. Sihanouk became increasingly depressed,

---

[4] The relations between the Vietnamese and the Cambodian Communists are described in J. Thomas Engelbert and Christopher Goscha, *Falling Out of Touch*, Clayton, Australia, in press, which draws heavily on Vietnamese archival materials.

and spent most of his time producing sentimental feature films, making speeches and entertaining foreign guests. At the same time, fearful of what might happen in Vietnam, he edged uneasily toward reopening diplomatic relations with the United States. These were renewed in 1969, and Sihanouk allowed a more or less pro-American government led by General Lon Nol to take office in Phnom Penh. In January 1970 he left the country, ostensibly for medical treatment, but many observers at the time viewed his departure as flight. Cambodia had become too complicated for him to rule single-handed, and so, while still identifying himself with the country, he walked away from it, perhaps half-expecting to be called back.

Two months later, while he was still abroad, the National Assembly voted to remove him as Chief of State. When Sihanouk learned of the coup, he was en route between Moscow and Beijing. When he arrived in China, his first impulse was to ask for political asylum in France, but Chou En-lai (Zhou Enlai) and others persuaded him to form a united front with communists from Vietnam, Laos and Cambodia, with a view to throwing out the Americans and the non-communist governments they supported in Indo-China. After forming the alliance, which spread the Vietnam War into Cambodia, the Prince became a figurehead ruler of a government in exile, taking up cosseted residence in Beijing. In Cambodia, the Communist Party swiftly took command of the resistance. In October 1970 the government in Phnom Penh renamed the country the Khmer Republic, with Lon Nol as its Chief of State. Many participants in the regime were former Democrats who had long resented Sihanouk's arbitrary rule. Others were military officers hoping to enrich themselves by their alliance with the United States.

For the next five years Cambodia was subjected to brutal American bombing, a civil war and Vietnamese invasions in the course of which hundreds of thousands of Cambodians, many of them civilians, were killed. By 1973 the so-called Khmer Republic controlled less than a quarter of the country. Politically, the republican government was never able to demonstrate its competence. Hundreds of thousands of refugees, fleeing combat and the US bombing, flooded into the cities of Phnom Penh and Battambang. Corruption flourished, and

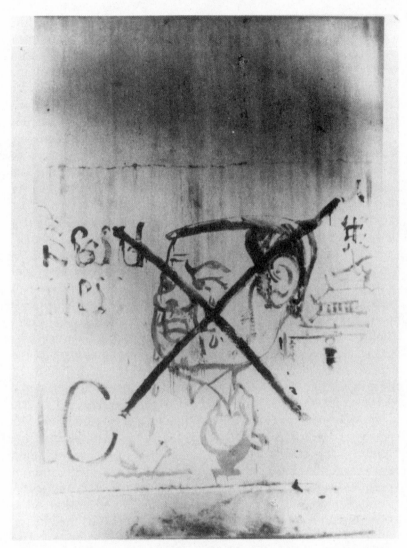

Plate 42   Poster showing head of Norodom Sihanouk, with graffiti, 1970. This followed his fall from power

to many Cambodians, particularly young people, the unseen enemy seemed to offer an attractive alternative to Lon Nol.

In 1970–1 North Vietnamese armed forces smashed Lon Nol's troops, which carried out no further offensives for the remainder of the war. Behind the shield formed by the Vietnamese, the Cambodian communists, long ago nicknamed 'Khmers Rouges' by Sihanouk, recruited new members and trained them in a rough and ready form of socialism. Some joined the movement mistakenly thinking they could restore Sihanouk to power, but most were drawn in by the communists' Utopian social agenda, which promised to sweep aside centuries of injustice inflicted on Cambodia's rural poor. In terms of social background, the movement mixed poor peasants with intellectuals from the towns, many of whom had been trained as school-teachers. The word 'communist', however, was never mentioned outside the party's inner circles, thus allowing the movement to seem different in orientation from Vietnam's party: more nationalistic and more Cambodian.

In 1971–2, several hundred Cambodian communists were sent down from Hanoi to aid the revolution (some of them had been in exile in Vietnam since 1954). They were suspected of Vietnamese sympathies and in 1972–3 most of them were secretly purged. By the end of 1972, when Vietnamese communist troops withdrew from Cambodia – as part of the cease-fire agreements reached in Paris by the Vietnamese with the Americans – the Khmer Rouge leadership was in the hands of those who, like Saloth Sar, had remained in Cambodia in the 1950s and 1960s and were antipathetic to Vietnam.

The war now pitted Cambodians against Cambodians. For two years conditions for combatants were brutal in the extreme. Neither side allowed prisoners to survive. American bombing in 1973 probably kept the communists from taking Phnom Penh, and certainly inflicted tens of thousands of casualties. A Khmer Rouge attack on the capital in 1974 also failed. In the zones under communist control, radical social arrangements, including the collectivization of land, were introduced. The Khmer Rouge were brutal to prisoners and severe in their dealings with everyone else. People in Republican zones, suffering runaway inflation, undernourishment, disease and the rampant corruption of the regime, hoped that the largely invisible Khmer Rouge would deliver peace and social welfare to all Khmers. Phnom Penh fell to the communists in April 1975, two weeks before their Vietnamese counterparts were able to occupy Saigon.

What happened in Cambodia over the next few weeks came as a shock to foreigners (those in Cambodia were driven out within a month), to Cambodia's urban population, and to anyone who had worked for the ill-fated Khmer Republic. The communists' clandestine radio boasted that with the 'liberation' of Phnom Penh, 'over 2,000 years of Cambodian history' had ended. The population of the city, exhausted by warfare, longed for reconciliation.

They were cruelly deceived. In victory, the communists were not magnanimous. Within a week all the towns and cities under Republican control were evacuated by force. Over two million men, women and children were driven into the countryside to take up their lives as agricultural workers, in accordance with a doctrine, derived from China, which held that poor peasants, and a handful of manual workers, were the only worthwhile members of society. In the exodus from the towns thousands of Cambodians died, and thousands more, particularly former soldiers, were secretly executed *en masse*. Other social policies that came into effect at this time abolished money, markets, organized religion, schools, private property and freedom of movement. Everyone was made to wear peasant costume, and came under the control of what the Khmer Rouge referred to as the 'organization' (*angkar*) – a handful of unseen party officials – whose often ambiguous commands were to be obeyed under pain of death.[5]

The leaders of the movement remained concealed. For several months, as the country was organized into new geographic zones with party officials in charge, and as 'new people' (evacuees) were absorbed, often painfully, into populations of 'base people' loyal to the regime, Saloth Sar and his colleagues held office under heavy guard in the abandoned capital.

In a constitution promulgated in January 1976, the state announced that its new name was to be Democratic

---

[5] Two excellent accounts of the Khmer Rouge era are: François Ponchaud, *Cambodia Year Zero*. New York: Henry Holt, 1978; and Elizabeth Becker, *When the War Was Over*. New York: Simon & Schuster, 1986. See also Michael Vickery, *Cambodia 1975–1982*. Boston, Mass.: South End Press, 1983; and Karl Jackson (ed.), *Cambodia 1975–1978: Rendez-vous with death*. Princeton, N.J.: Princeton University Press, 1989.

Kampuchea, and promised elections for a national assembly three months later. When these occurred, only 'base people' were allowed to vote, and slates of candidates, named by the party, were split among supposed peasants, soldiers and industrial workers. Among the candidates drawn from 'rubber plantation workers' was someone called 'Pol Pot', who became Democratic Kampuchea's prime minister. It was over a year before outsiders were able to identify this shadowy figure as Saloth Sar; Sar himself did not admit the connection until after he had been driven from power in 1979. When the new government took office Prince Sihanouk, who had returned from China in 1975 and up until this time had been nominally in charge of the country, was shunted aside and placed under house arrest.

The elections and the constitution were a public relations exercise for overseas consumption. Neither was referred to again in Democratic Kampuchea. Instead, Pol Pot and his most trusted colleagues swiftly set in motion a set of Utopian policies aimed at achieving socialism in Cambodia more quickly and more thoroughly than had been achieved anywhere else in the world. The short-term effect of these ideas was that over a million Cambodians died within months from malnutrition, overwork, wrongly treated diseases and execution. The policies were enshrined in an unpublished four-year plan, which sought to double Cambodia's agricultural output, especially in rice, in order to earn money from exports with which to pay for industrialization. It seems that the plan was a naïve and hasty copy of Chinese and Soviet models. Did Pol Pot know that these had failed? It is impossible to say, but it seems probable that, like his more radical counterparts in China, he believed that totally mobilized, totally indoctrinated peasants with 'bare hands' could construct a country that had never been constructed under earlier, 'feudalistic' regimes.

A key motto of Democratic Kampuchea was 'three tonnes per hectare', referring to a national target average yield of threshed rice. The goal was nearly three times as high as average yields in pre-revolutionary times. It was foolhardy, to say the least, for party officials to expect this kind of production in the aftermath of a civil war in an impoverished country that was filled with refugees and had no material incentives. By confusing the laws of history with their own wishful thinking, Pol Pot and his colleagues came close to destroying the country.[6]

Unsurprisingly, the four-year plan was in practice a disaster. Surpluses, where they existed, were siphoned off by the state, and the people who had grown them starved. Ill-conceived and poorly built irrigation works claimed thousands of workers' lives and wreaked ecological havoc. Thousands of other Cambodians succumbed to amateur 'medical' treatment meted out by untrained, self-confident adolescents. Others were executed for such offences as speaking foreign languages or foraging for food. Since Pol Pot and his colleagues were unable to conceive of these losses and disasters as connected with revolutionary policies or practice, and were committed to holding on to power at all costs, they blamed 'microbes' or 'traitors' inside the Party. Towards the end of 1976, a series of far-reaching purges was set in motion that took the lives of several thousand party members, who were accused of working for foreign intelligence services to undermine the revolution. The written 'confessions' of over 4,000 of these men and women have survived, and provide gruesome documentation for historians of the regime.

As Democratic Kampuchea tore itself apart, its leaders instigated a series of brutal cross-border raids into Vietnam, where they hoped to bestir the Cambodian minority and regain territory 'lost' to Vietnam centuries before. In this sense, the attacks, which were always brutal, were a failure, but until the end of 1977 they were not publicized by either side, nor were vigorous Vietnamese ripostes. The Communist Parties of Cambodia and Vietnam, on the surface at least, remained 'fraternal'.

In September 1977, Pol Pot made a state visit to China, where he was warmly welcomed as an official guest by Mao Tse-tung's successor, Hua Kuo-feng. A few days before his departure, in a long speech, Pol Pot finally admitted the existence of the Communist Party of Kampuchea, taking credit on the Party's

[6] For the text of the four-year plan, see David P. Chandler, Ben Kiernan and Chanthou Boua (ed. and tr.), *Pol Pot Plans the Future: Confidential leadership documents from Democratic Kampuchea, 1976–1977*. New Haven, Conn.: Yale University Southeast Asia Program, 1988, pp. 36–118.

Plate 43   Photographs of victims, Tuol Sleng, 1991

Plate 44   Democratic Cambodia cadre on the Thai border, 1979

behalf for the revolutionary successes which the speech proclaimed. The visit was probably spurred by Chinese approval
for Cambodian attacks on Vietnam, that was thought to have
taken the side of the USSR in the Sino-Soviet ideological conflict. Pol Pot came away with promises of increased military aid.
He may even have hoped for Chinese 'volunteers', although
they were not forthcoming. The war intensified when he returned to Phnom Penh; diplomatic relations between Cambodia
and Vietnam were broken off at the end of the year.

Throughout 1978 the leaders of Democratic Kampuchea
tried desperately to open up the country to outside recognition
while continuing both their war against Vietnam and the secret
purges inside the Party. The most far-reaching of the purges
killed thousands of men and women in the eastern part of the
country, bordering Vietnam, where Pol Pot blamed Vietnamese
military successes on Cambodian traitors. Hundreds of party
members, most of them soldiers, fled for their lives. They sought

Plate 45   Skulls: the killing fields

sanctuary across the border, where they were soon formed by the Vietnamese into a government in exile.

On Christmas Eve 1978 Vietnamese forces launched a massive invasion of Cambodia, claiming that the attack was being made by a Cambodian liberation front. Phnom Penh was evacuated by 6 January – Pol Pot fled to Thailand in a helicopter – and the Democratic Kampuchean regime disappeared almost overnight: Pol Pot had never trusted the population sufficiently to arm them in their own defence, and most Cambodians welcomed the invaders. In the place of Democratic Kampuchea the Vietnamese invaders installed a sympathetic government composed of Khmer Rouge defectors and Cambodians who had earlier sought refuge in Vietnam. The regime moved as quickly as it could, given its meagre resources, to restore institutions destroyed or abandoned under Democratic Kampuchea – in-

Plate 46   Drawing by Ra Bony, a boy in a refugee camp, 1982. A remembered image of two mountain warriors of Angkor Wat. They are tied together by the wrists. One is good, one bad; originally they inhabited the same body

cluding cities, money, schools, markets and freedom of movement. Political controls remained severe, and it became clear to
many that Vietnam's occupation of the country fitted into a
long-term strategic plan to join the components of Indo-China
into a Vietnam-dominated federation.

The disappearance of the Khmer Rouge, the widespread
famine, and uncertainty about Vietnamese intentions led hundreds of thousands of Cambodians to flee to Thailand in 1979
and 1980. Refugee camps were established in Thailand under
the auspices of the United Nations. By 1981, over 300,000
of these refugees had found permanent residence in France,
Australia, the United States and elsewhere. A similar number
remained in the refugee camps along the border and were fed by
the UN. Millions of their compatriots criss-crossed the country
looking for relatives and trying to regain their former homes.
In the process, few crops were planted and tens of thousands
starved.[7]

In the meantime, the remnants of Pol Pot's army, stumbling
across the border, were welcomed, fed and refitted by Thai
military authorities frightened by the possibility of a Vietnamese
invasion. Pol Pot also received support from the Chinese, who
remained allied to him, and indirectly from the United States,
which was eager to please China and to punish Vietnam both
for its invasion of Cambodia and for defeating the United
States. With such powerful allies Democratic Kampuchea held
on to Cambodia's seat at the United Nations, the only government in exile to do so, and Vietnam felt obliged to keep a large
army on Cambodian soil.

As testimony about the horrors of Democratic Kampuchea
reached the outside world via refugees and the regime in Phnom
Penh the United States and its allies sought to save face by
establishing a 'coalition' Cambodian government on the Thai
border, made up of the Khmer Rouge and factions loyal to
Prince Sihanouk (who in 1979 had returned to live in Beijing)
and one of his former prime ministers, Son Sann. To make the
coalition more palatable, it was claimed that the Communist
Party of Kampuchea was dissolved, but defectors from the

---

[7] For a vivid description of this period, see William Shawcross, *The Quality
of Mercy*. New York: Simon & Schuster, 1984.

Plate 47 Revolutionary poster, Phnom Penh, 1988

movement reported that its leaders remained in place and that Pol Pot was still in control. At the same time, it governed the people it controlled far less brutally than during its time in power. Among some Cambodians it gained a healthy reputation for its anti-Vietnamese stance and its relatively honest officials. The Phnom Penh government, in turn, continued to be isolated from international support and, more importantly, from the possibility of aid from countries outside the Soviet bloc.[8]

The stalemate began to alter in the later 1980s following the loosening of communist power in the Soviet bloc. One effect of the process was to deprive Vietnam and Cambodia of large amounts of Soviet aid. Vietnam was no longer able to sustain its army of occupation in Cambodia. Its last units were withdrawn in September 1989. Before their departure, the Phnom Penh regime introduced a series of popular reforms, perhaps hoping to stave off an insurrection. These included legalizing private

---

[8] For a perceptive analysis of Cambodia in the 1980s, see Michael Vickery, *Kampuchea*. London: Frances Pinter, 1986.

property, altering the flag and reinstating Buddhism as Cambodia's state religion. Although the government now claimed to be a 'liberal democracy', its unelected leaders remained in place and opposition parties were banned. Economically, Cambodia was quickly opened up to exploitation; hundreds of thousands of tons of timber and millions of dollars worth of gemstones were exported, without any controls, to Thailand and Vietnam, enriching foreign and local entrepreneurs often linked to opposing political factions.

The withdrawal of the Vietnamese, the opening up of the country and the end of the Cold War encouraged larger powers to seek a permanent peace settlement for Cambodia, and spirited negotiations began in 1989–90, culminating in the Paris Peace Accords of October 1991, whereby a new executive power was installed in Phnom Penh, with United Nations backing. The government *pro tem* consisted of the former anti-Vietnamese coalition plus the Phnom Penh regime. In theory, these uneasy bedfellows would disarm and co-operate while the United Nations prepared the country for 'free and fair' nation-wide elections in which the factions and new political groupings were entitled to participate.

Despite over $2 billion in UN administrative costs, consider-able good will, and hard work by UN officials and ordinary Cambodians – by mid-1993 nearly five million Cambodians registered to vote – the UN-sponsored peace plan was soon threatened by the Khmer Rouge's refusal to abide by the pro-visions they had agreed upon in Paris. The Khmer Rouge claimed, erroneously, that thousands of Vietnamese soldiers remained on duty in the country and, with more justice, that the UN had not been sufficiently harsh in its treatment of the incumbent regime, which was after all expected to provide the administrative infrastructure for the process. To back up its points, Khmer Rouge units assassinated over a hundred of what it called 'secret agents' – unarmed Vietnamese civilians – in random attacks throughout the country. The Phnom Penh government, meanwhile, intimidated workers for the new political parties, and campaigned vigorously against what it predicted would be a renewal of 'genocide' if any other political party was allowed to win.

In the event, the elections were peaceful. Over 90 per cent

of the registered voters went to the polls. The message they delivered was ambiguous. A royalist party led by Sihanouk's eldest son, Norodom Rannaridh, won seven more seats than the party formed by the incumbent government to contest the elections. For the first time in Cambodian history, a majority of Cambodians had voted against an armed incumbent government.

In the ensuing weeks, the two largest parties jockeyed for position, agreeing in the end to form a coalition government that would draft a new constitution. By the end of 1993 the constitution was in place and Cambodia had become a monarchy once again, with Sihanouk reinstalled as King. Sihanouk, who was seriously ill, accepted the honour with good grace, in spite, or perhaps because, of the fact that the monarch enjoyed no genuine political power. The King continued to live outside the country, returning for brief, ceremonial sojourns, while his son, Norodom Rannaridh, shared power as co-Prime Minister with the former communist Prime Minister, Hun Sen. The new government was recognized by countries that had shunned the preceding regime, and much-needed development aid began to arrive in substantial quantities. The country was still plagued by poverty, disease and corruption; by the continuing presence of Khmer Rouge guerrillas in the north and north-west; and by pressures from the outside world on its natural resources, which the Cambodians found difficult to resist. In early 1994, most analysts agreed that Cambodia was more at peace than it had been since the 1960s. It was certainly becoming more closely integrated into the rest of the region than it had been since before the arrival of the French.

Cambodian political history since the Second World War, and probably for a much longer period, can be characterized very broadly as a chronic failure of contending groups to compromise their positions or to share power with one another. These absolutist tendencies have deep roots in Cambodian tradition, as we have seen; in fact, they form one of the most perceptible continuities in two millennia of Cambodia's recorded history. Political pluralism in the late 1940s and early 1950s, extremely tentative in any case, was given scant encouragement by Sihanouk or the French, who urged the King to be more despotic. Sihanouk's dictatorial style, in turn, went unchecked throughout his years in power; it allowed no alternative styles of government, based on the unfamiliar concepts of pluralism or consensus (the latter word has no equivalent in Khmer), to develop. The Prince's failure to compromise and his harsh treatment of opponents encouraged them, when they had replaced him, to be uncompromising also. What was at stake, it seemed, was less the welfare of the people than to obtain access to theoretically unlimited power. In this sense, the Stalinist organization favored by Pol Pot can be seen in part as reflecting traditional and enduring Cambodian ideas of political control. In the 1960s, the tensions that developed between the opposition on the one hand and the Prince on the other, exacerbated by the Second Indo-China War, removed him from office and replaced him with a series of authoritarian regimes.

Although it is possible to study twentieth-century Cambodian politics from an indigenous perspective, it is crucial to recall that the country's location, topography and demographic weakness meant that, regardless of its internal politics, it was bound to be affected by events in Vietnam, and that sooner or later it would be engulfed by the Indo-China War. Cambodia's proximity to Vietnam affected its own communist movement and reduced any Cambodian government's capacity to maintain law and order. Cambodia's problematic psychological relations with Vietnam, rooted perhaps in nineteenth-century events, made it difficult for any Cambodian government, before 1979 at least, to form a genuine alliance with Vietnam or to confront it directly. Similarly, Vietnam, when facing Cambodia, has often found it impossible to formulate policies that do not contain a 'civilizing mission'.

Cambodian history often weighed heavily on its twentieth-century political figures. As we have seen, Sihanouk allowed his supporters to compare him favourably to Angkorian monarchs, and especially to Jayavarman VII. Ideas of Cambodia's past greatness also influenced General Lon Nol, who believed that in his holy war against Vietnamese 'unbelievers', virtuous Cambodian Buddhism, coupled with armed force, would inevitably triumph. Pol Pot was similarly misled. In his marathon 1977 speech, he remarked: 'If our people can build Angkor, they are capable of anything.' He seems seriously to have believed that his armies were capable (had they not been betrayed) of defeating the vastly more numerous Vietnamese.

The weight of the past on these three men, combined with the already noted tendency of the French to stress Cambodia's 'decline' and with a generalized distrust of the Vietnamese, has made it difficult for many Cambodians to come to grips with their own history, before and after 1945, with a view to making it respond to twentieth-century pressures and realities. Accustomed to blaming foreigners for Cambodian misfortunes – the Vietnamese are the favourite scapegoats – the quintessentially Khmer regimes of Sihanouk, Lon Nol and Pol Pot have escaped sustained indigenous analysis, except in terms of personalities, betrayals and cliques: the time-honoured 'explanations' that most Cambodians have been contented with in the political sphere. In other words, Cambodians seem reluctant to ask why these men came to power as they did, and to what extent their behaviour in office reflected aspects of Cambodian culture that were conducive to totalitarian rule.

Intense and widely shared conservatism, perhaps, makes Cambodians reluctant to back away from traditions that have repeatedly – one could almost say systematically – delivered suffering and injustice. These traditions, and the hierarchical personal relations enshrined in them, form much of the substance of Cambodia's 'two thousand years of history' and provide a way of examining the country that is less useful when applied to Thailand and Vietnam. Exactly why this should be so is problematic.

Much of Cambodia's uniqueness, in other words, may well spring from the deep continuities in its history and culture – examined in detail in this book – rather than from calculated or merely prudent responses to the deep, rapid and largely destructive influences of modern times. Pol Pot's revolution failed in large part because so many Cambodians, finding it irrelevant, were unwilling and unable to carry it out. A decade of Vietnamese occupation and experiments with a less-demanding form of socialism seem to have left no lasting marks. The so-called 'timelessness' of twentieth-century Cambodia, made up to a large extent of its self-referring frames of reference, has been part of its appeal to visitors and scholars alike for many years. But as Cambodia opens up whether willingly or not to the wider world, without sustained protection, it is uncertain if its inward-looking, family-orientated conservatism, so helpful in the past, will be sufficient for or of much help in its struggle to survive as an independent twentieth-century state.

Appendix I: Chronological Survey of Angkor's Rulers

Jayavarman II (*c.*770–*c.*834), normally regarded as the founder of Angkor, began his career as an exile and, returning to Cambodia, extended his dominion in a series of campaigns that led him from the lower Mekong to the north and west of the Great Lake. According to a much later inscription he had a series of capitals, the last being at Hariharālaya (Lolei), a few miles to the south-east of Siemreap. Claims to suzerainty over the Khmers by a Malay power were formally rejected when in 802, at Mahendraparvata in the Kulen hills, he consecrated the ideal of Khmer unity and independence. Historians used to date his reign from 802 to 850, but it now appears necessary to set it back at each end.

Jayavarman III (*c.*834–*c.*870): little is known about him except that he liked to hunt elephants. It is possible that his empire shrank, and was restored again by his successor.

The next king, Indravarman I (*r.* *c.*877–889/890), appears to have been linked to Jayavarman II's line, though his genealogical claims do not make the connection explicit.[1] He was responsible for the Preah Koh and the Bakong at Hariharālaya.

Yaśovarman I (*c.*889/890–*c.*910/912), whose accession may not have been peaceful, moved the capital to the north of where Siemreap now

---

[1] M. Vickery, Some remarks on early state formation on Cambodia. In *Southeast Asia in the 9th to 14th Centuries*, ed. D. Marr and A. Milner, Canberra: Research School of Pacific Studies, Australian National University, and Singapore: Institute of Southeast Asian Studies, 1986, pp. 95–115, at p. 104.

is, and where most later kings remained. His capital, Yaśodharapura, was centred on the Bakheng hill, which gives its name to the monument moulded to its peak, Yaśovarman's central shrine. His empire was claimed to extend to the south of Cambodia, to Champa, into Laos, and into Thailand. He was responsible for the great reservoir known as the Eastern Baray. Among other major works, he also built a massive embankment around his capital city and a causeway linking it to Hariharālaya.

Harsavarman I (*c.*910/912–*c.*923) came from Yaśovarman's immediate family. Possibly after the death of Yaśovarman the empire crumbled, with the kings at Angkor controlling a restricted area.

Īśānavarman II (*c.*923–*c.*928) is mentioned in some inscriptions: as far as these show, his empire may well have been confined to Angkor and the region of Battambang in the west.

Jayavarman IV (928–*c.*941) had a power base to the north of Angkor, at Koh Ker (referred to in an inscription as *Chok Gargyar*, 'Island of Glory'[2]). Here, at least since AD 922 (the date of an edict issued by him), he had been exercising power as a governor, vassal or rival of the previous king Īśānavarman II. He ruled over territories in Battambang, Siemreap, Kampong Thom, Kampong Cham and Ta Kev.

Harṣavarman II (*c.*941–944), Jayavarman's immediate successor, came to the throne in obscure circumstances, possibly amid conflict.

Rājendravarman II (944–*c.*968) restored Angkor after a period of neglect and consolidated the empire. He claimed descent from the rulers of Bhavapura, and brought together under his rule a number of territories not previously assimilated. His empire was claimed to extend to Vietnam, Laos, parts of Thailand, Burma and even China. In 950 he despatched an at least partly successful military expedition to Champa. His religious monuments include the Eastern Mebon and the Pre Rup.

Rajendravarman was followed by **Jayavarman V** (*c.*968–*c.*1000). Inconsistent versions of the date of succession to Rājendravarman may reflect strife. He built the Ta Kev monument at the western end of the

---

[2]   G. Coedès, *The Indianized States of Southeast Asia*, tr. S. Cowing. Canberra: Australian National University Press, 1968, p. 312, n. 46.

Eastern Baray as the centre of his capital Jayendranagarī. His younger sister married an Indian brahman Divākarabhaṭṭa from Mathurā.

Jayavarman's death was followed by several years of conflict between rivals. **Udayādityavarman I** (1002–1002) figures chiefly as a short-lived participant in an evidently very destructive contest for power at the capital. Udayādityavarman was followed at Angkor by Jayavīra-varman, who lasted until 1010; he however was never able to assert his control over the whole empire and was ousted in 1010; he is not usually reckoned in the list of kings.

The origins of **Sūryavarman I** (1002–1050) have been debated. It used to be thought that he was a usurper, and that he came from the west. His claims to the throne are not obviously worse than those of many other rulers generally regarded as legitimate, and his territorial base was in the east, on the Mekong. Beginning in 1000, he fought his way towards Angkor via the Dangreks and put an end to the reign of his predecessor at Angkor in 1010; the oath of allegiance sworn to him by his officials was dated AD 1011. Sūyavarman's monuments include four major *liṅga* shrines to north, south, east and west of the capital, and he was probably responsible for the Western Baray, the largest reservoir of all. Many inscriptions date from his reign, probably reflecting increasing competition for endowed land and the extension of the cultivated area.

The next ruler was **Udayādityavarman II** (1050–c.1066). Like other rulers, he becomes larger than life in the portraits of him offered by his inscriptions:

He excelled in seducing women to his will by his beauty, warriors by his heroism, sages by his good qualities, the people by his power, brahmans by his charity. Endowed with many noble qualities, when Sūryavarman went to the skies, this Prince of great energy was sworn universal monarch by his ministers.[3]

His temple mountain was the Baphuon, a great pyramid originally possessing a gilt tower. Udayādityavarman patronized the family of priests attached to the *devarāja* cult. The property bestowed upon the family at this time lay in the north-west of Cambodia, suggest-

---

[3]   A. Barth, *Inscriptions sanscrites du Cambodge.* Paris: Académie des Inscriptions et Belles-lettres, 1882, pp. 122–140; cited by L. P. Briggs, *The Ancient Khmer Empire*, Philadelphia, Pa: American Philosophical Society, 1951, p.168.

ing perhaps that migration and settlement were intensifying in the direction of Thailand.

During the reign of **Harsavarman III** (1066/1077–1080), according to Chinese sources, Angkor and Champa were jointly required to help China fight the Vietnamese. Subsequently there was war with Champa, in which the Chams claimed to have taken a city and offered prisoners and booty to a Cham national temple.

Jayavarman VI (1080–*c*.1107) came from a family said to have been ruling at Mahīdhara, possibly in Thailand, and his succession looks more irregular than most; he can be seen as the initiator of a new dynasty, sometimes identified as the Mahīdhara line. He was probably responsible for the great religious foundations at Phimai (up the Mun River in Thailand), where many Indian and local territorial gods, but especially the Buddha, were honoured.[4]

Dharanīndravarman I (1107–1112) was the older brother of the previous ruler; little is known about his short and doubtless unstable reign.

Sūryavarman II (1113–*c*.1150) is most famous as the builder of Angkor Wat, which was his central national shrine and probably contained the palace and administrative buildings within its enclosures. He was also active in war: successful campaigns against the Chams led to the installation of his own nominee on the Cham throne at Vijaya. It was during his reign that the Sung dynasty fled south; embassies were sent from Angkor to China in 1116 and 1120.

Dharanīndravarman II, the father of the later ruler Jayavarman VII, was credited in epigraphy with royal power; however, there is no evidence that he ruled at Angkor, and it is more accurate to place next on the list King **Yaśovarman II** (*c*.1150–*c*.1165), whose end, at the hands of the usurper Tribhuvanāditya, one of his officials, was probably violent.

Tribhuvanāditya's reign (*c*.1165–1177) is obscure. It is possible that his palace was at the site of the subsequent Preah Khan temple complex, which contains a shrine to the god Tribhuvanavarmeśvara.

---

[4] However, it has been questioned whether the original dedication was to the Buddha, or to a local god. See C. Jacques, *Angkor*. Paris: Bordas, 1990, p. 108.

His reign ended when a Cham fleet made its way unexpectedly up the Tonle Sap to the Great Lake and scored a rapid and devastating victory that gave power at Angkor to the Cham ruler Jaya Indravarman IV.

The Chams were soon expelled by **Jayavarman VII** (1181–*c*.1218), the main features of whose reign are detailed above. After expelling the Chams he fought his way to dominance and inaugurated his reign as Khmer emperor. His empire extended to the lower Mekong, into Laos to the north, and into the Khmer parts of Thailand. He constructed a new capital city, Angkor Thom, centred on the Bayon shrine which had a Buddhist icon and whose towers were decorated with faces of the *bodhisattva* Avalokiteśvara. He built 102 'fire-houses' and constructed roads linking Angkor with the outer parts of the kingdom. The chronology of the end of his reign is quite obscure.

Little is known about his successor, **Indravarman II**, whose reign lasted until 1243.

Jayavarman VIII (1243–1295) sponsored the last known royally endowed temple, for the benefit of the priest Jayamangalārtha, said to have lived to the truly ripe age of 104. There is evidence of a phase of resurgent Hinduism that inspired the defacement of some of Jayavarman VII's Buddhist sculpture, and it is thought that this unusually intolerant episode of Hindu fundamentalism took place in the reign of Jayavarman VIII, although it has been suggested that Indravarman II might have been responsible, and that he could possibly have been the leper king of folk memory.

Indravarman III (*c*.1295–1308) was reigning at the time of the visit of Chou Ta-kuan, who offers a great deal of concrete information about Angkor at the time. He reports wars against Thai invaders; in subsequent reigns the problem became worse. However, for the time being, Angkor was still the centre of a bustling kingdom.

The record of subsequent kings quickly becomes shadowy and confused, and most of it is dependent upon the contradictory accounts offered by Thai and Cambodian court chronicles composed much later.

Appendix II: The Periodization of Religious Art and Architecture

The evolution of Khmer religious art passed through a series of phases that spanned four centuries and more; the Bayon marked the last major stage of development. Here is a summary of the stages of Angkor's architecture as identified by the research of French scholars, each stage representing a precisely defined style:[1]

Kulen, corresponding to the reign of Jayavarman II who, as noted above, left almost no architecture commissioned by himself; but the period was marked by a substantial number of religious foundations whose architecture and sculpture incorporated significant adaptations of the art of 'Chen-la'.

Preah Koh, named after the group of memorial shrines founded by Indravarman at Hariharālaya; the basic elements of the Angkorian monumental repertoire were established in this period, with the temple mountain, the rectangular enclosing wall, the 'library' buildings in the enclosure, the gateway towers and so forth.

Bakheng, at the end of the ninth century and early in the tenth, marked especially by the monument on the hill of that name which fixed the symbolic centre of the realm of Yaśovarman, founder of the

---

[1] On these stages, see P. Stern, *Les Monuments du style khmer du Bayon et Jayavarman VII.* Paris: Presses Universitaires, 1965; H. Parmentier, *L'Art khmer classique.* Paris: Ecole française d'Extrême-Orient, 1939; G. de Coral-Rémusat, *L'Art khmer, Les grands étapes de son évolution.* Paris: Van Oest, 1940, pp. 108–117; J. Boisselier, *Le Cambodge.* Paris: Picard, 1966; R. Dumont, Les styles de l'art khmer. In C. Jacques, *Angkor,* Paris: Bordas, 1990, pp. 174–83.

city that remained the site of most subsequent Angkorian capitals. The style was marked by rich architectural symbolism at the expense of an abundance of sculptural detail.

Koh Ker, in the earlier tenth century and partly concurrent with the preceding phase, with which it shared many features. Koh Ker was the site of Jayavarman IV's capital to the north of Angkor.

Pre Rup, late in the same century, named after the temple-mountain built by Rājendravarman on the southern side of the Eastern Baray; the same ruler, who returned the capital to the Yaśodharapura site, built also a temple pyramid on an artificial island in the middle of the Eastern Baray – the Eastern Mebon.

Banteay Srei, named after the cluster of shrines built in 967, described above; it warrants the identification of a separate style on account of its extremely rich sculptural decoration as well as its highly distinctive architectural conception, in which everything is miniaturized.

The **Khleangs,** late tenth and early eleventh centuries. The style is named after gallery buildings in the palace enclosure, but it is widely represented by religious foundations, especially the Ta Kev. The Ta Kev, begun in 975 by Yaśovarman V, marks the convergence of the main elements of the Angkorian temple mountain. An innovation was that its superstructure was almost entirely of sandstone. It has a group of five sanctuary towers standing upon a three-tier pyramid. This in turn stands on two concentric platforms, and there are two enclosing walls interrupted by entry pavilions at the mid-points. One enclosing wall sustains a continuous vaulted gallery, an innovation maintained in subsequent temple-mountains.

The **Baphuon,** named after the temple mountain of Udayādityavarman II in the middle of the eleventh century. This monument, richly decorated with religious art honouring Viṣṇu, offers various developments in the treatment of sculptural themes above doorways, but is specially distinctive in the steepness of its sides, a feature that led to the early collapse of the retaining walls.

Angkor Wat, at the end of the eleventh and in the early twelfth centuries. It is represented by a large number of temples in different parts of the Khmer territory, and combines luxuriant detail with a strong sense of proportion. Bas-relief is particularly rich in this period. The great vaiṣṇavite temple of Sūryavarman II after which the style is named is described in chapter 14.

The **Bayon,** the late twelfth and early thirteenth centuries. It is the last phase before the steep decline in royally sponsored architecture that set in after Jayavarman VII; yet so much was done by this monarch that many have found it impossible to attribute it all to the one period. There was little by way of stylistic innovation, although the Bayon itself, with its gigantic faces set like monster clock dials upon the four sides of the fifty or so towers (many now collapsed), has a central shrine built upon a complex and rather confusing plan; it too is described in chapter 14, along with the imposing walls and gateways of the great city of Angkor Thom.

Bibliography and Guide to Further Reading

General Works on Cambodian History and Traditional Culture

The most recent general history is D. P. Chandler's *A History of Cambodia*, Boulder, Col., and Oxford: Westview Press, 1992, which surveys the entire course of Cambodian history. Apart from this, general works on Cambodia are hard to find. Most are in French, and most are now out of print. Cambodia is well served, however, in general histories of South-East Asia, of which the most recent is *The Cambridge History of Southeast Asia*, 2 vols, ed. N. Tarling, Cambridge: Cambridge University Press, 1992. In French, S. Thierry, *Les Khmers*, Paris: Seuil, 1964, offers a brief, beautifully written account of early history and traditional culture.

Art and Architecture

This subject is served by a number of large and often sumptuously illustrated books on the religious art and architecture before and during the period of Angkor. A recent valuable production, with the bonus that it contains a detailed scholarly summary of Cambodian history up to the end of Angkor, is C. Jacques, *Angkor*, Paris: Bordas, 1990. Other well-illustrated coffee-table books include Bernard Groslier and Jacques Arthaud, *Angkor: Art and Civilization*, London: Thames & Hudson, 1966; and Donatello Mazzeo and Chiara Silvi Antonini, *Monuments of Civilization: Ancient Cambodia*, London: Cassell, 1972.

Among more specialized scholarly monographs, important is J. Boisselier's, *Le Cambodge*, Paris: Picard, 1966. Other major studies, laying the foundations for our knowledge of the history of Cambodian art, are: P. Stern, *Les Monuments du style khmer du Bayon et Jayavarman VII*, Paris: Presses Universitaires, 1965; H. Parmentier, *L'Art khmer classique*, Paris: Ecole française d'Extrême-Orient, 1939; G. de Coral-Rémusat, *L'Art khmer: Les grands étapes de son évolution*, Paris: Van Oest, 1940.

The subject is served by articles in learned journals; before about 1970, most appeared in the *Bulletin de l'Ecole française d'Extrême-Orient*, which has long been the main repository of research on early Cambodia. An important example is P. Stern, Diversité et rythme des fondations royales khmères, *loc. cit.*, 44 (1954), pp. 649–87. More recent articles include the intriguing if controversial reinterpretations of the symbolism of Angkor Wat in R. Stencel et al., Astronomy and cosmology at Angkor Wat, *Science*, 193 (1976), pp. 281–7; and E. Morón, Configuration of time and space at Angkor Wat, *Studies in Indo-Asian Art and Culture*, 5 (1977), pp. 217–67.

Culture, Society and Economy

On the Cambodian population, a detailed survey of South-East Asian peoples is F. Lebar, G. Hickey and J. Musgrave, *Ethnic Groups of Mainland Southeast Asia*, New Haven, Conn.: Human Relations Area Files, 1964. This is now outdated in some respects; for a summary of more recent research into the origins of South-East Asian peoples, see P. Bellwood, The Austronesian dispersal and the origin of languages, *Scientific American*, 265, no. 1 (July 1991), pp. 88–93, and his chapter on 'Southeast Asia before history', in N. Tarling (ed.), *The Cambridge History of Southeast Asia*, Cambridge: Cambridge University Press, 1992, vol. 1, pp. 55–136.

Historical geography is explored by B.-P. Groslier, Pour une géographie historique du Cambodge, *Les Cahiers d'Outre-Mer*, 104 (1973), pp. 337–79. There are articles bearing on traditional Khmer society in K. Hutterer (ed.), *Economic Exchange and Social Interaction in Southeast Asia: Perspectives from prehistory, history and ethnography*, Ann Arbor, Mich., University of Michigan Press, 1977; and a still pertinent interpretation of the influence of Indian culture upon mainland South-East Asian society, originally published in French in 1933, is P. Mus, *India Seen from the East: Indian and indigenous cults in Champa*, ed. and tr. I. W. Mabbett and D. P. Chandler, Clayton, Victoria: Monash University Centre of Southeast Asian Studies, 1975.

A major study of traditional culture and its origins, often neglected but full of interesting material (and speculative interpretations), is E. Porée-Maspero, *Etude sur les rites agraires des Cambodgiens*, 3 vols, Paris: Mouton, 1962-9. Folk culture as embodied in oral tradition is presented by S. Thierry, *Etude d'un corpus de contes cambodgiens*, Paris and Lille: Librairie Honoré Champion, 1978; and Khing Hoc Dy, *Contribution à l'histoire de la littérature khmère*, 2 vols, Paris: l'Harmattan, 1990-2. There are fascinating insights into beliefs about the supernatural in Ang Chouléan, *Les Etres surnaturels dans la religion populaire khmère*, Paris: Cedoreck, 1986; and A. Forest, Cambodge: pouvoir du roi et puissance de génie, in Forest (ed.), *Cultes populaires et sociétés asiatiques: Appareils cultuels et appareils de pouvoir*, Paris: l'Harmattan, 1991, pp. 185-223.

On urbanization, a substantial study of the rise of royal cities in South-East Asia, offering a richly documented religious interpretation, is Paul Wheatley's *Nāgara and Commandery*, Chicago, Ill.: Department of Geography, University of Chicago, 1983. Commerce in the Angkorian period has not been much studied, but see K. Hall, Khmer commercial development and foreign contacts under Sūryavarman, *Journal of the Economic and Social History of the Orient*, 18, no. 3 (1975), pp. 318-36; and the same author's chapter, Economic history of early Southeast Asia, in *The Cambridge History of Southeast Asia*, vol. 1, Cambridge: Cambridge University Press, 1992, pp.183-275.

Agriculture

On rural life, the classic study of traditional Khmer farmers is J. Delvert, *Le Paysan cambodgien*, Paris and the Hague: Mouton, 1961; this book, based on research carried out in the 1940s and 1950s, is full of detailed information about all aspects of rural society. On the nature of agriculture in the Angkorian period, and the problems associated with its interpretation, much of what is known stems from the work of Bernard Groslier, including his La cité hydraulique angkorienne. Exploitation ou surexploitation du sol? *Bulletin de l'Ecole française d'Extrême-Orient*, 66 (1979), pp. 161-202; also his Agriculture et religion dans l'empire angkorien, *Etudes rurales*, nos 53-6 (1974), pp. 95-117, and parts of a work based largely on sixteenth-century Iberian sources, *Angkor et le Cambodge au XVIe siècle d'après les sources portugaises et espagnoles*, Paris: Presses Universitaires de France, 1958. More recently, though, revisionist views have been advanced; see particularly W. van Liere, Traditional water management in the lower Mekong Basin, *World Archaeology*, 11, no. 3 (1980), pp. 265-80; Yumio Sakurai, Tank agriculture in

South India: an essay on agricultural Indianization in Southeast Asia, in *Transformation of the Agricultural Landscape in Sri Lanka and South India*, ed. S. D. G. Jayawardena, Kyoto: Kyoto University Center for Southeast Asian Studies, n.d., pp. 117–58; and F. Grunewald, A propos de l'agriculture dans le Cambodge mediéval, *Asie du Sud-est et Monde Insulindien*, 13, nos 1–4 (1982), pp. 23–38.

Prehistory

Cambodia itself has afforded few opportunities for archaeological research on the spot in recent years, but a great deal has been done on the prehistory of neighbouring countries. An important recent synthesis is C. F. Higham's *The Archaeology of Mainland Southeast Asia*, Cambridge: Cambridge University Press, 1989. The chapter by P. Bellwood, Southeast Asia before history, and his article on The Austronesian dispersal, both cited above, are also valuable. The subject is served by many of the articles in R. B. Smith and W. Watson (eds), *Early South East Asia: Essays in archaeology, history and historical geography*, New York: Oxford University Press, 1979. There are many monographs and journal articles on the prehistory of the region, mostly in English; one on Cambodia itself, in French, is Roland Mourer's Préhistoire du Cambodge, *Archéologia* no. 233 (1988), pp. 40–52. Others, principally on Thailand and Vietnam, include works by such scholars as H. Loofs-Wissowa, Donn Bayard, Elizabeth Moore and others, as cited in the notes to the text of this book.

On the archaeology of the historical period, C. F. Higham's work, already noted, has substantial sections on the archaeological evidence, particularly for Angkor. There are many relevant articles also in Smith and Watson, *op. cit.* The important site of Oc Eo in the Mekong delta, associated with 'Fu-nan', was excavated by L. Malleret; see his *L'Archéologie du delta du Mekong*, 4 vols, Paris: Ecole française d'Extrême-Orient, 1959–63.

Overviews of Early History

The classic history of the region in the pre-colonial period is G. Coedès's *Les Etats hindouisés d'Indochine et d'Indonésie*, rev. edn, Paris: Boccard, 1964, translated into English by S. Cowing as *The Indianized States of Southeast Asia*, Canberra: Australian National University Press, 1968. Despite the progress of research since Coedès's time, this work, based upon pioneering research, remains the most important summary of early South-East Asian history. The author's *The Making of South-East Asia*, trans. H. M. Wright, London: Routledge & Kegan Paul, 1966, covers the same ground, with a greater emphasis on social and cultural history; and a work intended for a wider readership, designed to correct popular misconceptions about Cambodian history, was Coedès's *Angkor: An introduction*, tr. E. Gardiner, Hong Kong: Oxford University Press, 1963. A major synthesis of knowledge about Cambodian history up to the end of Angkor, still valuable because of its richness of detail, is L. P. Briggs's *The Ancient Khmer Empire*, Philadelphia, Pa: American Philosophical Society, 1951. More recent research is embodied in a multitude of articles and monographs; some collections of papers about South-East Asia contain significant contributions on Cambodia, for example D. Marr and A. Milner (eds), *Southeast Asia in the 9th to 14th Centuries*, Singapore: Institute of Southeast Asian Studies, and Canberra: Research School of Pacific Studies, Australian National University, 1986.

Primary Sources

These fall almost entirely into two categories: the inscriptions associated with temples, and accounts based on reports by foreign visitors, particularly Chinese.

The study of the inscriptions of Cambodia was one major part of Coedès's life's work, and he brought most of the extant inscriptions together in his magisterial *Les Inscriptions du Cambodge*, 8 vols, Paris: Ecole française d'Extrême-Orient, 1937–66. This work is supplemented by the work of Claude Jacques. Most of the articles on Cambodian epigraphy appear in the *Bulletin de l'Ecole française d'Extrême-Orient*. For example, an important inscription containing evidence about eleventh-century religious and social organization, as well as a summary of earlier reigns, comes from Sdok Kak Thom and was published by G. Coedès and P. Dupont, along with two other inscriptions, in Les stèles de Sdok Kak Thom, Phnom Sandak et Prah Vihar, *Bulletin de l'Ecole française d'Extreme-Orient*, 63 (1943–6), pp. 57–134.

Chinese accounts of parts of South-East Asia include I-ching, *A Record of the Buddhist Religion as practised in India and the Malay Archipelago*, tr. J. Takakusu, Oxford: Clarendon Press, 1896, an account of travels by a Buddhist pilgrim, with brief references to the Khmer kingdoms. Chou Ta-kuan, *Mémoires sur les coutumes du Cambodge de Tcheou Takouan*, tr. P. Pelliot, Paris: Ecole française

d'Extrême-Orient, 1951, is a particularly vivid and detailed description of Angkor at the end of the thirteenth century, while it was still
prosperous and flourishing. Two sources with brief and problematic
references to the Khmers are Ma Tuan-lin, *Ethnographie des peuples
étrangers à la Chine*, tr. Le Marquis d'Hervey de Saint-Denys, vol. ii,
Geneva: Georg, 1883; and Chau Ju-kua, *Chau Ju-Kua: His work on
the Chinese and Arab trade in the 12th and 13th centuries*, tr. F. Hirth
and W. W. Rockhill, St Petersburg: Imperial Academy of Sciences,
1911.

Periods and Problems: Works Based largely on Inscriptions

Inscriptions are the main source for the history of Cambodia before
the fall of Angkor, and most research on this period has been based on
them. Some collections of papers, such as the works already mentioned edited by Smith and Watson and by Marr and Milner, contain
significant contributions on Cambodia. The scholar most active in
the field of Cambodian epigraphy is C. Jacques, whose *Angkor*, cited
above, contains the results of much original historical research as well
as being an illustrated guide to art and architecture. To represent his
articles, it must suffice to mention Nouvelles orientations pour l'étude
de l'histoire du pays khmer, *Asie du Sud-est et monde Insulindien,
Cambodge I*, 13, nos 1–4 (1982), pp. 39–58, which calls for a new
way of looking at the ancient Khmer kingdoms and identifies new
directions for research. Also used in the present work is his unpublished manuscript (written for seminar purposes), Histoire pré-
angkorienne du pays khmer. Another active scholar using epigraphic
sources is Michael Vickery, author of various studies of the Angkorian
and 'Chen-la' periods: for example, his The reign of Sūryavarman I
and royal factionalism at Angkor, *Journal of Southeast Asian Studies*,
16, no. 2 (1985), pp. 226–44. He has also written a major study of
Cambodia before Angkor; at the time of writing it is being prepared
for publication by the Centre of Southeast Asian Studies, Monash
University, Clayton.

Much attention has been given to the nature of kingship in Angkor;
see for example H. Kulke, *The Devarāja Cult*, tr. I. W. Mabbett,
Ithaca, N.Y.: Cornell University Southeast Asia Program, Data Paper
no.108, 1978; C. Jacques, The Kamraten Jagat in ancient Cambodia,
in Karashima Norbu (ed.), *Indus Valley to Mekong Delta: Explorations in epigraphy*, Madras: New Era Publications, 1985) pp. 269–
86; Nidhi Aeusrivongse, Devarāja cult and Khmer kingship at Angkor,
in K.R. Hall and J.K. Whitmore (eds), *Explorations in Early Southeast*

Asian History: The origins of Southeast Asian statecraft, Ann Arbor, Mich.: University of Michigan, Center for South and Southeast Asian Studies, 1976, pp. 107–48; M. Vickery, Some remarks on early state formation in Cambodia, in D. Marr and A. Milner (eds), *op. cit.*, pp. 95–115; and H. Kulke, The early and the imperial kingdom, ibid., pp. 1–22. A study of political institutions is S. Sahai, *Les Institutions politiques et l'organisation administrative du Cambodge ancien*, Paris: Ecole française d'Extrême-Orient, 1970.

On the use of inscriptions for information about the physical environment, see Judith Jacob, The ecology of Angkor: evidence from the inscriptions, in P. A. Stott (ed.), *Nature and Man in South East Asia*, London: School of Oriental and African Studies, 1978.

Periods and Problems: Works Based Largely on Foreign Accounts

Chinese visitors were the chief source of information written by outsiders. P. Pelliot's Le Fou-nan, *Bulletin de l'Ecole française d'Extrême-Orient*, 2 (1902), pp. 248–303, although written so long ago, still remains the major source for the 'Fu-nan' period. P. Wheatley, *The Golden Khersonese*, Kuala Lumpur: Oxford University Press, 1966, reviews and quotes extensively all the foreign sources (particularly Chinese) for the ancient political geography of South-East Asia. B.-P. Groslier, *Angkor et le Cambodge au XVIe siècle d'après les sources portugaises et espagnoles*, Paris: Presses Universitaires de France, 1958, uses sixteenth-century Iberian accounts.

Cambodia after Angkor

The period immediately following the end of Angkor is particularly obscure. There are some travellers' accounts, such as Gabriel Quiroga de San Antonio, *Brève et Véridique relation des événements du Cambodge*, tr. A. Cabaton, Paris: Leroux, 1914. Modern studies include the following: D.P. Chandler, Folk memories of the decline of Angkor in nineteenth-century Cambodia: the legend of the leper king, *Journal of the Siam Society*, 67 (1979), pp. 54–62; May Ebihara, Societal Organization in 16th and 17th century Cambodia, *Journal of Southeast Asian Studies*, 15, no. 2 (1984), pp. 280–95 (and see other articles in the *Symposium on Societal Organization in Mainland Southeast Asia prior to the 18th Century*, to which this is a contribution); M. Vickery, *Cambodia after Angkor: The chronicular evidence for the fourteenth to sixteenth centuries*, Ann Arbor, Mich.: University Microfilms, 1977; M. Vickery, The 2/k125 fragment: a lost chronicle of Ayuthaya, *Journal of the Siam Society*, 65, no. 1 (1977), pp. 1–80, at p. 61.

For Cambodian classical literature, the *Reamker* and the normative poems known as *chhbab* have been fluently translated into French by the renowned Cambodian linguist, Saveros Pou. See *Une guirlande de cpap*, 2 vols, Paris: CEDORECK, 1988; and *Ramakerti*, Paris: Ecole française d'Extrême-Orient, 1977. See also Khing Hoc Dy, *Contribution à l'histoire de la littérature khmère*, Paris: l'Harmattan, 1990.

Cambodian chronicle histories from 1594 to 1677 have been ably translated into French: Mak Phoeun, *Chroniques royales du Cambodge de 1594 à 1677*, Paris: Ecole française d'Extrême-Orient, 1981. See also B.-P. Groslier, *Angkor et le Cambodge au XVIe siècle d'après les sources portugaises et espagnoles*, Paris: Presses Universitaires de France, 1958.

For an analysis of post-Angkorian art styles, see M. Giteau, *L'Iconographie du Cambodge post-angkoréen*, Paris: Ecole française d'Extrême-Orient, 1975.

The most detailed study of nineteenth-century pre-colonial Cambodian history is David P. Chandler, *Cambodia before the French: Politics in a tributary kingdom, 1794–1848*, Ann Arbor, Mich.: University Microfilms, 1974.

The early stages of French colonialism are fruitfully examined in Milton Osborne, *The French Presence in Cambodia and Cochinchina: Rule and response*, Ithaca, N.Y.: Cornell University Press, 1969. For a readable account of the Mekong River expedition, see Milton Osborne, *River Road to China*, New York: Liveright, 1975. For the early twentieth century, see Alain Forest, *Le Cambodge et la colonisation française: Histoire d'une colonisation sans heurts*, Paris: l'Harmattan, 1980.

The only detailed history of Cambodia between 1945 and 1990 is David P. Chandler, *The Tragedy of Cambodian History: Politics, war and revolution since 1945*, New Haven, Conn.: Yale University Press, 1991. See also Marie-A. Martin, *Cambodia: A shattered society*, Berkeley, Cal.: University of California Press, 1994. Prince Norodom Sihanouk's memoirs, *Souvenirs doux et amers*, Paris: Fayard, 1982, are colourful, but should be used with caution. For the trajectory of Cambodian radicalism between 1945 and 1975, see Ben Kiernan's pathbreaking study, *How Pol Pot Came to Power*, London; Zed Books, 1985; and David P. Chandler, *Brother Number One: A political biography of Pol Pot*, Boulder, Col., and Oxford: Westview Press, 1992.

American involvement in Lon Nol's Cambodia is treated scathingly in William Shawcross, *Sideshow: Nixon, Kissinger and the destruction of Cambodia*, New York: Simon & Schuster, 1979; while the best overall histories of the revolutionary period that followed are probably: Michael Vickery, *Cambodia 1975–1982*, Boston, Mass.: South End Press, 1983; and Elizabeth Becker, *When the War was Over*, New York: Simon & Schuster, 1986. See also Karl Jackson (ed.), *Cambodia 1975–1978: Rendez-vons with death*, Princeton, N.J.; Princeton University Press, 1989; and David Chandler, Ben Kiernan and Chanthou Boua (eds and trs), *Pol Pot Plans the Future: Confidential leadership documents from Democratic Kampuchea, 1976–1977*, New Haven, Conn.: Yale University Southeast Asian Studies, 1988. Serge Thion, *Watching Cambodia*, Bangkok, 1993, is an absorbing collection of essays written over a twenty-year period. For post-1979 developments, see Nayan Chanda, *Brother Enemy*, New York: Harcourt Brace Jovanovich, 1986; Grant Evans and Kelvin Rowley, *Red Brotherhood at War*, London: Verso, 1990; and Michael Vickery, *Kampuchea*, London: Francis Pinter, 1986. On the issue of genocide, see Ben Kiernan (ed.), *Genocide and Democracy in Cambodia*, New Haven, Conn.: Yale University Southeast Asia Program, 1993. For an assessment of contemporary cultural issues, see May Ebihara, Judith Ledgerwood and Carol Mortland (eds), *Cambodian Culture since 1975: Homeland and exile*, Ithaca N.Y.: Cornell University Press, 1994.

Index

administration, 165;
Cambodian provincial,
230; organization of,
166–7; under
Rajendravarman, 100
Aeusrivongse, Nidhi, 118
agriculture, 14, 30–1, 33–4,
139–55; at Oc Eo, 68–9;
prehistoric origins of,
44–8; suitable
environments for, 33,
35–6; and urbanization,
58
Airāvata (mount of Indra),
189, 195, 200
Alexander the Great, 2
Amarendrapura, 91
America, Cambodia
bombed by, 244
Amitābha (Buddha of
infinite light), 202
Ānanda temple, 185
Ananta (cosmic serpent),
201
Anavatapta (mythical lake),
206
Ang, Chouléan, 110, 123

angkar ('organization'), 247
Angkor: agriculture in,
147–55; archaeology of,
50; decline of, 212–17,
219; empire of, 98, 100;
reference of term, 12,
95–6
Angkor Thom, 98, 194–5,
207
Angkor Wat (newspaper),
234, 236, 237
Angkor Wat, 103, 105,
120, 122, 187, 190–3;
architectural period, 267
Aninditapura, 91
apsaras (nymph), 197
Arab sources, 85–7
archaeology: of Angkor, 50;
of Burma, 63; of China,
52, 53, 56; of 'Fu-nan',
67–8; of Thailand, 41,
49, 54
architecture; in Angkor,
183–97; Indian
prototypes, 19; and myth,
18, 184
armies, 156